Intelligence

Investigation, Community, and Partnership

Intelligence

Investigation, Community, and Partnership

Clive Harfield

MSc, LLM, MPhil, PhD
Warwickshire Police
John Grieve Centre for Policing and Community Safety

and

Karen Harfield

BSc (Hons)
Superintendent, Warwickshire Police

OXFORD
UNIVERSITY PRESS

OXFORD

UNIVERSITY PRESS

Great Clarendon Street, Oxford, OX2 6DP,
United Kingdom

Oxford University Press is a department of the University of Oxford.
It furthers the University's objective of excellence in research, scholarship,
and education by publishing worldwide. Oxford is a registered trade mark of
Oxford University Press in the UK and in certain other countries

Published in the United States of America by Oxford University Press
198 Madison Avenue, New York, NY 10016, United States of America

British Library Cataloguing in Publication Data

Data available

Library of Congress Cataloging in Publication Data

Data available

ISBN 978-0-19-923003-7

For Bryn

Preface

This contribution to the Blackstone's Practical Policing series follows the philosophy of the series by seeking to move beyond the sort of guidance that might appear in a policy document or doctrine manual to the consideration of practical issues in a wider context. Hence this volume juxtaposes practical experience, and where appropriate policy guidance, with academic commentaries to reflect upon and illustrate both the complexity but also the potential in good intelligence management.

At times the authors have been faced with the chicken-and-egg dilemma because information collection and intelligence management is a cyclical process and a judgment had to be made about the order in which material should be discussed because a number of options were available. It is hoped that the reader will find logic and assistance in the order that has been selected. At times it has proved useful to reiterate material that appears elsewhere in the book in order to ensure that each chapter can be read individually as well as in conjunction with the whole volume.

Intelligence, which it is argued is a profession in its own right within policing, oversteps the functional boundaries of law enforcement to engage partner agencies whose roles and remit also contribute to community safety and the reduction of harm. To have written a book that spoke to all partner agencies in detail was beyond the scope of this present commission. Here the focus is on intelligence work within the police service but within the context of policing in its widest, multi-agency sense. Partner agencies it is hoped, as well as police practitioners, will gain insight into police intelligence work and how it relates to their own role. Similarly it is hoped that third parties such as the academic community will be given food for thought in what follows.

About This Book

It is easy for all of us now, more than 40 years on to sift slowly through the relevant records, neatly arranged in chronological order, and ask ourselves, with the additional benefit of hindsight, why clues were missed, why appreciations were faulty, why incorrect decisions were taken. Those who have never experienced it should not forget the 'the fog of war' factor, the atmosphere of urgency, the pressures the strain, day after day, week after week, year after year, they try to solve the problems and complete the jigsaw puzzle—or rather puzzles because in a world war, no single problem can be considered in isolation: there are dozens of them each calling for swift and most of them immediate action. The more senior the individual concerned the more likely it is that he will have to switch his attention at any time during the day—or night from one end of the world to the other, from the land to the sea or to the air, from the tactical situation to the long-term implications, from the possible reactions of the enemy to the behaviour of allies. Nothing is simple, nothing is certain, but everything is important.

Patrick Beesly *Intelligence and Decision Making*, 1990, pp 317–8

It is a great pleasure to introduce this significant and timely contribution to an important aspect of current thinking about policing at a time of great challenges for and to the service. For many years I have been using the heroic, late Patrick Beesley's books and article to inform my police intelligent decision-making. This book builds on my learning from him.

There are many ways of breaking down the emergence of intelligence led policing. Here I have wilfully side-stepped some secrecy issues and have chosen a number of milestones to show where I think my friends and colleagues Karen and Clive Harfield's excellent second book fits into intelligence thinking. The fundamental point is that they help deal with Patrick Beesley's concerns. The significance of Beesley (if that needs spelling out in an almost daily environment of alleged police intelligence failures) is that he identified for me and for all of us the role of academics, as analysts, alongside operational officers in the submarine tracking room during successful intelligence operations in the 'fog of war'.

The early 1960s saw the wider development of protean and protogenic intelligence branches in response to what Mary McIntosh called the *Changes in the Organization of Thieving* (1971), which identified for investigators the opportunities available to gather intelligence about the planning and preparatory efforts in project crimes.

This learning was further informed by David Powis's work on reforming informant management. Powis was supreme at holding commanders accountable for their actions as a method of handling harm and risks. I acted as his staff officer during part of this period. His work underpinned Covert Human Intelligence Sources thinking in the new regime created by the Regulation of Investigatory Powers Act 2000.

The policing of Northern Ireland, in which military and police thinking developed together on minimising extreme risks, also contributed to reforms in architecture, strategy, tactics, handling, controls, authorities, record keeping, co-ordinating, and tasking groups and interagency intelligence-led working. Sir Kenneth Newman returned to the Metropolitan Police from the RUC via the police staff college. He bought with him thinking about 20th century business models of planning and performance, Problem Oriented Policing, and Policing by Objectives, leading to the Force Intelligence Development Steering Committee amongst many other initiatives. This latter saw the translation of Powis' thinking about informers, analysis, and profiling promoted into mainstream policing.

David Phillips had long been an inspiration to me after hearing him include military models of planning and intelligence into learning about football disorder at a lecture at the Police Staff College. On succeeding Paul Condon in Kent as Chief Constable in 1993, he introduced an increasing range of intelligence tools at every level of policing. In parallel, in the early 1990s Kent and the Met were jointly reviewing the application of all intelligence tools force-wide. This led to the intelligence reforms arising from the Stephen Lawrence inquiry, including the role of academics.

Intelligence was a direct product of Peter Imbert's values and standards 'Plus' Program in the Metropolitan Police because of the practical application of intelligence to evidence and leadership issues disclosed from the Evidence Project Implementation Committee and applied locally in the Crime Investigation Priority Project. This period also saw the development of analytic and reasoning tools to study risk, health, safety and welfare, and human rights.

In this regard the creation of the National Drugs Intelligence Unit, precursor to the National Criminal Intelligence Service (NCIS), was particularly significant because it promoted nationally the importance of, and good practice in managing, informants, surveillance, multi-level undercover operations, analysis, which in turn prefaced money laundering investigation, and asset tracing and seizure. In NCIS Brian Flood and Roger Gaspar then did a great job of highly creative synthesising in deriving the National Intelligence Model not just from all the learning from the aforementioned but also from the wider debates that had occurred around each milestone.

And this is where we arrive at Clive and Karen's present contribution, a continuation of the journey initiated by McIntosh. Their first book, *Covert Investigation* (OUP, 2005), was described by one reviewer as the first book dedicated to covert policing; this present volume will widen the debate. It will engage practitioners from all agencies with the progressive professional focus on risk and harm reduction; and with the wider academic debate on police intelligence issues. For the academic audience it provides insight into intelligence practicalities.

It will help deal with some of the sillier arguments about intelligence failures and will be a step change for informing those who want a human rights compliant effective intelligent led policing system that can handle risk and manage and limit harm.

John G.D. Grieve CBE QPM
Professor Emeritus London Metropolitan University
Senior Research Fellow University of Portsmouth
Independent Monitoring Commission Northern Ireland

Acknowledgements

The police careers of both the authors have included roles in intelligence management as well as gathering information through covert means for intelligence analysis. Both have worked in partnership with law enforcement and other agencies in the UK and with foreign colleagues. Such experiences have been invaluable in writing this book and so our first thanks go to all the colleagues, within the police service and without, with whom we have worked and who, vicariously, have informed and influenced the content that follows.

To Professor Allyson MacVean and Professor Emeritus John Grieve QPM, London Metropolitan University, our thanks for their practical as well as intellectual support. As ever, staff at the National Police Library provided excellent service in supplying articles and books. The privilege of Research Reader access to the library at the University of Warwick also contributed to the successful completion of this work.

And a particular 'thank you' to our editors at Oxford University Press, Peter Daniell, Lindsey Davis, and Jodi Towler: for the commission; for their encouragement; for their guidance; for their patience when the day job disrupted the writing schedule; and, not least, for lunch!

Contents

Contents

APPENDICES

Table of Cases

Table of Legislation

UK Statutory Instruments

International Conventions

List of Tables

List of Figures

Special Features

This book contains several special features intended to assist the reader.

Case studies

To provide illustrative examples of certain points and issues, both real and hypothetical case studies have been used.

Definitions

Where appropriate definitions of concepts and case law are provided.

Figures

Some information core concepts have been illustrated in diagrammatic form for ease of presentation.

Further information and reading boxes

These features direct readers towards sources cited in the text, and to additional material that will amplify and elaborate the content of this book.

Key notes

Information requiring particular emphasis is summarized in key points.

Tables

Some information core concepts have been tabulated for ease of illustration and presentation.

Glossary Including Useful Websites

All website url details correct at September 2007

4x4 System for grading intelligence based on evaluation of source and intelligence content. Used widely in Europe and formerly in the UK.

5x5x5 System for grading intelligence used in the UK in which the source, the intelligence content and dissemination restrictions are all evaluated.

ACPO Association of Chief Police Officers of England, Wales and Northern Ireland.
<http://www.acpo.police.uk/>

ACPO (S) Association of Chief Police Officers for Scotland.
<http://www.scottish.police.uk/main/acpos/acpos.htm>

ACRO ACPO Criminal Records Office. ACPO has assumed the responsibility of being the Central Authority for Criminal Records Exchange, facilitating the exchange of criminal records within the EU primarily, and with other international partners as infrastructures and negotiations permit.

ANI Access Northern Ireland. Northern Ireland equivalent of the CRB, being established during 2007.

ANPR Automatic number plate recognition. A system used in temporary roadside equipment or via CCTV to identify vehicle registration plates and so trace suspect vehicles or vehicles believed to be being driven untaxed, uninsured or without MOT. Can be used in conjunction with PNC markers.

ASBO Anti-social Behaviour Order. Created under section 1 Crime and Disorder Act 1998, empowering local authorities or police can seek court imposition of an ASBO as an alternative form of intervention to criminal prosecution. The procedure is a civil, rather than criminal, process. However, breach constitutes a criminal offence.
<http://www.uk-legislation.hmso.gov.uk/acts/acts1998/19980037.htm>
See also <http://www.homeoffice.gov.uk/anti-social-behaviour/>
<http://www.homeoffice.gov.uk/rds/pdfs2/hors236.pdf>

Assets (NIM) The NIM recognizes four categories of assets: knowledge, system, source, and people.

BCS British Crime Survey, undertaken biannually on behalf of the Home Office, in which victimisation is studied rather than reported crime. Usually indicates that much more crime is committed than is reported to the police.

BCU Basic Command Unit, sometimes labelled Operational Command Unit (OCU). A police administrative unit at sub-force level with geographical responsibility for delivering local policing, usually headed by a Superintendent or Chief Superintendent.

BIA The Border and Immigration Agency, which assumed the responsibilities of the former Immigration and Nationality Directorate prior to the reorganization of the Home Office in 2007.
<http://www.ind.homeoffice.gov.uk>

Bichard Inquiry Sir Michael Bichard was appointed by the Home Secretary to enquire into child protection measures, record keeping, vetting and information sharing in Humberside Police and Cambridgeshire Constabulary—the Bichard Inquiry—following the murder of Jessica Chapman and Holly Wells. His report, *The Bichard Inquiry Report* (House of Commons Paper HC653, June 2004) together with follow-up reviews of progress made on his recommendations, can be accessed at <http://www.homeoffice.gov.uk/pdf/bichard_report.pdf>

British Crime Survey (BCS) Open source material of relevance in strategic assessments and other contextual analysis. A biannual survey of victims which helps assess fear of crime and provides comparative data by recording how much crime has not been reported to the police.
<http://www.homeoffice.gov.uk/rds/bcs1.html>

Butler Inquiry A *Review of Intelligence on Weapons of Mass Destruction* (House of Commons Paper HC898, July 2004) was undertaken by a Committee of Privy Counsellors chaired by The Rt Hon The Lord Butler of Brockwell. It can be assessed at <http://www.butlerreview.org.uk>.

CDRP Crime and Disorder Reduction Partnership (termed a Community Safety Partnership (CSP) in Wales). Created by section 17 of the Crime and Disorder Act 1998, amended by section 97 of the Police Reform Act 2002 and now to be understood within the context of amendments brought into effect by section 22 of and Schedule 9 to Police and Justice Act 2006. Membership comprises the local council (District, Unitary or County as applicable); the Chief Officer of Police; the relevant Probation Committee; every police authority, every fire authority, every English Primary Care Trust and every Welsh health authority any part of whose area lies within the CDRP; and other such responsible authorities as may be designated.
CDA 1998 <http://www.opsi.gov.uk/acts/acts1998/19980037.htm>
PRA 2002 <http://opsi.gov.uk/acts/acts2002/20020030.htm>
PAJ 2006 <http://www.opsi.gov.uk/acts/acts2006/20060048.htm>
(Explanatory Notes <http://www.opsi.gov.uk/acts/en2006/2006en48.htm>)

CHIS Covert human intelligence source (eg informer, under-cover officer, test-purchase operative, decoy officer), authorisation of whose activities is required under RIPA.

CIS Customs Information System. EU database for customs organizations.

Community intelligence Defined by ACPO/Centrex as 'Local information which, when assessed, provides intelligence on issues that affect neighbourhoods and informs both strategic and operational perspectives in the policing of local communities. Information may be direct or indirect and come from a diverse range of sources including the community and partner agencies'.
ACPO *Practice Advice on Tasking and Co-ordination* 2006, p 21.

Comparative Analysis (NIM) Analytical technique intended to identify serial or patterned behaviour through similarities or, for the purposes of elimination, discrepancies.

Control Strategy (NIM) The outcome of Strategic Tasking & Co-ordination—a strategic document devised to set the strategic direction for the organization (force, agency) or sub-unit (BCU). An element of the NIM.

CPIA Criminal Procedure and Investigation Act 1996 proscribes regime for pre-trial disclosure of evidence, intended to ensure defendants have access to all relevant evidence. Provisions for non-disclosure of unused and sensitive material such as intelligence reports.
<http://www.uk-legislation.hmso.gov.uk/acts/acts1996/1996025.htm>

Crime Pattern Analysis (NIM) Analysis of reported crimes to identify trends, linked incidents, and crime hot-spots.

Crime audit Section 6(2) of the Crime and Disorder Act 1998 required CDRPs to undertake a review of the levels and patterns of crime and disorder in their areas prior to formulating a crime and disorder reduction strategy. These reviews were colloquially termed crime audits. The Police and Justice Act 2006 has amended section 6 of the CDA entirely and now the manner in which crime and disorder strategies are to be formulated is to be prescribed by Regulations under the new section 6(3).

Crime Series Crimes that are thought to be committed by one offender or a defined group of offenders on the basis of similar execution or intelligence indicating a connection.

Crime Trend A broad pattern of crime (eg increase or decrease over time) as indicated either by reported crime or through victim surveys.

Criminal Business Profile (NIM) Detailed analysis of how a criminal or criminal group is conducting its criminality.

CRB Criminal Records Bureau. Manages disclosure of previous convictions for pre-employment checks.
<http://www.crb.gov.uk>

CRISP Cross Regional Information Sharing Project. A consortium of local police forces collaborating to share local intelligence, adopted within the IMPACT programme as an interim solution en route to the fully functional PND. Aborted in early 2007 due to Home Office budgetary constraints.

CSP Community Safety Partnership. The term used in Wales to describe a CDRP. See CDRP above.

DAF Disclosure Application Form—standard form used by CRB upon which Registered Bodies may request police information about individuals.

Disclosure Certificate Issued to applicant and Registered Body upon completion of CRB check.

Disclosure Scotland Equivalent of CRB in England and Wales and ANI in Northern Ireland.

Disclosure Service Provided by CRB, the Scottish Criminal Records Office and the police service, pursuant to Part V of the Police Act 1997.

Disclosure Unit Police staff, often located within the FIB, responding to disclosure requests.

DMM Daily management meeting. Conducted on BCUs, to determine and prioritise daily business within the context of objectives set by the fortnightly Tasking & Coordination meeting.

DSU Dedicated Source Unit. It is ACPO recommended good practice, following on from RIPA, section 29, that those persons who now fall within the definition of a CHIS but who were formerly termed 'informers', should now be managed by unit of specially-trained handlers and controllers. Previously the handling and management of informers was undertaken by individual officers. The rationale for the recommended good practice is founded upon the desire to improve professional standards and reduce the risk of corruption.

DPA Data Protection Act 1998
<http://www.uk-legislation.hmso.gov.uk/acts/acts1998/19980029.htm>

Demographic/Social Trend Analysis (NIM) Analysis of the population, including changes in demographic profile and other social factors, in a given area intended to inform planning for law enforcement and other public sector requirements.

ECHR European Convention on Human Rights and Fundamental Freedoms, Council of Europe, 1950 given UK domestic effect in the HRA (see below).
<http://www.echr.info>
    See also <http://www.echr.coe.int>—European Court of Human Rights

Enforcement Priorities Linked to Intelligence and Prevention Priorities. Derived from the Control Strategy and intended to direct the use of resources towards achievement of the Control Strategy.

EU European Union
<http://europa.eu>

Eurodac EU fingerprint database used solely to identify asylum seekers. All asylum seekers aged over 14 years have their fingerprints taken as part of the asylum request procedure.

<http://ec.europa.eu/justice_home/key_issues/eurodac/eurodac_20_09_04_
en.pdf>

Eurojust EU institution located in The Hague. Facilitates information exchange and provides mutual legal assistance support to prosecutors in joint operations involving two or more EU Member States.
<http://eurojust.europa.eu/>

Europol EU institution established under the Europol Convention 1995 and located in The Hague. Co-ordinates information exchange and intelligence support to investigators in joint operations involving two or more EU Member States.
<http://www.europol.europa.eu/>

Evaluation The process of assessing the value and accuracy of information, or the capability and reliability of a source of information. In terms of results analysis, evaluation is the measuring of outcomes and the analysis of methods used, tactics deployed and strategies adopted in any given prevention, intervention, or enforcement response.

FLINTS Forensic Lead Intelligence System. Developed by West Midlands Police and shared access with neighbouring forces. A database to assist in collation of intelligence and evidence in order to link suspects to a scene. Depends upon all crimes being entered as well as hard evidence and intelligence.

FSS Forensic Science Service
<http://www.fss.org.uk>

GCHQ Government Communication Headquarters.
See <http://www.gchq.gov.uk/>.

GPMS Government Protective Marking Scheme within which documents are determined to be (in ascending order of sensitivity) 'not protectively marked', 'restricted', 'confidential', 'secret' or 'top secret'.

HMIC Her Majesty's Inspectorate of Constabulary. Conducts inspections of individual force performance and practice and also thematic inspections across the service. See:
Police Act 1996
<http://www.opsi.gov.uk/acts/acts1996/1996016.htm>
Police and Justice Act 2006
<http://www.opsi.gov.uk/acts/acts2006/20060048.htm>
(Explanatory Notes <http://www.opsi.gov.uk/acts/en2006/2006en48.htm>)
Also <http://inspectorates.homeoffice.gov.uk/hmic/> for access to HMIC reports.

HOLMES Home Office Large Major Enquiry System. Computerised system to assist in management of information and evidence in large-scale investigations. Updated recently as HOLMES2.
<http://www.holmes2.com/holmes2/index.php>

Hot spots Geographical concentrations of particular incidents, eg street robberies, traffic accidents, anti-social behaviour

HRA Human Rights Act 1998. Gives domestic effect to UK obligations under the European Convention on Human Rights and Fundamental Freedoms 1959 (Council of Europe).
<http://www.uk-legislation.hmso.gov.uk/acts/acts1998/19980042.htm>

Hutton Inquiry Lord Hutton was commissioned by the Secretary of State for Constitutional Affairs to conduct an inquiry into the death of Dr David Kelly, a government scientist and expert on WMD. This was not a post mortem inquiry but considered aspects of intelligence and media reporting. The *Report of the Inquiry into the Circumstances Surrounding the Death of Dr David Kelly CMG* (House of Commons Paper HC247, January 2004) is accessible at
<http://www.the-hutton-inquiry.org.uk>

IBB Independent Barring Board, created under section 1 of the Safeguarding Vulnerable Groups Act 2006, to establish and maintain a children's barred list and an adults' barred list under Schedule 3 of that Act. Individuals are entered upon the barred lists upon evidence of conduct that endangers or presents a threat of harm to children or vulnerable adults.

ICS Integrated Children's System. Supports work of Social Services in childcare issues.

IMPACT Intelligence Management, Prioritisation, Analysis, Coordination & Tasking. The government programme for improving national police intelligence capability through implementation of the Bichard Inquiry recommendations.

Information All forms of information which the police gather or obtain and then document and process. Includes intelligence.

Intelligence Defined by ACPO/NCPE as 'information that has been subject to a defined evaluation and risk assessment process in order to assist with police decision-making'.
ACPO/NCPE *Practice Advice on Tasking and Co-ordination* 2006 p 108.

Intelligence Community Generally defined as national agencies working in the intelligence arena (eg MI5, MI6, GCHQ, Defence Intelligence Service) but which could include police Special Branch, given its national coordination and close operational links with MI5.
See <http://www.intelligence.gov.uk/>.

Intelligence Priorities Linked to Enforcement and Prevention Priorities. Derived from the Control Strategy and intended to direct the use of resources towards achievement of the Control Strategy. These are the actions identified as fulfilling the intelligence requirement that is needed to inform any given crime or disorder intervention or enforcement.

Intelligence Products (NIM) NIM recognizes four types of product: strategic assessments; tactical assessments; subject profiles (originally called target profiles); and problem profiles. These four products are produced by intelligence unit analysts to inform tactical and strategic tasking and coordination.

Intelligence requirement Characterized by the gap between what is known and what is not known. In other words, what investigators and partners need to find out.

Interpol Non-governmental association of police agencies established 1923, and reconstituted 1956. Assists in information/intelligence exchange between foreign law enforcement agencies but has no operational jurisdiction of its own.
<http://www.interpol.int>

IPE (R) Intelligence, Prevention, and Enforcement. Categories for priority requirements to be set out in the control strategy on the basis of the strategic assessment. A number of police forces have added the fourth category, R, to designate reassurance priorities.

ISC Intelligence and Security Committee, established by the Intelligence and Security Act 1994 to examine policy, administration and expenditure in relation to MI5, MI6 and GCHQ. It also has oversight of the Joint Intelligence Committee. Members are appointed by the Prime Minister in consultation with other political party leaders. The redacted reports of the Committee are published on its website.
<http://www.cabinetoffice.gov.uk/intelligence/>

JIC 1) In the context of UK national intelligence machinery and the WMD debate, Joint Intelligence Committee: a committee within the Cabinet Office providing ministers and officials with coordinated interdepartmental intelligence assessments.
<http://www.intelligence.gov.uk/central_intelligence_machinery/joint_intelligence_committee.aspx>
2) In the context of agency partnership working,
   a. Special Branch officers working alongside customs and immigration at ports of entry, Joint Intelligence Cell.
   b. Neighbourhood policing and Safer Neighbourhood Teams working in collaboration with other local agencies, Joint Intelligence Cell.

Knowledge assets Documents that inform best practice amongst practitioners and partners. For example: statute and case law; codes of practice; manuals of guidance; Home Office Circulars; organizational policies and procedures.

Knowledge Products (NIM) Knowledge products are the documented learning and good practice that support the intelligence profession. The NIM, being a documented business process, is itself a knowledge product. Other examples include statute and case law, training, procedural manuals and doctrine, and intelligence-sharing protocols.

Level 1 Local level criminality and/or policing provision, defined by force or BCU boundaries.

Level 2 Cross-border level criminality and/or policing provision, defined by problems or criminality that transcends a single BCU or force/local authority area.

Level 3 National/International level, defined by criminality (usually serious and organised crime) and/or policing provision that operates on a national/international scale.

LPA Local Police Area—in some forces this is the term used to describe the sub-divisional unit of a BCU.

LPP Local Policing Plan. Statutory requirement of police authorities under section 6ZB of the Police Act 1996 as amended by the Police and Justice Act 2006. PA 1996 <http://www.opsi.gov.uk/acts/acts1997/1997050.htm>
PJA 2006 <http://www.opsi.gov.uk/acts/acts2006/20060048.htm>
(Explanatory Notes <http://www.opsi.gov.uk/acts/en2006/2006en48.htm>)

MAPPA Multi-agency Public Protection Arrangements. Required by section 67(2) of the Criminal Justice and Court Services Act 2000, obliging Chief Constables jointly with their local probation board (in combination 'the responsible authority') to assess and manage the risks posed by 'relevant sexual or violent offenders and other persons who, by reason of offences committed by them (wherever committed), are considered by the responsible authority to be persons who may cause serious harm to the public'. Other agencies required to co-operate with the MAPPA responsible authority are: Social Services; Primary Care Trusts, NHS Trusts and Strategic Health Authorities; Youth Offending Teams; local housing authorities; registered social landlords; local educations authorities; electronic monitoring providers; Jobcentres.
<http://www.uk-legislation.hmso.gov.uk/acts/acts2000/20000043.htm> for the Act.
    For further information on MAPPA see:
<http://www.probation.homeoffice.gov.uk/output/Page30.asp>.

Market Profiles (NIM) Analysis of criminal markets (eg drug-dealing, disposal of stolen goods) to inform intervention tactics and strategies and tasking and coordination.

MI5—Security Service National intelligence agency with a primary focus on defending the UK from terrorism, extremism, and espionage.
See <http://www.mi5.gov.uk/>.
Also Security Service Act 1989
<http://www.opsi.gov.uk/acts/acts1989/Ukpga_19890005_en_1.htm>
and Security Service Act 1996
<http://www.opsi.gov.uk/acts/acts1996/1996035.htm>.

MI6—Secret Intelligence Service National intelligence agency with a primary focus on acquiring intelligence overseas on behalf of the British Government.
See <http://www.sis.gov.uk/output/Page79.html>.

Also Intelligence Services Act 1994 <http://www.opsi.gov.uk/acts/acts1994/Ukpga_19940013_en_1.htm>.

MOPI Management of Police Information

See ACPO *Guidance on the Management of Police Information* (NCPE Centrex 2006)

Statutory Code of Practice issued under ss 39 and 39A of the Police Act 1996 and reproduced in the appendices to this volume.

NAFIS National Automated Fingerprint Identification System. For an evaluation of its operation see *The Processing of Fingerprint Evidence after the Introduction of the National Automated Fingerprint Identification System (NAFIS)*. Home Office Online Report 23/04 at

<http://www.homeoffice.gov.uk/rds/pdfs04/rdsolr2304.pdf>

NBM National Briefing Model. Derived from the NIM. Further information available in ACPO *Guidance on the National Briefing Model* (Centrex/NCPE, Wyboston, 2006).

NCPE National Centre for Policing Excellence. Established as part of the Central Police Training and Development Authority (Part 4, Criminal Justice and Police Act 2001) and absorbed into the National Policing Improvement Agency (section 1 Police and Justice Act 2006). Compiles and publishes good practice doctrine for policing.

Neighbourhood priorities Issues of most concern to a local community or neighbourhood (howsoever defined), identified through community engagement by Neighbourhood Policing Teams.

Neighbourhood profile Created by the Neighbourhood Policing Teams and recording general information about the neighbourhood including key individuals such as community leaders, employment profile, and significant locations. Should inform the strategic assessment in order for potential risks and threats to be identified and addressed within the control strategy.

Neighbourhood Watch Government initiative to foster community spirit and problem-solving in reducing crime.
See <http://www.crimereduction.gov.uk/nbhwatch.htm>.
Also <http://www.neighbourhoodwatch.net/>.

Network Analysis (NIM) Analysis of the associations and interactions between different individual criminals or criminal organizations. Understanding the strengths and weaknesses of such networks identifies opportunities for intervention or infiltration.

NHC National HumInt Centre. HMRC's national centre for human intelligence: eg CHIS-generated intelligence.

NIM National Intelligence Model. A business process intended to provide a framework within which intelligence, prevention, and enforcement priorities are identified and actioned.

The Code of Practice relating to NIM is in the appendices to this volume and is available online.

See ACPO guidance at <http://www.acpo.police.uk/asp/policies/Data/nim2005.pdf>.

NIM Minimum Standards Jointly developed as a good practice and inspection benchmark by ACPO, HMIC, and other partners. Chief Constables are required under the NIM Code of Practice to have implemented NIM to at least the minimum standards.

NIU HMRC's National Intelligence Unit.

NPIA National Policing Improvement Agency. Became operational in 2007, incorporating Centrex, NCPE and the Police Information Technology Organization. <http://www.npia.police.uk>

OCTF Overseas Crime Task Force. Created in 2007 to address international exchange of conviction information.

OCU Operational Command Unit. Alternative label for BCU.

Operational Intelligence Assessments A review process intended to ensure that intelligence/investigation remains focused on primary objectives.

PCSO Police Community Support Officer (also known as a Community Support Officer (CSO)). Police staff with minimal enforcement powers, whose function is to provide high visibility patrolling. See Part 4 of the Police Reform Act 2002, as amended by the Police and Justice Act 2006.
Police Reform Act 2002
<http://www.opsi.gov.uk/acts/acts2002/20020030.htm>
(Explanatory Notes <http://www.opsi.gov.uk/acts/en2002/2002en30.htm>)
Police and Justice Act 2006
<http://www.opsi.gov.uk/acts/acts2006/20060048.htm>
(Explanatory Notes <http://www.opsi.gov.uk/acts/en2006/2006en48.htm>)

People Assets One of the four assets recognized by the NIM. Defined as the right people with the right skills in the right roles.

PESTELO Mnemonic framework model for conducting environmental scanning used to identify emerging trends or issues and potential risks or threats under the following categories: Political, Economic, Social, Technological, Environmental and Organisational.

PLAICE Risk assessment model developed within the Metropolitan Police Service to aid analysis of potential/existing risks specifically in relation to covert operations. A suggested alternative to PPPLEM. Mnemonic based on the following risk categories: Physical, Legal, Assets, Information technology, Compromise, Environment. See R Billingsley 'Risk management: is there a model for covert policing?' *Covert Policing Review* [2006] 98–109.

PLX Police Local Cross-check. Joint ACPO/CRB/PITO initiative intended to facilitate better enhanced disclosure in pre-employment conviction checks.

PNC Police National Computer. Contains information about wanted and convicted persons, lost and stolen property. Linked to the Schengen Information System.

PND Police National Database. At time of writing the planning for this is underway. Recommended by the Bichard Inquiry as a means of ensuring police and partners have access to intelligence about crime and criminals outside their immediate geographical jurisdictions and areas of responsibility. Final architecture and functionality yet to be determined. Key element of the IMPACT programme.

POP Problem-oriented policing: the concept that through SARA analysis (see below) policing can adopt a problem-solving approach to community safety.

See H Goldstein *Problem-Oriented Policing* (McGraw-Hill, New York, 1990); also A Leigh, T Read, and N Tilley *Problem-Oriented Policing: BritPop* (Police Research Group, Crime Detection and Prevention Series Paper 75, Home Office, London, 1996).

POVA Protection of Vulnerable Adults List, maintained by the Department for Education and Skills, documenting persons deemed unsuitable to work with vulnerable adults.

PPPLEM Risk assessment model developed by Deputy Assistant Commissioner John Grieve (Metropolitan Police Service) to aid analysis of potential/existing risks; preliminary to drafting of a risk management strategy. Mnemonic based on the following risk categories: Police/Public, Physical risks, Psychological risks, Legal risks, Economic risks, and Moral risks.

Prevention Priorities (NIM) Linked to Enforcement and Intelligence Priorities. Derived from the Control Strategy and intended to direct the use of resources towards achievement of the Control Strategy through tactics such as preventative analysis, ANPR, CCTV, and collaboration with Neighbourhood Watch.

Problem Profiles (NIM) One of the four intelligence products. Detailed description of a given problem (eg crime series, hot-spots) and associated intelligence enabling lead investigators, SIOs or BCU commanders and partner agencies to identify the most appropriate intervention tactics.

PVS Passport Verification Service.

QAF Quality Assurance Framework. Devised as a CRB compliance tool to set standards for police disclosure units.

Registered Bodies Organizations permitted by the CRB to make pre-employment checks via the disclosure service.

Rehabilitation of Offenders Act 1974 Provides that certain criminal convictions become 'spent' after a specified period and permits disclosure of convictions to an applicant applying for roles working with children or vulnerable adults. The accompanying ROA 1974 (Exceptions) Order defines those jobs which are exempt from ROA provisions.

(Pre 1988 statute texts are not yet available online.)

Results Analysis (NIM) Reflective evaluation of whether a given intervention tactic or strategy has achieved the desired outcome in order to learn lessons of success or failure. Ideally should be undertaken both during and at the end of intelligence, prevention and enforcement operations with the learning then being stored in a searchable and retrievable form in an appropriate form of 'organizational memory'.

RIPA Regulation of Investigatory Powers Act 2000, provides statutory authority for all covert investigation other than interference with property (for which see Part III, Police Act 1997).

    See <http://www.uk-legislation.hmso.gov.uk/acts/acts2000/20000023.htm>.

    See also Police Act 1997, Part III, for statutory authority to interfere with property, which is often necessary to conduct intrusive surveillance: <http://www.uk-legislation.hmso.gov.uk/acts/acts1997/1997050.htm>.

Risk Analysis (NIM) Analysis of the risks posed by individuals or crime types or of other risks faced by the public or organizations, intended to inform tasking and coordination prioritization and operational planning.

SARA An analytical model which forms a crucial element of POP (see above). The mnemonic represents Scanning, Analysis, Response and Assessment, with assessment being another way of labelling results analysis.

SCRO Scottish Criminal Records Office.

Schengen Information System Also known as SIS. Established under Articles 95, and 97–100 of the Schengen Convention 1990. Records information concerning wanted persons, missing persons, extradition, surveillance of persons and objects, and missing/stolen objects. Linked to PNC so that any officer making a check with the PNC automatically also checks the SIS. Likewise, law enforcement officers in the 27 EU Member States (together with Schengen associate States: Norway, Iceland, and Switzerland) checking their PNC equivalent will automatically check the relevant categories of information alerts on the UK PNC. SIS II currently being debated and developed. Intended to have the capacity to record additional information including biometric data.

Secret Intelligence Service See MI6 above.

Security Service See MI5 above.

SID Scottish Intelligence Database.

Signal Crimes Any crime or episode that influences public perception about their safety and so induces a change in behaviour.

    See M Innes and N Fielding (2002) 'From community to communicative policing: signal crimes and the problem of public reassurance' *Sociological Research Online* 7/2 at <http://www.socresonline.org.uk/7/2/innes.html>. Also ACPO (2005) *Practice Advice on Professionalising the Business of Neighbourhood Policing* NCPE Centrex, p 24.

SIO Senior Investigating Officer.

Sirene Gateway mechanism to the Schengen Information System. The UK Sirene bureau was formerly housed within NCIS and is now located within SOCA. The Sirene bureau undertakes all international communication relating to the SIS.

SIS /SIS II See Schengen Information System (above).

SMART Acronym describing the characteristics required in performance target-setting: Specific, Measurable, Achievable, Relevant, and Timely.

SOCA Serious Organised Crime Agency (UK), became operational on 1 April 2006. See <http://www.soca.gov.uk>.
  Relevant legislation at <http://www.uk-legislation.hmso.gov.uk/acts/acts2005/20050015.htm>.

Source assets One of the 11 areas of assessment criteria for NIM implementation, for example appropriate resources and procedures for dealing with victims and witnesses; prisoners; Crimestoppers; CHIS; undercover/test purchase officers; forensic data; surveillance product.

Strategic Assessment (NIM) One of the four NIM intelligence products, produced by intelligence unit analysts in order to inform and drive strategic tasking and coordination.

Subject Profiles (NIM) One of the four NIM intelligence products, produced by intelligence unit analysts pursuant to control strategy priorities or emerging high risk issues in order to assist lead investigators, SIOs, or BCU commanders and partner agencies in identifying the most appropriate intervention tactics. Formerly known as Target Profiles.

SWOT Strengths, Weaknesses, Threats, Opportunities: a framework for environmental scanning and for identifying organizational capacity and capability gaps.

System assets One of the 11 areas of assessment criteria for NIM implementation. For example physical security; security policies (confidentiality, vetting, integrity standards); implementation of sterile corridor concept; authorities processes and documentation management systems in place; effective briefings; effective debriefings; interagency information sharing protocols.

Tactical Assessments (NIM) One of the four NIM intelligence products, produced by intelligence unit analysts in order to inform and drive tactical tasking and coordination.

Tactical Menu Options for intervention divided into four themes: targeting offenders; management of hot-spots; investigation of linked/serial incidents; and implementation of crime prevention measures.

Tactical Options These are divided into three generic areas of activity: prevention, intelligence, and enforcement.

Tactical Plan The outcome of the weekly Intelligence Unit Meeting: 'the collective term for the prevention, intelligence and enforcement plans that form part of the problem or subject profile.'
ACPO/NCPE *Practice Advice on Tasking and Co-ordination* 2006 p 82.

Tasking and Coordination (NIM) Occurs at both the strategic and tactical levels within the NIM.

The strategic tasking and co-ordination considers the strategic assessment in order to set a control strategy (at either BCU or force level) within which context tactical tasking and co-ordination takes place. It prioritizes the intelligence requirement and resource allocation.

Tactical tasking and co-ordination is informed by the fortnightly tactical assessment. Prioritizes intervention (based on tactical options) pursuant to the overall control strategy. Reviews and amends as required the intelligence requirement.

Target Profiles (NIM) See Subject Profiles above.

VBS Vetting and Barring Scheme. Addresses Bichard Recommendation 19 for the registering of those who wish to work with children or vulnerable adults. Registration signifies that there is no known reason to prevent an individual working with these groups. Established under the Safeguarding Vulnerable Groups Act 2006.

ViSOR Violent and Sex Offenders Register.

WMD Weapons of Mass Destruction.

1

Intelligence in Context

1.1 **Introduction**

In their previous collaboration, *Covert Investigation*, the first book within the Blackstone's Practical Policing Series, the present authors drew upon their operational and managerial experience within the Police Service to address an obvious gap in the available literature. They wrote the book that they needed as covert investigation practitioners and would have bought if it had already been written. In this collaboration they are once again drawing upon their own practitioner experience but in a different context because there is a significant body of literature (including practitioner doctrine and good practice guidance) on the subject of intelligence, written from a variety of perspectives. The thematic select bibliography at the end of this volume is but a small sample of what is available. How much of it is ever accessed by practitioners is a moot point. For the curious and committed, university degrees are now offered in intelligence studies and counter-terrorism intelligence in particular has, unsurprisingly, attracted considerable practitioner, academic and, above all, political attention since the watershed events in New York of 9 September 2001.

The brief for this volume was to write a book on intelligence for policing practitioners. The authors interpreted that as policing with a small 'p': policing in its widest sense of regulating behaviour and activity in order to achieve general safety and well-being. Just as the police service is actually a minority provider of policing services, so police officers are a minority of those involved in policing. This book is not an attempt to replicate, reproduce, or replace the Police Service doctrine and guidance produced by the National Policing Improvement Agency (NPIA) and its precursor constituent elements (although where appropriate that doctrine and guidance has been cited). Although written by police practitioners drawing upon their operational experience, this book speaks to the wider policing family that includes not only the extended police family of support staff including Police Community Support Officers (PCSOs) but also partner agencies. In doing so, it is to be hoped that those outside the family yet interested in the subject area, for instance the academic audience and the wider community, will also find this a thought-provoking contribution to the intelligence literature.

The writing of this book has been an exercise in reflective thinking and the documenting of experiential learning. As such the final product goes beyond what was originally envisaged when the original proposal was submitted for peer review and is the better for it. The lesson of which the authors have been repeatedly reminded whilst endeavouring to compact the essence from a vast subject area into the available word limit, is that intelligence is not about information gathering; it is about information management. Organizations that structure their capability around information gathering rather than information management will quickly discover that capability to acquire information does not correspond with capacity to manage or use that information. A crucial trap to be avoided is that of 'naïve empiricism': the belief that more information will automatically lead to individuals and organizations becoming better informed (Gill 2000: 211).

The technology labelled 'Echelon', for instance, captures all communications sent via satellite, copying them to computerized analytical systems scanning for key words, which identify communications of interest for human analysts to examine and follow up as required. Passive data acquisition through electronic banking, CCTV systems, door entry swipe card systems, to name but a few, generates information overload (Sheptycki 2004). Undoubtedly authorities are better informed (simply because they have access to ever-increasing amounts of information), but the 'vast volume' of data that it is now possible to gather as information is capable of paralyzing analytical effort when trying to translate it into intelligence (Andregg 2007: 59).

So it is about intelligence as a function of information management that this book has been written. It does *not* purport to be the definitive practitioner guide. The subject area is too vast for that to be attempted in this sort of book (or perhaps in any other sort of book). But it does seek to broaden practitioner horizons with relevant academic commentary of which they might not otherwise be aware. By the same token, it may assist academics to engage with an extended practitioner perspective that is not necessarily captured through research interviews or observational fieldwork.

This book aims to provide a context for intelligence for those working in or studying the myriad of functions that fall under the umbrella label of policing. No apology is made for using police operational experience as a foundation for this work, but every effort has been made to highlight relevance beyond the Police Service. The practitioner audience envisaged for this book is not confined to police officers.

The structure of the book begins, in academic parlance, with a literature review of thematic inspections and some reflective thinking that has been undertaken in a variety of public inquiries into the function of intelligence. Having thus set the scene to illustrate why what follows is important, there is a discussion of what is understood by the label 'intelligence'; what sources of information are available to feed into the intelligence process; and the business process that has been defined for the police service enthusiastically, and perhaps erroneously, termed the National Intelligence Model. The discussion then moves on to the legal framework within which information gatherers and processors operate before considering the risks involved in such work and how these might be managed and mitigated. The book concludes with consideration of how intelligence-led interventions might be planned, the processing of intelligence, and it concludes with a reflective framework which can assist organizations and individuals with intelligence responsibilities to check their implementation of intelligence-led activity. These are all areas of learning that the authors have encountered during their own roles within the policing intelligence profession. The sub-title to this volume attempts to encompass the breadth of possible perspectives on intelligence in order to engage with particular audience communities amongst practitioners and academics. There are others of course, but title convention precludes further itemization. Suffice it to say that investigation and problem-solving, community safety, and partnership-working are the backdrop against which the thematic chapters are set.

'Intelligence-led policing', like all sound-bites, has its limitations when trying to convey concepts and understanding. The word *'intelligence'* does not necessarily enjoy a consensus of meaning (ch 3 below, and see also Sohi and Harfield, forthcoming). *'Led'* invests in the concept of intelligence an authority and a certainty that it may not always warrant. *'Policing'*, as already alluded to, is an all-embracing term for a variety of activities performed by a variety of agencies. Yet it is generally interpreted exclusively, in reference to the activities of the public Police Service, rather than as a reference to all public and private entities involved in activities that would be covered under the umbrella of policing label (the private policing and security sector is larger in terms of personnel employed than the public Police Service for example (Johnston 1992)).

The events leading up to the invasion of Iraq, together with subsequent episodes in the 'war against terror', have exposed intelligence work to public debate in unprecedented fashion. In the glare of publicity intelligence has been shown to be wrong, incomplete, misinterpreted, or to have been used in an unwarranted way. Political decisions about military intervention in foreign sovereign regimes may seem far removed from day-to-day community safety and policing through partnership but in the mind of the public, 'intelligence' is 'intelligence' (and often 'spying') no matter what the theatre of operations and its use discredited (rightly or wrongly) in one arena reflects adversely on the intelligence profession elsewhere (see also Andregg 2007). Why then, would anyone think that 'intelligence-led policing' was a good idea?

1.2 **Intelligence-Led Policing?**

What is intelligence-led policing in any case? As a phrase it seems to have been coined during a period of sustained reform of UK police reform in the 1990s but as a general concept, as the quote below illustrates, it has a more ancient pedigree.

Further information and reading

Police work is impossible without information, and every good officer will do his best to obtain reliable intelligence, taking care at the same time not to be lead away on false issues. Information must not be treasured up, until opportunity offers for action by the officer who obtains it, but should be promptly communicated to a superior, and those who are in a position to act upon it. Not only is this the proper course of action to take, in the public interest, but it will be certainly recognised, both by authorities and comrades, promoting esteem and confidence, which will bring their own reward.

(Vincent *Police Code and General Manual of the Criminal Law,* 1881, 202)

At its simplest, 'intelligence-led' conveys the relatively obvious notion that policing activity (be it focused on community safety, the investigation of crime, the regulation of trading standards, the collection of customs and excise, or organizational priorities expressed in terms of intelligence requirement, prevention, enforcement, and reassurance) should be informed and directed rather than undertaken randomly: so far, so much common sense.

What have emerged in the last decade are practitioner, policy-maker, and academic discourses about how best intelligence and policing should be structured. In a joined up world one might have expected a single discourse with contributions from all three participant groups but unfortunately that is not how the literature reads.

The debate sits within a wider context. Information, particularly in digitized form, has become the new economic and social driving force—as well as a policing tool capable of greater exploitation than ever before (Petersen's introduction to and description of the science of surveillance technologies, for instance, runs to over 1000 pages, 2007). To adopt and adapt an archaeological taxonomy of tool type, humanity has moved on from the Stone Age, the Bronze Age, the Iron Age and the Steam Age into the Information Age. As society changes so, too, must the policing of it. Intelligence-led policing would appear to be, in part and in its widest sense, about harnessing and structuring that potential.

Besides potential, practicalities also have to be addressed. The era of intelligence-led policing emerged from the era of new managerialism. For some intelligence-led policing is therefore primarily about meeting performance targets whilst achieving value for money and achieving more from resources, which, many people argue, are not keeping pace with rising demand. Doubts about whether intelligence-led policing is or is not a performance management regime, at least in the eye of those with governance responsibilities, will be quickly dispelled on reference to a paper jointly authored and published by the Home Office and Association of Police Authorities—*Police Performance Management: Practical Guidance for Police Authorities* (2006). 'NIM [the National Intelligence Model] is a business process for policing activity. . . . Police authority members and officers should have some familiarity with the principles of NIM, and, in particular, the Strategic Assessment, because of their important role planning and driving operational performance' (Home Office/APA 2006, 15). If police authority members and officers happen to be reading this book alongside the *Practical Guidance*, it is to be hoped that they will acquire 'some familiarity' with all the other issues pertinent to intelligence-led policing, of which the NIM is but a small part.

Others, including a leading architect of the current age of intelligence-led policing, attribute a far narrower meaning. In a 1998 lecture delivered at the police college Bramshill, attended by the authors, Sir David Philips (then Chief Constable of Kent County Constabulary) argued that the role of intelligence-led policing lay in supporting criminal detection and in rehabilitating and raising the occupational status of the detective who, in Sir David's opinion as expressed at the time, had been rather denigrated by the focus on uniformed community

policing during the 1980s and early 1990s. In this guise intelligence-led policing is presented as serving and supporting the evidence-gathering by detectives
that will achieve successful prosecutions. Such an interpretation brings with
it perceptions of a hierarchical relationship which has organizational cultural
implications, which can result in unintended consequences.

Sir David Philips makes the point that criminals are rendered vulnerable by
the fact that their criminality is rarely random. If behaviour is not random then
it is patterned. From this structure and from the movement of criminals, their
lifestyle, capability, and intent may be inferred and so intervention options
identified. In this interpretation intelligence-led policing is about identifying
criminal capability, assessing criminal intention, and then managing interventions against these two features in a timely fashion. It is an approach that could
be adapted by other enforcement and regulatory agencies responsible for investigating specific offending. But is such a narrow focus making the best use of
intelligence?

Three rather different takes in intelligence-led policing are discussed. And
these are just examples to illustrate the possible tiers of interpretation. They do
not constitute a definitive and exclusive catalogue.

1.3 Is there an Intelligence Profession within Policing?

It is possible to view the Police Service as a collection of professions: community/
neighbourhood policing; roads policing; criminal investigation; scene examination to name some of the more obvious. Other agencies whose functions include
activities that fall under the umbrella of 'policing' have their own professions.
Given that policing is supposed to be intelligence-led, and that police forces in
England and Wales are supposed to have implemented the NIM, it might be supposed that an intelligence profession has come into existence. There is evidence
to suggest that it has not.

It follows that an organization that aspires to be intelligence-led should invest
appropriately in equipment and specialist training for intelligence staff and at
least awareness training for their colleagues. Frontline staff regularly engaging
with the public, from whom most intelligence will be gleaned, will need to be able
to employ user-friendly systems to facilitate the capture and recording of intelligence. Such investment is not always apparent. In one policing organization, and
following the much-heralded implementation of the NIM, training for specialist
intelligence unit staff was initially ranked 248th in a list of training priorities
whilst intelligence awareness training for frontline staff featured not at all. Policy
without resources becomes mere rhetoric, in which circumstance frontline staff
can only derive knowledge and learning tacitly through their peers.

Intelligence-led policing as a means of achieving value for money has already
been discussed. How intelligence units are staffed and resourced can seriously
undermine value for money. For example, specialist computer training is required

for intelligence staff: because they will be working with a number of different restricted access databases including the Police National Computer (PNC). Such training incurs cost. Anecdotal evidence from different police forces indicates that intelligence departments are sometimes seen as a convenient place in which temporarily to situate staff confined to 'light duties'. This form of human resource management incurs significant additional costs for the intelligence department and the organization as a whole. Either the staff temporarily assigned will have to be trained on the myriad systems, which will incur a repeated direct cost for little return, or else they will have to try to perform their temporary duties without the necessary training being provided (and consequently without access to some of the restricted databases), in which case there will be two forms of immediate opportunity cost:

- reduced capacity and capability in the processing of information into intelligence within the department; and
- reduced output for both proactive and reactive investigators for whom the intelligence department is a source of both information and intelligence.

There are consequences for staff welfare and morale which generate a longer-term opportunity cost. Neither the temporarily assigned staff unable to carry out all the work required, nor the permanent (and presumably trained) staff of the intelligent department who will have to carry the extra burden of reduced skills capability, respond well to such circumstances, a further drain on motivation and productivity. Members of staff who do not feel valued are unlikely to add value themselves.

In terms of equipping intelligence units with appropriately-trained and skilled staff, this evidence suggests that intelligence has yet to be widely viewed as a profession within the police service.

Such an interpretation is reinforced with the research into the work of analysts within the Police Service undertaken by Cope and discussed in greater detail in Chapter 9.1 below. To this anthropological data may be added further anecdotal evidence corroborated through repeated instances. One Basic Command Unit intelligence manager was advised by a senior officer not to 'stay more than a few months in intelligence as it won't look good on your CV, nor will it contribute anything useful to your next [promotion] board. You won't be able to tick any of the promotion boxes by working in intelligence'. Others performing similar intelligence roles revealed that this advice had been offered to them as well. For a service supposedly intelligence-led, this is hardly a positive promotion by senior managers of the role of intelligence. Yet, funnily enough, colleagues both senior and junior in rank apparently felt it necessary to prepare for their own promotion boards by visiting intelligence department managers for a briefing on the NIM and what the intelligence department did, which reveals that it was an area of policing that they thought they ought probably to mention in a promotion board, but about which such information as had been provided by the organization had previously failed to grab their attention.

Taken together all this is evidence of a lack of professional understanding. By definition therefore the concept of an intelligence profession within the Police Service is not well established. In some cases this lack of understanding is documented in the most ironic of ways: for instance, in one organization staff appraisal performance criteria measured intelligence unit and dedicated source unit staff (informant handlers) in terms of arrests made, case files sent for prosecution and prisoner interviews conducted. None of which are functions that intelligence or dedicated source unit staff would expect to perform amongst their routine duties. If human resources departments do not understand the work of intelligence staff or, worse, define it in terms of activities actually undertaken by other professions within the police service, little wonder that intelligence may not yet enjoy the status of a profession.

This highlights a further issue. Intelligence-led policing is not just something the intelligence unit or the proactive investigation unit undertakes. The rhetoric demands that the whole organization undertakes or supports intelligence-led policing. If the support services are not geared to supporting intelligence-led policing (and inappropriate appraisal frameworks are an indicator that they are not), the organization will struggle to deliver intelligence-led policing. To this theme the book returns in Chapter 10 below.

This book seeks to promote a better understanding of the role of the intelligence profession within policing. By extension, it hopes to promote a similar improved understanding amongst partner agencies that will be working with police forces.

1.4 **Promoting the Professional Ethic**

Promoting understanding in order to achieve professional recognition can be reinforced through acknowledging professional standards that have to be met. Here the police service has a number of ready-made frameworks to assist and it is important to distinguish between intelligence work that supports policing and intelligence work that supports aggressive military action for instance where the rules of engagement are rather different (Andregg 2007). Policing does not operate in a world where the ends justify the means.

Some of the ready-made governance frameworks that apply to policing will also encompass partner agencies working with the police. First, there is the Police Code of Conduct. Secondly there is the statutory framework regarding the acquisition and use of information, discussed in greater detail in Chapter 6 below. Thirdly, there is the overarching framework of human rights legislation in which intelligence work operates (see C Harfield and K Harfield, *Covert Investigation* (Oxford University Press, Oxford) ch 1).

Intelligence processing and management requires a secure professional environment, and a professional approach to risk management (discussed in Chapter 7 below) naturally gives rise to appropriate arrangements.

Promoting the professionalism of intelligence work within the Police Service involves more than just using the NIM business process (see Chapter 5 below). It involves recognizing the skills required to gather information and analyse intelligence and investing in them. It involves recognition of the fact that intelligence is a holistic discipline to which the whole organization contributes and in which all staff have a role to play directly or indirectly.

The governance of intelligent management does not simply reside within statute law. Senior executives in organizations utilizing intelligence management have responsibility for ensuring the appropriate and professional use of information gathering and intelligence analysis. Chapter 10 below offers for consideration a possible framework upon which to base intelligence governance within individual organizations.

In terms of establishing and consolidating intelligence professionalism, some basic principles, drawn from informal discussions with a variety of colleagues in different jurisdictions, can be proposed for further debate:

1. Intelligence work must be lawful, for a legitimate purpose, necessary, and proportionate.
2. Staff throughout the organization must be appropriately aware, trained, and equipped for their role within the intelligence management process (be it information gathering through general activities and routine interaction; information gathering through directed intelligence operations including covert operations; analysis; management; or strategic policy-making).
3. Security and confidentiality are essential in establishing an effective and professional intelligence environment.
4. Organizational and partnership activity should be based on knowledge of problems and their context, to which understanding intelligence contributes.
5. Intelligence serves no purpose if it is not used.
6. The effective use of intelligence as a tool requires objectivity and open-mindedness on both the part of the analyst and the subsequent user.

1.5 **Conclusion**

Information-gathering and the subsequent analysis to generate intelligence does not operate with a vacuum. The current (2007) political expectation of the police service in the UK is that it will be intelligence-led. This is reinforced with a prescribed business process called the National Intelligence Model (see Ch 5 below) that police forces in England and Wales are expected to have implemented and which other agencies are encouraged to adopt. A statutory framework for information acquisition, processing, and retention structures the work, defining remit and responsibilities. Promoting the professionalism necessary in intelligence work involves recognition of the fact that intelligence is a holistic discipline to which the whole organization contributes and in which all staff have a role to play directly or indirectly.

Is intelligence-led policing the future? A new phrase is beginning to enjoy some currency: knowledge-based policing. It has been used in connection with combating serious and organized crime (senior director, Serious Organized Crime Agency, personal communication 2005) and with improving community policing (Assistant Chief of Police, Norway, 2007). Time will tell whether this is just a new sound-bite or whether it is a concept with substance. It is possible, like intelligence-led policing, that it will come to mean different things to different people. But the fact that various practitioners are talking about knowledge-based policing as the next step beyond intelligence-led policing indicates increasingly widespread recognition that intelligence-led policing as it is currently understand and implemented can be enhanced and improved upon.

As a label knowledge-based policing could serve to demystify. The 'intelligence' label, inevitably, brings with it connotations of James Bond and the world of spies. A number of advocates argue that intelligence-led policing could do worse than adopt a militaristic approach to intelligence, although intelligence to support war effort seems, on the face of it, an inappropriate approach to policing peaceful society. Knowledge is a term that could embrace partners more readily in problem-solving and resolution delivery, especially those partner agencies who would not necessarily identify with the concept and imagery of 'intelligence'. 'Knowledge-based harm reduction' or 'knowledge-based community safety' could be terms more embracing still.

As a contribution to the debate it is suggested here that knowledge-based policing could be viewed as a mode of intervention interaction. As a business process for policing, the NIM envisages three generic strategic priority requirements arising from each strategic assessment: enforcement, intelligence, and prevention. These are derived from three key policing (in its widest, multi-agency sense) activities which generate intervention options: investigation, community-engagement, and partnership. Figure 1.1 illustrates the relationships between the strategic priority requirements and the activities generating intervention options as a mode of intervention interaction. In the overlapping shaded area, the combination of requirements and intervention options will be drawing upon a breadth of experience, expertise, capacity, and capability that policing ceases to be an intelligence-led discovery process and becomes a knowledge-based resolution process.

It could be argued that here the discussion is one of semantics, but perception is all-important in promoting acceptance and understanding. A decade into the era of intelligence-led policing, there is enough evidence in various forms to suggest that the police service has not yet fully embraced the intelligence profession. If a different form of words encourages new ways of thinking, then the delivery of more effective policing to achieve safer communities and reduce the risk of harms will benefit.

And intelligence is not so much a way of working as a way of thinking. This book seeks to introduce to practitioners and partners at all levels, the breadth of consideration involved in intelligence work within policing. It starts with a decade of lesson learning.

Figure 1.1 Mode of intervention interaction

The shaded area signifies the combination of effort and intervention that comprises knowledge-based policing/community safety.

Further information and reading

Andregg M 'Intelligence ethics: laying a foundation for the second oldest profession' in L Johnson (ed) *Handbook of Intelligence Studies* (Routledge, London, 2007) 52–63

Cope N 'Intelligence-led policing or policing-led intelligence?' *British Journal of Criminology* 44 188–203 (2004)

Gill P *Rounding Up the Usual Suspects? Developments in Contemporary Law Enforcement Intelligence* (Ashgate, Aldershot, 2000)

Johnston L *The Rebirth of Private Policing* (Routledge, London, 1992)

Petersen J *Understanding Surveillance Technologies: Spy Devices, Privacy, History and Applications* (2nd edn, Auerbach Publications, Boca Raton, New York, 2007)

Sheptycki J 'Organizational pathologies in police intelligence systems: some contributions to the lexicon of intelligence-led policing' *European Journal of Criminology* 1 307–32 (2004)

Sohi K and Harfield C 'Intelligence and the Division of Linguistic Labour in C Harfield, A MacVean, J Grieve, and D Phillips (eds) *The Handbook of Intelligent Policing: Consilience, Crime Control, and Community Safety* (Oxford University Press, Oxford, 2008)

Outside the Pyramid: Intelligence in Practice

2.1 **Introduction**

The need to undertake reflective thinking has been a feature of many of the police training courses attended by the authors. It is firmly embedded in the gospel of good management and good practice. In the form of results analysis, reflective thinking is written into the National Intelligence Model (NIM). Yet generally it seems to be a practice that often succumbs to time pressures imposed by the 'jobs waiting' queue in the control room and by the ceaseless emerging of new issues or spontaneous incidents requiring command attention: desirable rather than essential. Results analysis, of course, is not an end in itself. The conclusions drawn must be fed back into the planning of future activity. The next results analysis then questions what has been done differently and whether it has worked. And so the reflective cycle begins again.

In recent years some very public reflective thinking about intelligence issues has been forced upon the police service and other agencies in the form of independent enquiries following trauma and tragedy, or arising from widespread public suspicions given voice in the media concerning the nature and use of intelligence in informing the political decision to invade Iraq in 2003. Reliance on inquiries as a vehicle for reflection is less than satisfactory. Such learning about intelligence inevitably inclines to the specific and episodic rather than holistic and evolutionary contemplation, and it creates the vulnerability that responses to address specific issues raised by a particular inquiry may by-pass wider matters of contextual relevance. This chapter seeks to capture the salient points from various recent official reports and inquiries into the use and application of intelligence in its various forms, as a foundation for reflection underpinning the discussions in subsequent chapters. Starting with the work of HMIC on intelligence issues, the chapter then considers the work of independent inquiries.

2.2 **HMIC Reports on Intelligence Issues**

Her Majesty's Inspectorate of Constabulary (HMIC), for 150 years the body ensuring good practice in policing, has only concentrated effort on intelligence issues in the last 10 years. Three relevant thematic reports are discussed here, and in each section the paragraph references relate to the particular report at that time under discussion.

2.2.1 **In the beginning:** *Policing with Intelligence* **(1997)**

With the benefit of a decade's hindsight, HMIC's report *Policing with Intelligence* (1997) may seem today a little naïve. That the authors felt it necessary to make one particular assertion in the report is certainly noteworthy: 'it is widely acknowledged that law enforcement operations are far more likely to be effective if directed by accurate information' (paragraph 1.13). The inclusion of what might now be considered at best a clichéd conventional wisdom if not the downright obvious, suggests that at the time—1997—this may still have been an argument that needed to be made in some quarters. A document of its time, *Policing with Intelligence* represented the first attempt within the police service to start to articulate a definitive concept of intelligence-led policing from the various ideas on the subject that were circulating in the 1990s. In that respect it was groundbreaking.

It was also direction setting, as might be expected of an HMIC thematic inspection, within a context that demonstrated three significant, defining characteristics.

The first of these was the then imminent embodiment of two innovations, the National Criminal Intelligence Service (NCIS) and the National Crime Squad (NCS), founded upon the premise that these two brand new independent organizations would manifest intelligence-led policing. With their creation came the need to cement their working relationship as national entities with a police service otherwise entirely local, to the point almost of being parochial, in character. Hence the report conceptualized intelligence in terms of a pyramid hierarchy of police organizational structures rather than in terms of policing functions (paragraphs 2.1 and 2.2), emphasizing that 'the logical apex of this pyramid is not law enforcement agency territory at all, but is rather the work of national governments who co-operate on the basis of negotiated treaties'.

Secondly, in following the lead of four Audit Commission reports (*Tackling Crime Effectively*, vols I and II 1994, 1996; and *Tackling Patrol Effectively* 1996; which themselves built on the earlier *Helping with Enquiries* 1983) HMIC situated the concept of intelligence-led policing firmly within the context of the contemporary government crusade for public sector reform and enhanced managerialism in the police service (paragraphs 1.19–1.21). Performance measures were the means recommended by HMIC 'to reflect the importance of the concept, as the philosophy of intelligence driven activity expands into all areas of policing' (paragraph 6.6, see Table 2.1 below). This might be described, more accurately, as intelligence-led management rather than intelligence-led policing.

Thirdly, HMIC accepted the military context of intelligence as the framework model for policing intelligence. This was achieved almost subliminally through a literary device—the preface quote. The quote used by HMIC comes from a Chinese military strategist Sun Tzu and is detailed in the case study box below. As quoted the reference appears apposite, even seductive, but it is an interpretative translation. Two other translations are included below by way of comparison. A number of lessons can be drawn from this. Intelligence, as will be seen in Chapter 3, might be viewed as information translated through analysis. Translations vary, allowing flexible interpretation. Reader beware! Given the purpose of the quote as used in *Policing with Intelligence*, how likely is it that HMIC would have used either the Clavell or Sawyer translations (see case study below)? Their interpretations are subtly different and not as well suited to the purposes that HMIC wanted to put the quote to.

And whilst there is no need to reinvent the wheel, is it always appropriate to borrow paradigms from entirely different functional theatres? Military intervention and policing are very different functions, as typified by the need in post-conflict reconstruction (eg Kosovo, Sierra Leone, East Timor) for the military to hand over to civilian police detachments once the 'hot war' is over and peace needs to be created or supported. With adopted paradigms come adopted presumptions. And even if the intention is to *adapt* a paradigm, rather than *adopt*, those not privy to the original intention might subsequently assume adoption and the presumptions that come with it, rather than realize that adaptation was intended and with it, a new set of presumptions. Paradigm and presumption influence perception and interpretation. With a stretch and political spin, 'the war against terrorism' and the 'fight against organized crime' might directly borrow military interventions but is an intelligence paradigm developed for war the most appropriate approach to adopt in informing community safety and neighbourhood policing through partnership and consent?

Case study—Borrowing an intelligence paradigm

HMIC prefaced *Policing With Intelligence* with the following quote, attributed to Sun Tzu *The Art of War* (ca 490 BC/2,500 BP), although HMIC did not cite the edition or translation source.

> Hence, in the work of the entire force:
> Nothing should be regarded as favourably as Intelligence;
> Nothing should be as generously rewarded as Intelligence;
> Nothing should be as confidential as the work of Intelligence.
> Subtly, very subtly, nowhere neglect the use of Intelligence. It is called the Divine Web. It is the treasure of the Ruler.

In the translation edited by James Clavell (*The Art of War: Sun Tzu*, Hodder & Stoughton, London, 1981) the same passages, drawn from Chapter XII, 'The Use of Spies', are rendered rather differently.

> v 14—Hence it is that with none in the whole army are more intimate relations to be maintained than with spies. None should be more liberally rewarded. In no other business should greater secrecy be preserved.
> [...]
> v 18—Be subtle! Be subtle! And use your spies for every kind of business.

Likewise Ralph Sawyer's translation (*The Art of the Warrior: Leadership and Strategy from the Chinese Military Classics*, Shambhala, Boston, 1996, 120):

> Thus of all the Three Armies' affairs no relationship is closer than with spies; no rewards are more generous than those given to spies, no affairs are more secret than those pertaining to spies. [. . .] It is subtle, subtle! There are no areas in which one does not employ spies.

The original Chinese script is open to considerable interpretation so that the case can be argued for any of the above translations—the authors are grateful to John Grieve for exploring this issue for us and for sharing his knowledge and expertise on Sun Tzu. Perhaps unintentionally what HMIC has done by choosing the translation it did, abbreviating and conflating the text, is illustrate how information can be variously interpreted into intelligence that can deliver very different messages. It is a salutatory, if unwitting, lesson in using intelligence.

What were the implications of these founding characteristics?

The authoritative weight of an HMIC thematic inspection report is significant. The explicit and implicit paradigms and presumptions defined in *Policing with Intelligence* have strongly influenced police thinking about intelligence for a decade. In doing so, other avenues of approach or consideration may have been forestalled or abandoned as the conventional wisdom was created. It begs the question, how much unfettered thought went into intelligence-led policing at the outset?

In promoting the conceptualization of intelligence as conforming to the police organizational pyramid hierarchy—a concept familiar enough to a disciplined, rank-based service—was HMIC unwittingly sowing the seeds of constrained thinking? Such a model certainly places the police service as subordinate to the Security Service and Secret Intelligence Service at the top of the pyramid when in fact the latter two organizational functions, being significantly different from policing (and having only a tangential statutory responsibility to assist in *serious and organized* crime if required), should perhaps have located them as lateral partners (see figure 2.1). A consequence of this vision was that when the Security Service and Secret Intelligence Service came to review the national intelligence environment and the contribution of the police service to criminal intelligence, the police service was in a disadvantaged position in terms of responding to the very strong criticism of police intelligence made by the other agencies (the *Spedding Report*: 'Spedding Report highlights intelligence turf wars that stop gangs being brought to justice' The Independent 28 August 2001). It could be argued that the *Spedding Report* provided part of the founding rationale for the subsequent abolition of NCIS and its merger with other agencies into the Serious Organised Crime Agency (SOCA) led by a former MI5 Director General.

Figure 2.1 The national intelligence infrastructure pyramid as perceived in 1997

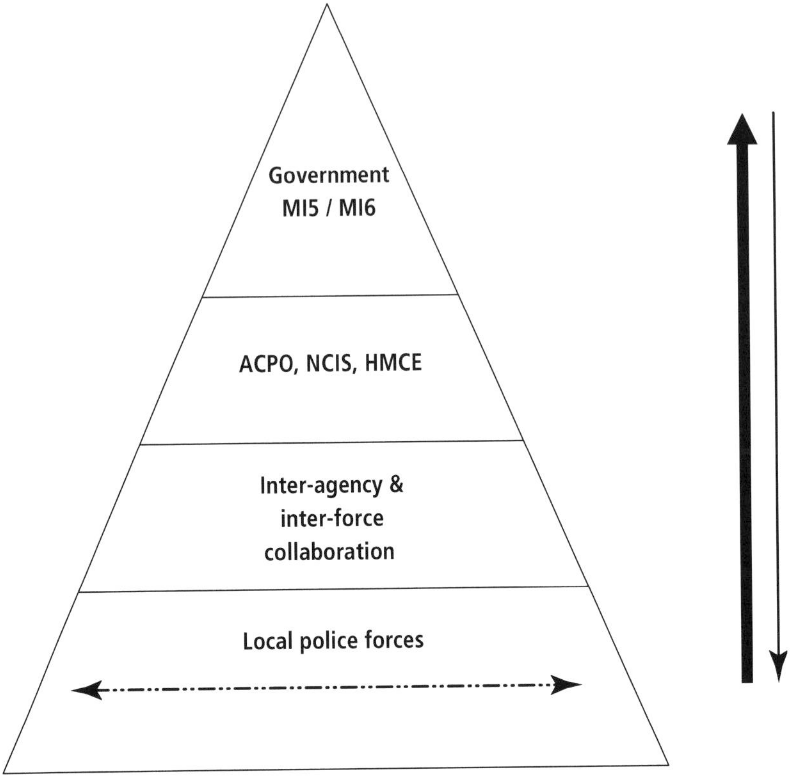

Government
MI5 / MI6

ACPO, NCIS, HMCE

Inter-agency &
inter-force
collaboration

Local police forces

Perceived information flows in a rigid pyramid hierarchy. Most intelligence flowing upwards. Some downward dissemination. Inconsistent lateral exchange.

Looking down the hierarchy rather than up, *Policing with Intelligence* focused on promoting and selling the benefits of NCIS, and to a lesser extent the NCS, to the wider police service. The political need to do this is understandable given the radical innovation of national policing agencies. But consequently there may be perceived a disproportionate emphasis in the report on intelligence issues in relation to serious organized crime when compared with the almost coincidental references to intelligence for local policing. There is no reference at all to 'community intelligence'.

The immediate and diverting effect was not only to conceptualize intelligence in terms of police force structures rather than in terms of policing function but also to establish at the outset that police service intelligence functions not focused on the detection of (serious) crime were lower down the hierarchy of apparent importance than criminal intelligence, even though the detection of crime was just one of several significant policing functions contributing to overall community safety, and one that historically has occupied less police time than other policing functions.

HMIC made the point explicitly that there was a need for two-way communication vertically and laterally within the pyramid structure (paragraph 2.1) but a pyramid being the shape it is, there is significant distance, and consequently greatest communication vulnerability, between the elements at the top and the bottom and the elements at either side of the horizontal strata. Information flows in a hierarchy tend to be upwards rather than downwards. They tend to be confined to single agencies: the pyramid does not seem a helpful model with which to promote partnership working. Lateral communication channels are at their greatest stretch (with greatest gap potential), at the widest point of the pyramid, the exchange of intelligence between local policing areas between police and local partner agencies; the community safety level where most intelligence exists and the greatest need (and partnership) potential for intelligence exchange resides. The current dilemma in 2007 about how to engage the national security agencies with local community intelligence in order to understand and counter radicalization associated with the al-Qaida terrorist movement is a consequence of the de facto communication inhibitors created by the pyramid conceptual model of intelligence management. To this example of the vertical intelligence communication gap can be added the horizontal example about communication failings in the vetting of Ian Huntley prior to his appointment as school caretaker at Soham (see discussion of the *Bichard Report* below). In examining the role of Special Branch, HMIC found both lateral and vertical communication gaps both within Special Branch, between Special Branch offices, and between Special Branch, police colleagues, and partners (HMIC *A Need to Know* 2003, paragraphs 2.59, 3.35).

That there should be de facto inhibitors defying the multi-directional information flows envizaged by HMIC is in part due to the mixed organizational culture of a UK police service divided into at least 52 component parts (the public police forces) even before specialist police forces and other public agency partners are factored into the equation. HMIC recognized that the independence and autonomy of forces 'was bound to result in diversity in procedures', although it was hoped the report would 'encourage' the standardisation of good practice (paragraph 1.25). Nowhere was this prescience proved more accurate than in the subsequent implementation of the NIM (see Ch 5 below).

Policing and community safety incorporates functions beyond the detection of criminal offences and identification of offenders. Intelligence for policing and community safety goes far wider in concept than intelligence for criminal detection. Yet it was criminal intelligence upon which HMIC focused with the very first paragraph of the executive summary:

> Good quality intelligence is the lifeblood of the modern police service. It allows for a clear understanding of crime and criminality, identifies which criminals are active, which crimes are linked and where problems are likely to occur. It enables valuable resources to be targeted effectively against current challenges and emerging trends, ensuring the best opportunities for positive intervention and maximum value for money. (*Policing with Intelligence* 1997, p 1)

Such an approach was entirely consistent with Audit Commission messages about effective policing through enhanced detection dating as far back as 1983 and *Helping with Enquiries*, which advocated focusing on the prolific criminal not the crime. (This focuses performance effort on achieving detections—and sanctioned detections in particular—which alone will not achieve the reduction in harm that government is seeking to measure through the recent interim police performance assessment framework the first results from which were published in October 2007.)

Not unnaturally, intelligence came to be associated with the delivery of performance indicators through this approach. Once established in the police psyche, this perception, reinforced by other facets of managerialism, added to the structural issues in constraining thinking about intelligence, its purpose, potential, and the role of partnership. That paradigm is only now being challenged with the drive towards renewed emphasis on community policing in the form of ward-based Neighbourhood Policing Teams. Although *Building Communities, Beating Crime* (Home Office 2004) has no specific section devoted to intelligence, it stresses the role of intelligence in 57 references, three of these specifically about community intelligence which is described as fundamental for the prevention and reduction of crime as well as its detection, and documents the significance of the NIM in local policing on a further 23 occasions.

The recommendations made by HMIC in *Policing with Intelligence* (see Table 2.1 below) make no mention of local policing or community intelligence. The focus is on structure (particularly at the cross-border level and regional tasking and coordination), on the tasking of specialist support units (which would tend to be confined to major investigations), on measuring performance and on asset recovery from organized crime.

This, then, was the cultural foundation, if not the philosophical and theoretical foundation, of the emerging intelligence profession within policing. From the outset intelligence was presented, despite occasional lip service to its future potential in all aspects of policing, (paragraph 3.36), as being principally focused on the investigation of serious crime and significant criminals. Such activity is of course a key element of policing, but it is not the only element of policing. And in terms of partnership working and community safety, such an approach potentially excludes those partner agencies not involved in gathering evidence of crime for use in criminal prosecution because it is not geared to any other form of authoritative intervention.

Table 2.1 HMIC recommendations in Policing with Intelligence (1997, paragraph 6.6)

- Supporting the concept of a 'force director of intelligence', with ownership of criminal intelligence, *recommends* that the role should be fulfilled by an officer of Assistant Chief Constable rank. This officer, probably already holding the crime/operations port folio within force, would be ideally placed to drive intelligence issues and to action matters requiring inter-force co-operation by consultation with their counterparts.

- *Recommends* that all forces adopt the practice of using formal tasking criteria for the deployment of specialist support units, and introduce costing and evaluation of operations completed.

- Commends the work done to develop the National Informants Database and *recommends* that a strategy should be devised, in conjunction with National Police Training, HMC&E and the ACPO Crime Committee to enhance understanding and awareness of its capabilities.

- *Recommends* forces devise and introduce criteria to measure performance in respect of the crime intelligence functions, to reflect the importance of the concept, as the philosophy of intelligence driven activity expands into all areas of policing.

- Believes that the service must put in place a structure that will address the problems posed by cross border crime and *recommends the* establishment of Regional Tasking and Co-ordinating Groups in all regions

- *Recommends* a review of the arrangements for recovering assets obtained from criminal activity to allow specific large-scale investigations to be contracted out to forensic accountants and auditors. This would involve an element of financial 'pump-priming' to launch and fund any enquiry until assets began to be recovered. Thereafter, the investigation would continue on a self financing basis, with the investigators' fees being a percentage of the total assets recovered , paid from the assets seized after initial start-up costs had been reimbursed. The balance remaining would go to the Treasury. Treasury Rules would need to be adapted to facilitate the process.

- *Recommends* legislation be devised to target the realized assets of top level criminals and the legal companies they use to launder their profits. The goal would be to require persons suspected of involvement in organized crime, who have proven significant criminal links and who are shown by financial investigation to have great wealth but no legitimate means of income, to account to a Court for their assets, with the burden of proving legitimacy on the person whose commercial affairs were being examined.

As will be seen in Chapter 5, although the NIM theoretically is not confined to the business processes supporting criminal intelligence, the early cultural emphasis on crime detection and performance management set in train by *Policing with Intelligence* has continued to prevail, the paradigm only recently being challenged by the relaunch of community policing through neighbourhood policing teams and workforce modernization that is advancing the pluralization of local policing delivery.

The immediate lesson from this report was that the police service had to get serious about managing and using intelligence to assist crime detection. The long-term lesson informs us how the intelligence profession within the police service arrived at where it is today. Understanding these cultural origins should help inform adaptation and transformation strategies in developing police intelligence so that it better supports all policing functions.

2.2.2 **Scientific and technical intelligence:** *Under the Microscope* **(2002)**

In its thematic inspection of police scientific support services, HMIC devoted an entire chapter promoting the intelligence value to be derived from forensic examination and evidence and another to the management of technical resources including surveillance support.

Of strategic and policy concern was HMIC's discovery 'that the advice contained in *Policing with Intelligence* seems not to have been widely followed', (paragraph 6.10). Five years after the initial thematic report and two years after the introduction of the NIM, there was the strong impression that the police service had still not fully bought into the concept of intelligence-led policing. Indeed, their 1997 recommendations notwithstanding, in some forces HMIC found that intelligence was a matter left largely to the individual BCUs to organize with negligible interaction with either HQ or across administrative boundaries, thus confining intelligence to localized effort and, it might be inferred, only parochial success (paragraph 6.12).

At an operational and tactical level, with the notable exception of the West Midlands Police, HMIC found 'little evidence of a clear understanding of the importance of scientific support to intelligence and vice versa' (paragraph 6.8). Scenes of crime investigators exhibited little awareness of their potential intelligence contribution and saw themselves as situated outside the intelligence loop, whilst intelligence officers demonstrated 'very poor' awareness of forensic capability (paragraphs 6.20–6.21, 6.24). Five out of six forces lacked understanding of the forensic science intelligence opportunities and so missed them (paragraph 6.18). The targeting of scenes of crime investigations through intelligence was confined to a few isolated and innovative BCUs (paragraphs 6.25–6.26).

Even within the cultural construct that emphasized criminal investigation over other policing functions, there was little understanding of what intelligence-led policing might actually encompass.

The notable exception identified by HMIC was West Midlands Police and the computer system it developed to assist in the management of evidence and the linking of suspects with scenes. The force's Forensic Lead Intelligence System (FLINTS) 'has the capacity to link suspects with crimes that otherwise may not have been linked . . . provided all crimes are entered onto the database' together with relevant evidence (paragraphs 6.32 and 6.33). It is the comparison of evidence and intelligence on a single database that creates the added value of this system. The caveat, as with any tool, is that it is only as good as the person using it. If relevant information is not input, it will not be available for comparison.

Under the Microscope went on to consider technical support in intelligence gathering (Chapter 7), identifying four categories of technical support:

- devices enabling visual surveillance
- devices enabling audio surveillance
- devices enabling object location and tracking
- devices enabling communication interception.

Any one of these, subject to the relevant statutory authorities and the strict limitations on the interception of communications, could be deployed across the tactical menu: visual observation, remote monitoring and recording, covert techniques, and specialist sensitive techniques. HMIC noted that in many forces the utilization of such tactics and supporting technical equipment was in its infancy and that there had been no general guidance since a 1984 Home Office Circular prescribing deployment authority levels. The time was right, HMIC concluded, to draw up national standards.

2.2.3 Special Branch: *A Need To Know* (2003)

Intelligence gathering 'is the core activity of Special Branch' (paragraph 3.33). In HMIC's first ever inspection of Special Branch, whose primary function is intelligence-gathering rather than detecting crime or problem-solving, the police service's inconsistent attitude towards intelligence-led policing was highlighted once more.

The structural location of Special Branch within the police service is complicated. Each police force has a Special Branch for which it is answerable to the chief constable. But Special Branch also serves to extend the reach of the national security and intelligence agencies into local domestic communities and through partnership tasking in support of its own function, MI5 has always had a de facto coordination role both in intelligence acquisition and dissemination. HMIC 'was concerned that, in some instances, bilateral relationships between individual Special Branches and the Security Service are stronger than those with neighbouring forces. This can result in limited passage of information between adjacent Special Branches and over reliance on the Security Service to act as a national information distribution centre' (paragraph 2.59). Since the 2003 inspection, a Special Branch national coordinator role has been created within the police service supported by regional Special Branch coordination offices (a development that directly follows on from some of the inspection findings).

How does this multiplicity of masters and tasking fit with the NIM? Frankly it does not: a reality recognized by HMIC who advocated a 'pragmatic' approach and suggested that 'considerable flexibility should be exercised in the application of NIM to Special Branch' (paragraphs 1.15 and 2.49). The issues revolve around subject matter and resources. Each force Special Branch has a different capacity and capability depending upon the resources available within the force for investment in Special Branch work. Despite a uniformity of mission across the different Special Branch offices, HMIC found 'significantly less consistency' in terms of unit size, management structure, resource allocation, operational capability, and intelligence management (paragraph 2.73, and see also 3.33). Some force Special Branches are sufficiently well-resourced to be able to apply NIM processes within the branch and execute tasking accordingly. But in the majority of forces access to specialist skills such as covert surveillance has to be shared between all departments within the force. The NIM processes provide a vehicle for prioritizing competing applications for support and the issue for Special Branch is whether or not to risk exposing a particular interest or intelligence operation through participation in the force NIM resource allocation procedure. HMIC found real dilemmas in a number of forces about this issue. Inevitably, separating Special Branch from the force NIM process undermines the value of the process in terms of intelligence coordination and enhancing cross-border/cross-departmental working. It removes the N from NIM and means that intelligence-led policing can never be truly holistic.

At the same time, the recognition in recent months that community cohesion, interaction and intelligence has an even greater role to play in countering the sort of terrorism evident in the UK since the London bombings of July 2005 (HM Government *Countering International Terrorism: The United Kingdom's Strategy* Cm 6888, TSO, London, 2006), means that never has it been more important for Special Branch to engage with neighbourhood policing teams which is probably best achieved through the NIM process in order to avoid unwitting compromise through confusion and lack of coordination.

The NIM also has the potential to enhance the coordination of partnership working. Collaboration with partner agencies has met with varied success for Special Branch. In some ports Joint Intelligence Cells (JIC) have been established with customs and immigration colleagues but the success of these ventures was directly proportional to the commitment of all agencies to such enterprises (paragraphs 2.34; 3.76). Partners' roles 'are not necessarily complementary' and 'a range of issues [have] to be resolved to enable JICs to become the accepted and effective norm' (paragraph 2.34). Structural issues intrude again: partner agencies internal administrative boundaries are often regional in scope, limiting contiguity with force-based Special Branches and complicating the practicalities of partnership working.

Given that intelligence gathering is the core activity for Special Branch, the inspection conclusion that inadequate intelligence management (including IT support) was 'a major shortcoming in Special Branch capability and effectiveness', particularly post 9/11 (paragraph 2.104), is of significant concern. If the intelligence management systems are not in place, then performance evaluation adds little value. Thinking on this issue had moved on from the general call for more performance management in 1997 to the 2003 recognition of the 'obvious concerns around utilising quantitative data in assessing performance' (paragraphs 3.93; 3.97). One intelligence containing 10 pieces of information could easily be reconfigured as 10 separate reports for counting purposes. And there is no meaningful way to assess performance when many months might be taken to gather and analyse information leading to just one intelligence report that prevents multiple harms in thwarting a terrorist attack. The need remains to ensure that intelligence work is properly tasked and effectively carried out, contributing to beneficial outcomes. The Special Branch (inspection) highlighted how complicated performance management is in the intelligence theatre, especially if there is a need to divorce Special Branch from the NIM machinery employed throughout the remainder of the service.

In the aftermath of the July 2005 bombings, an inquiry conducted by the Intelligence and Security Committee found that many of the issues around disparate capacity and capability, and therefore competence, within Special Branches remained, evidenced by the imprecise nature of targets and objectives coupled with the lack of defined standards to be achieved in counter-terrorism support (*Report into the London Terrorist Attacks on 7 July 2005*, Cm 6785, TSO, London, 2006, paragraphs 132–3).

2.2.4 The picture painted by HMIC inspection

Taken as a whole, these three thematic inspection reports chart aspects of developing thinking in relation to intelligence-led policing. In 1997 HMIC proposed a relatively limited definition of intelligence-led policing that focused on crime and criminal detection. Such a perspective was consistent with the prevailing performance management wisdom. Through the auspices of a thematic inspection of scientific support five years later (by which time the NIM had been launched), it became apparent that progress towards even this closely defined interpretation of intelligence-led policing was not as significant as might have been anticipated or hoped for, and that the police service was essentially missing a trick in failing to recognize the intelligence potential inherent in forensic evidence. The use of technical equipment in the gathering of intelligence was limited, although in part this can be explained by the fact that covert investigation had only recently been placed on a statutory footing meaning that many forces were only just beginning to develop a capability and capacity for such investigative and intelligence work. Intelligence capacity and capability are the *raison d'être* of Special Branch and this thematic inspection raised important questions about the extent to which intelligence-led policing can be an holistic approach given the specialist nature of the work undertaken by Special Branches which has to dovetail with yet simultaneously remain discrete from other policing functions. Other general lessons emerging from the Special Branch report are that added value and return will be proportionate to investment made—a lesson that translates across all aspects of intelligence in policing—and the reminder that successful intelligence partnership working is difficult to achieve if the partners do not have a common purpose. An HMIC inspection of CDRPs and their intelligence management would be an informative comparative study in this respect.

There have been no thematic inspections focusing on intelligence since 2003 but implementation and operation of the NIM now comes within the baseline assessment model of force inspection. At time of writing the latest publicly available data is the baseline assessment of 2006 which reveals that of the 23 business area categories in the analysis framework, NIM implementation ranks 13th, having been 11th the year before. The evidence of the baseline assessment framework analysis is that the service is currently achieving more success in leadership, traffic policing, and performance management than it is in operating the NIM business process. Whilst the detection of crime has not ceased to be a policing priority, with the 2004 White Paper, *Building Communities, Beating Crime*, renewed emphasis was placed on neighbourhood policing and problem-solving: functions that benefit from good intelligence support just as much as crime detection and which rightly deserve to be considered within a wider definition of intelligence-led policing. The overall service performance in respect of neighbourhood policing and problem-solving was ranked 21st. The framework analysis rankings merely reflect relative success in different business areas. Forces are graded in each business area as excellent, good, fair, or poor. The overall gradings for the 43 English and Welsh forces are detailed in Table 2.2 below.

Table 2.2 2006 Baseline assessment grades in two business areas

	Excellent	Good	Fair	Poor
NIM implementation	2	22	19	0
Neighbourhood policing and problem-solving	1	20	18	4

Further information and reading

HMIC *Policing With Intelligence: Criminal Intelligence–A Thematic Inspection On Good Practice* (HMIC, London, 1997). Available online at <http://www.nationalarchives.gov.uk>

HMIC *Under The Microscope* (HMIC, London, 2002). Available online at <http://inspectorates.homeoffice.gov.uk/hmic/inspections/thematic2/utm/>

HMIC *A Need To Know: HMIC Thematic Inspection of Special Branch and Ports Policing* (HMIC, London 2003). Available online at <http://inspectorates.homeoffice.gov.uk/hmic/inspections/thematic2/antk/>

2.3 **Case-Based Intelligence Lessons**

In the last 15 years specific episodes or issues have given rise to a number of reviews of aspects of investigation and intelligence. These key reports are now considered to draw out relevant intelligence lessons. The material divides itself into two broad groups: reviews arising from specific crimes (the murders of Stephen Lawrence, 1993; Victoria Climbié, 2000; Holly Wells and Jessica Chapman, 2003; and Naomi Bryant, 2005; the terrorist attacks in London, 2005) and reviews from more general issues (fraud and suspicious activity reporting; and the role of intelligence prior to the 2003 invasion of Iraq).

2.3.1 **The MacPherson Inquiry**

The painful general conclusions and lessons about institutional racism learnt during the MacPherson inquiry into the murder of Stephen Lawrence seem sometimes to overshadow the specific issues in relation to investigating major crimes that were also identified during the inquiry; particular lessons just as significant as the wider issue of institutional racism. There were many intelligence failings both preceding and during the murder investigation. From the investigation issues can be extrapolated lessons about what should have gone before, which provide a benchmark against which to test how successful intelligence management has become since the creation of roles and systems to support implementation of the NIM.

The intelligence failings fall into a number of themes. In the immediate response to the attack, MacPherson found cause to criticize the failure of senior officers to ensure that house-to-house and other enquiries were promptly conducted on the night of the murder to ascertain intelligence that would inform fruitful lines of inquiry (*The Stephen Lawrence Inquiry*, paragraphs 12.31 and 12.40: all subsequent paragraph references cited in this section are to the MacPherson Report unless otherwise stated).

As the investigation developed 'such research and intelligence gathering as did take place was sporadic and delayed. There was no separate research unit in the investigation team' and despite the names of the prime suspects coming repeatedly to attention 'no concerted action [was] taken to discover whether corroborating information could be obtained from other sources' (paragraphs 7.11–7.12). Even if the capacity to undertake intelligence support to the investigation had been provided, the senior investigating officer's lack of familiarity with HOLMES (Home Office Large Major Enquiry System), the major investigation information support data management software, meant that the potential to manage receipt of intelligence and initiate actions upon such receipt was significantly impeded (paragraph 14.4). This highlights the need for major inquiries to be supported by a dedicated intelligence team and appropriate information management systems.

Lack of intelligence support capacity and SIO faith in HOLMES were not the only intelligence inhibitors during the investigation. Attitudes, including institutional racism, blinkered investigators to potential lines of intelligence and evidential inquiry. Indeed, MacPherson found that the 'obdurate attitude' of some officers towards the racist nature of the murder led to a failure to follow up intelligence amounting to 'neglect' (paragraphs 19.36–19.37).

The failure to follow up opportunities to generate new intelligence was matched by an equal failure to utilize the intelligence already in possession of investigators. One element of the intelligence gap matrix (discussed in more detail in Chapter 8 below) is information already gathered but 'lost' in the system that can be categorized under the label 'don't know what we do know'. This particular type of intelligence gap was evident throughout the Lawrence murder investigation. Again, institutional racism was identified amongst the underlying causes of failure. 'The view of many of the team that the murder of Stephen Lawrence was not solely motivated by racism may well be reflected in [the] failure to obtain readily available local intelligence' (paragraph 20.14). Two sources of information already in the possession of the police were the local intelligence collator's card index and the Racial Incident Unit (RIU) card index. Both indices were available for consultation in the same office at Plumstead police station. The collator's index contained rather more useful information than the RIU index and there was evidence to suggest that much of the information in the hands of the RIU was retained in the memories of the two officers in the unit rather than committed to a readily accessible archive (paragraphs 35.12–35.14). The growing inadequacy of the card index as an intelligence tool had been more than sufficiently demonstrated during the Yorkshire Ripper serial murders investigation in the late 1970s and early 1980s. The Home Office had funded the development of HOLMES as a direct consequence of that lesson. But that lesson was only applied in the context of major inquiries. In the mid 1990s, computerization of local intelligence records (to render the data more secure and easier to search) was apparently still not universal. This was a systemic failing, one that even the coroner in the Lawrence case felt obliged to comment on (paragraph 42.35).

Thus the seeds of intelligence failure had been sown before Stephen Lawrence was murdered. The final, more general, intelligence lesson from this inquiry report relates to community intelligence and constitutes a failing both before and during the investigation. 'None of the five suspects in the Stephen Lawrence murder had cards in the Racial Incident Unit index. The reason for this is that until the Stephen Lawrence murder there were no identifiable crimes committed by the suspects which were infected with racism' (paragraph 35.12). The fundamental failing of an intelligence system based solely on criminal investigation is that those who successfully evade detection will not feature in it. A system informed only by police-generated data (crime reports, arrest records, charge sheets, prosecution files) will only ever reveal part of the picture. The five prime suspects may not have been recorded in the RIU index, but there was more than enough intelligence within the local community and amongst partner agencies to have warranted urgent investigation when the suspects' names repeatedly came to notice during the murder inquiry (paragraphs 7.10–7.13; 45.18). But community intelligence had not been systematically harvested, nor partner agency intelligence about the community systematically exchanged: '. . . liaison with the local organizations and improvement of intelligence gathering might well have assisted in the early stages of the investigation of Stephen Lawrence's murder' (paragraph 29.54).

Further information and reading

MacPherson W *The Stephen Lawrence Inquiry* Cm 4262, (The Stationery Office, London, 1999). Available online at <http://www.archive.official-documents. co.uk/document/cm42/4262/4262.htm>.

See also ACPO *Murder Investigation Manual* (Wyboston: NCPE/Centrex, 2006), which illustrates the role intelligence can play in the investigation of murder as a continuous thread informing inquiries and therefore how lessons from the Stephen Lawrence inquiry have come to influence current good practice guidance.

2.3.2 **The Victoria Climbié Inquiry**

Victoria Climbié was admitted to North Middlesex Hospital on 24 February 2000, bearing 128 separate injuries, deformed, malnourished. The next day she died, aged eight years and three months. On 12 January 2001 her great-aunt, Marie-Therese Kouao and Carl John Manning were convicted of Victoria's murder.

Victoria Climbié was known to be a child at risk by three housing departments, four Social Services departments, two Metropolitan Police child protection teams, two hospitals and a specialist centre run by the National Society for the Prevention of Cruelty to Children.

The public inquiry examining what could have been done to prevent her death identified 12 key opportunities for intervention, and numerous other opportunities (Laming 2003, paragraph 1.17). The 'gross failure of the system' was 'inexcusable' (Laming 2003, para.1.18).

The system failed because of ineffective partnership working and inadequate information exchange between agencies. The inquiry found evidence of:

- poor record-keeping;
- a failure to share information;
- a lack of clarity in information that was exchanged;
- undue delays in referring concerns to partner agencies;
- a failure to investigate referrals properly;
- a lack of will to invest in establishing effective partnerships; and

- a failure of such partnership working as did take place to be conducted on the basis of equality between different agencies bringing different expertise and knowledge to the partnership.

Throughout the 400 pages of the report, recurring themes are the need for effective management of inter-agency working and for accurate and timely information sharing. With ever greater emphasis on partnership working, this catalogue of failings makes explicit, if indeed that was ever necessary, where systemic vulnerabilities lie. It is for subsequent initiatives to learn these lessons the better to underpin future intelligence-led partnerships. Could these circumstances happen again? There are in England and Wales, at the time of writing, 150 Social Services departments, 30 health authorities, and 43 police forces . . .

Further information and reading

Paragraph 1.43—Improvements to the way information is exchanged within and between agencies are imperative if children are to be adequately safeguarded. Staff must be held accountable for the quality of the information they provide. Information systems that depend on the random passing of slips of paper have no place in modern services. Each agency must accept responsibility for making sure that information passed to another agency is clear, and the recipients should query any points of uncertainty. In the words of the two hospital consultants who had care of Victoria:

'I cannot account for the way other people interpreted what I said. It was not the way I would have liked it to have been interpreted.' (Dr Ruby Schwartz)

'I do not think it was until I have read and re-read this letter that I appreciated quite the depth of misunderstanding.' (Dr Mary Rossiter)

The fact that an elementary point like this has to be made reflects the dreadful state of communications which exposed Victoria to danger.

Laming, Lord *The Victoria Climbié Inquiry* Cm 5730 (The Stationery Office, London, 2003). Also available online at <http://www.victoria-climbie-inquiry.org.uk>.

2.3.3 The Bichard Inquiry

The circumstances in which Ian Huntley, an individual who had aroused frequent suspicion as to the threat he posed to young girls, was able to secure employment as a school caretaker that ultimately led to him murdering Soham schoolgirls Holly Wells and Jessica Chapman were scrutinized at the request of the Home Secretary by Sir Michael Bichard. Bichard was asked to examine in particular child protection measures, record keeping, vetting, and information sharing in Humberside Police and Cambridgeshire Constabulary. Some of the intelligence failings identified by Bichard echoed themes from the MacPherson inquiry. Vetting to assess Huntley's suitability to work at a school failed to identify pre-existing serious concerns that he posed a threat to children.

In respect of intelligence management within Humberside Police Bichard found 'six major failures to gather and manage intelligence' (Bichard report paragraph 2.5: all subsequent paragraph references cited in this section refer to the Bichard report unless otherwise stated).

- Failure to use the principal intelligence database (known locally as CIS Nominals, see information box below) properly (paragraphs 2.7–2.17)
- Failure of the intelligence recording system (2.18–2.30)
- Failure to use CIS Crime properly (2.31–2.34)
- Failure to use the Child Protection Database and Child Protection Units properly (2.35–2.45)
- Failure to share information between Humberside Police and Social Services (2.46–2.48)
- General confusion and lack of awareness surrounding data protection, record retention, review, and deletion (2.49–2.72).

Further information and reading

CIS, the Criminal Information System, was a Humberside Police local database with two functions: CIS Nominals, the core tool containing information about persons who came to police notice, and CIS Crime which was a database of crimes reported, recorded, detected and disposed of. In respect of Huntley, most of the information recoded on CIS Crime had been wrongly entered (paragraph 2.5).

For further explanation of these databases see Appendix 3, Bichard M *The Bichard Inquiry Report* HC 653 (The Stationery Office, London, 2004). Available online at <http://www.homeoffice.gov.uk/pdf/bichard_report.pdf>.

Underlying all of the above was failure in staff awareness. Despite the emergence of the intelligence-led policing concept since the time of Stephen Lawrence's murder, and despite the promulgation of the NIM since 2000, Bichard found a general lack of intelligence awareness amongst Humberside Police officers and staff, including amongst managers running units the work of which depended on good intelligence. 'Police officers' active involvement in the intelligence recording process should have been routine . . . it was anything but' (paragraph 2.24). '. . . officers did not fully appreciate the value of intelligence, or the importance of their role in ensuring that it was properly recorded. Management failed to identify and address the problem' (paragraph 2.30).

If, as Humberside Police accepted during the inquiry:

- patterns of behaviour are important in crime generally and are particularly important in the context of sexual offences;

- knowing about past allegations could be extremely important in informing decision making in any particular case; and
- the ability to identify developing behaviour patterns depends on the availability of easily accessible records about past contacts,

then failure to ensure officers and staff are fully aware of intelligence practices and that they are familiar with intelligence systems inevitably means that the organization's ability to deliver, or to contribute towards partnership delivery of, community safety is significantly inhibited. In the case of Huntley there was a failure to identify a pattern of behaviour that, had they known about it, may well have prompted the education authorities in Cambridgeshire not to employ Huntley. Only with a proper appreciation and awareness of intelligence issues will the right information be collected and recorded to constitute 'direct' intelligence, leading to the accumulation of knowledge that will enable analysts to identify patterns of behaviour and other 'secondary' intelligence.

Equally there was a lack of mutual awareness about each other's systems between Humberside Police and Social Services. Social Services, whose Social Services Information Database (SSID) was a national system, lacked any means for checking past contacts with an alleged abuser because their records were structured around abused children rather than alleged abusers. Social Services therefore had no capability of responding to intelligence requests about an offending individual's antecedents (paragraphs 2.46–2.48; 2.137–2.139).

In respect of Cambridgeshire Constabulary Bichard identified the following mistakes in information handling (paragraph 2.146):

- An error was made in entering Huntley's date of birth in the Child Access Database.
- An error was made in the PNC check, which was only carried out against the name of 'Ian Nixon', and not against that of 'Ian Huntley'.
- An error was almost certainly made in failing to send a 'foreign force' fax to Humberside Police (where an applicant for vetting indicated previous residence in another force area, the vetting force should make enquiries about the applicant with the other relevant force).
- An error was almost certainly made in failing to scrutinize the Police Check Form before closing off the file to ensure that any 'foreign force' faxes which should have been sent had been.
- In the very unlikely event that a fax was sent, an error was made in closing the file before any reply had been received.

At the systemic level, Cambridgeshire had failed to anticipate the increase in applications for vetting checks following the instigation of the Criminal Records Bureau (CRDB). The Cambridgeshire CRB had not been sufficiently well managed and managers had failed to notice that individual operators were working inconsistently in carrying out vetting checks. Consequently its ability effectively to engage in intelligence exchange with partner agencies was compromised.

Looking at the police service as a whole, Bichard noted that there was general confusion about data protection responsibilities in respect of intelligence retention and that each force had different local guidelines on this matter despite national guidance issued by ACPO. The 'precise content varied widely. On occasion, local forces had a different approach to that contained in the national guidance' (paragraph 3.81). In relation to force IT systems for managing information and intelligence Bichard was unable to complete a national picture so diverse were the constituent elements but was able to identify certain characteristic features:

> There was, and remains, no uniformity of approach. Each of the 43 police forces has a variety of IT systems, which are used for a variety of different purposes. The interfaces between systems at local force-to-force level are almost non-existent. Even within forces, the interface between systems has been patchy at best. While not all functions or applications necessarily need to be linked *between* police forces, this is *not* the case with intra-force applications. Improvements in this unhappy position are limited, although in some instances, such as the PNC, the capacity is available to store and distribute reliable information nationally between forces. (paragraph 3.63)

For Bichard the lessons included:

- the urgent need for a national IT-based intelligence database; and
- the need for national standards for record creation, retention, review, deletion and information sharing, including a Code of Practice.

(Bichard Inquiry Report Recommendations 1 and 8–11)

The IMPACT project was initiated by the Home Office to give effect to many of the Bichard recommendations, including that for a national intelligence database and improvements in IT capability in other areas of the criminal justice system. It is intended to match information from six police databases (crime, intelligence, firearms, child protection, custody, and domestic violence) with all types of crime (HMG, *Fraud Review: Final Report*, The Stationery Office, London, 2006, paragraph 4.41). It is a project beset with funding shortfalls and 'technical issues' that have necessitated significant delivery goals and timetable revisions (*Bichard Inquiry Recommendations: Fourth Progress Report*, 2007, pp 5–6).

Definition of IMPACT

Intelligence Management, Prioritization, Analysis Coordination and Tasking

---

ACPO has also issued two guidance documents: retention guidelines in respect of PNC records and guidance on the management of police information. A Code of Practice on Police Information Management was published in 2005 and must be implemented across the police service by 2010 (see Appendix B below).

Bichard made no specific recommendations about police training for all officers and staff in order to enhance intelligence awareness and skills but his report clearly identified the need for better training, and in this respect echoed the need inherently identified within the context of the MacPherson Inquiry.

Further information and reading

ACPO *Retention Guidelines for Nominal Records on the Police National Computer*, (ACPO, Kings Worthy, 2006)

ACPO *Guidance on the Management of Police Information*, (NCPE/Centrex, Wyboston, 2006)

ACPO *Data Protection: Manual of Guidance* (ACPO, London, 2006)

Bichard M *The Bichard Inquiry Report* HC 653 (The Stationery Office, London, 2004). Available online at <http://www.homeoffice.gov.uk/pdf/bichard_report.pdf>

Home Office *Code of Practice on the Management of Police Information* (NCPE, Wyboston, 2005)

Home Office *Bichard Inquiry Recommendations: Fourth Progress Report* (The Stationery Office, London, 2007). Available online at <http://www.bichardinquiry.org.uk>

Wate R 'Responding to the Public Inquiries: lessons learnt from the Bichard Inquiry' *The Journal of Homicide and Major Incident Investigation* 2/2 41–51 (2006)

2.3.4 HMI Probation Inquiry into the management of Anthony Rice

Released in November 2004 under Life licence supervision following a conviction for rape in 1999, Anthony Rice went on to commit a serious assault on a lone female in Southampton in April 2005 and then to murder Naomi Bryant in Winchester in August 2005. In respect of both these offences, Rice's connection with the former only coming to light after his arrest for the latter (Rice review, paragraph 9.2.16), he was convicted in October 2005 and sentenced to two terms of life imprisonment, having already been recalled to prison under the terms of his Life licence. At the time the 2005 offences were committed Rice was under the joint supervision of Hampshire Constabulary and the Hampshire Probation Service pursuant to Multi Agency Public Protection Arrangements (MAPPA). Following internal reviews within Hampshire Constabulary and Hampshire Probation Service, these agencies jointly requested HMI Probation to undertake an independent review to identify lessons to be learnt. If supervision within the community of dangerous offenders upon release is to be viable, then good intelligence and information management is crucial in MAPPA partnerships. The review by HMI Probation is published and in the public domain. At the time of writing the possibility of civil litigation remains.

Further information and reading

HMI Probation *An Independent Review of a Serious Further Offence case: Anthony Rice* (HMIP, London, 2006). Available online at <http://inspectorates. homeoffice.gov.uk/hmiprobation/inspect_reports/serious-further-offences/ AnthonyRiceReport.pdf>.

HMIP recorded that 'it is very much to the credit of the Hampshire MAPPA authorities that they took the initiative to approach this Inspectorate direct to request an independent review of this case' (Rice review, Foreword, p 2).

What emerges from the reflections of this salutary independent review is a better understanding of the broad range of intelligence necessary to support a MAPPA partnership. It is now recognized that it is not enough merely to know an offender's antecedents, associates, and places frequented. Nor is it sufficient to know an offender's *modus operandi* in relation to the committing of individual offences. For successful MAPPA management, in addition to the above, it is necessary to understand an offender's behaviour in such detail that trigger events can be identified and intervention initiated well before an offender reaches the stage in his pattern of behaviour where a violent and/or sexual offence is committed.

The recognition of trigger events and emerging behaviour depends on a cumulative intelligence picture being drawn from the information available to individual MAPPA partners being shared so as to facilitate better-informed decisions.

Key decisions in the case of Rice included decisions to relocate him from a Category B prison to a category D prison (paragraph 1.2.2); housing him in a hostel ill-equipped in terms of staff capability for managing such a dangerous offender (paragraph 6.10.3; 10.2.7–10.2.9); and relaxing restrictions on Rice's movements (eg alcohol prohibition, curfew, and boundary restrictions) when he breached the conditions of his hostel residency (paragraphs 8.2.16–8.2.17; 8.3.5; 9.2.6; 10.3.6–10.3.7). Although information was in existence and in the possession of various agencies (prison, police, and probation services) that may have informed alternative decisions in each of the above instances, not all relevant information appears to have been available to the decision-makers at the time decisions were made. For instance, although the London Probation Service had completed a 'good quality' assessment of Rice (following his period of residence there) and had passed their assessment to the Hampshire Probation Service, the latter agency did not share that assessment with MAPPA partners, leading to a 'deficient' management plan for Rice. Similarly, the police, whilst completing an assessment of Rice's inclination to commit sexual offences, failed to include in this assessment his history of violence (paragraph 10.3.2). These missed opportunities followed on from a failure to draw to the attention of the Parole Board, Rice's conviction history of offending against children and a failure on the part of the parole board to recognize and challenge that there was insufficient evidence to warrant Rice's reclassification from Category B down to Category D.

Case study—Anthony Rice

It was a misjudgement by the MAPPA not to ensure that they had both received and accessed the fullest information, and by these means made the fullest possible assessment of Rice's *Risk of Harm*. (paragraph 10.3.3)

... an extended team can work very well when they combine successfully to produce an effective managed resettlement plan, but it can also happen that shared responsibility slips easily into a muddle of mistaken assumptions and diffused responsibility when not well managed. (paragraph 10.2.7)

HMI Probation *An Independent Review of a Serious Further Offence case: Anthony Rice* (HMIP, London, 2006)

Offender assessments are documented on the Probation Service's OASys database. 'OASys is the best available aid to identifying in a consistent and systematic way the individual High and Very High Risk of Harm offenders who are more likely to commit [a Serious Further Offence] than other current offenders' (paragraph 11.12). But like 'all such tools its value depends largely on the skill of the people using it as well as the efficiency of the IT system it runs on' (paragraph 11.12). Significant progress has been made in the information management technology available to agencies responsible for securing community safety since the card index at Plumstead police station, but with new technology comes the need for revised training not only in the systems themselves but also in the new ways of working made possible by the systems and through which their full potential will be realized. This lesson echoes both the MacPherson and the Bichard inquiries.

HMI Probation discovered a 'succession of specific mistakes, misjudgments and miscommunications at all three phases of Anthony Rice's Life sentence [which] had a compounding effect that amounted to what [HMIP] called a *cumulative failure*' (paragraph 11.2).

In partnership working, almost by definition, other agencies will have intelligence unique to their role that will nevertheless be important and of added value when considered alongside the intelligence held by partner agencies. Partnership had worked up to a point but Rice as an individual presented particular challenges to the system and his case exposed a reliance on, and failure to challenge, assumptions about other agencies' intelligence access and interpretation, as well as failures to exploit all available information and intelligence already in possession of the relevant agencies. Once again, agencies (certainly as a partnership and possibly on an individual basis) did not know what they knew. Had they done so, decisions might have been made differently.

2.3.5 **The London terrorist attacks of July 2005**

The key question studied by the Intelligence and Security Committee (ISC) in relation to the terrorist attacks in London on 7 and 21 July 2005 was could they have been prevented? Had intelligence forewarning the attacks been missed or misinterpreted? At the time the report was tabled before Parliament investigations arising from the attacks were still subjudice and so the report was necessarily constrained in its considerations. Nevertheless it contains lessons of general application in intelligence work.

The ISC concluded that intervention and prevention might have been possible if different investigative decisions had been taken during 2003–2005 (*Report into the London Terrorist Attacks*: paragraphs 56–7. All paragraph references cited hereafter in this section refer to that report unless otherwise stated). The issue for the intelligence services and the police had been one of prioritization for limited resources. Although different action priorities might have opened up opportunities for early intervention, under the prevailing circumstances the priorities that were investigated were reasonable and understandable.

Action prioritization is a dilemma for all decision-makers. It depends upon the best available intelligence and reasonable assessment. Where more than one interpretation of any given intelligence is possible, decision-makers will have to make a judgment call about which interpretation to prioritise and action, or whether a further intelligence operation should be commissioned to fill intelligence gaps. It is for intelligence staff to highlight to the decision-makers that an assessment has led to more than one interpretation and which interpretation, if any, is less vulnerable to uncertainty. It is for decision-makers to make the judgment call about what action to take.

This leads onto a second important lesson identified by the ISC. The committee expressed concern that:

> [t]he threat level system and alert state systems are confusing not only to the public but also, more worryingly, to practitioners themselves. In evidence to the Committee, the Director General of the Security Service said it had become clear as a result of July that the varying different alert state schemes were a cause for confusion among officials, Ministers and parts of the [Critical National Infrastructure]. Crucial decisions are taken on the back of these systems–there is little point in producing detailed assessments if those for whom they are intended do not understand the system behind them. *There must be clarity of the various systems and levels, and a shared understanding of both design and purpose among users of the system.* (paragraph 86)

Equally, community safety and protective services partners and practitioners employing the NIM or OASys, for instance, must ensure their common understanding of the language and its meaning in relation to intelligence work if partnership, or even individual operations within a single agency, is to be successful.

The third lesson of general applicability is one that, as will be seen below, emerges from similar intelligence reviews. The July 2005 attacks 'highlighted the limits of . . . current knowledge of the activities of Islamist extremists in the UK, and of their links abroad' (paragraph 111; see also 112, 131, 135). The realization dawned that potential terrorists were not drawn from those already with criminal convictions (a common characteristic of Irish terrorists from both sides of the community) but were individuals radicalised within their own communities. Thus criminal intelligence, as a starting point, was insufficient. Much more community intelligence is required to understand the phenomenon of radicalization and to identify emerging terrorist conspiracies. The potential implications are significant. As will be seen in the discussion of the NIM (Chapter 5), the police service has not developed or utilized the concept of community intelligence as much as it might have. The concept would seem to have great potential for neighbourhood policing and CDRP work, as well as for domestic counter-terrorism. If community intelligence were to be developed primarily in the latter context, it might become difficult simultaneously or subsequently to develop neighbourhood policing community intelligence simply because such work will have become associated with counter-terrorism protective services rather than with less dramatic aspects of community safety.

Further information and reading

Intelligence & Security Committee *Report into the London Terrorist Attacks on 7 July 2005* Cm6785 (The Stationery Office, London, 2006). Available online at <http://www.cabinet-office.gov.uk/intelligence>.

See also Home Office *Threat Levels: The System to Assess the Threat from International Terrorism* (The Stationery Office, London, 2006). Available online at <http://www.intelligence.gov.uk/upload/assets/www.intelligence.gov. uk/threatlevels.pdf>.

2.4 Intelligence Lessons from a Wider Context

Case-based lessons are founded upon mistakes or people and procedures being challenged in unanticipated ways. Often this is the only way in which certain lessons will become manifest and the learning identified. Alongside the specific cases considered above have been more general reviews of intelligence work in a variety of contexts.

2.4.1 The government's fraud review 2006

The establishment of the Asset Recovery Agency (Proceeds of Crime Act 2002, s 1) with its powers to instigate civil recovery of assets derived from criminal activity, marked a significant enhancement to the official armoury against profit-motivated crime. It also expanded the demand for and potential supply of intelligence relating to crime, the organization of profit-motivated crime and the realization of criminal profits. HM Government commissioned a review of fraud investigation, reporting jointly to the Chief Secretary of the Treasury and the Attorney General. The review noted that although the use of criminal intelligence had always been central to policing, the concept of intelligence had expanded to incorporate a more strategic view of intelligence and the role it could play as well as the more traditional perceptions of intelligence contributions to operational planning and tactical choices (Fraud Review paragraph 4.31: subsequent paragraph citations in this section are to this report unless otherwise stated).

In the chapter on 'Reporting Fraud', the Review examined the role of intelligence at some length (Chapter 4, particularly the section commencing at paragraph 4.31). Financial crime, comprising fraud and money laundering, suffers its own particular type of intelligence gap: 'the capacity to organise, categorise, sift, store and analyse information on fraud at a national level is not a responsibility any law enforcement organization currently has' (paragraph 4.36). The state of fraud intelligence 'varies enormously' and depends upon individual forces investing resources in its investigation (paragraph 4.37), even though it has not been a priority crime for local forces as identified through Home Office targets and objectives. It is also a form of criminality that easily and often transcends police force boundaries, thus rendering effective investigation and intelligence gathering vulnerable to the absence of both individual effort and regional cooperation in this theatre of criminality.

In assuming many, although not all, of the functions once undertaken by the National Criminal Intelligence Service (NCIS), the Serious Organized Crime Agency (SOCA) has the function of gathering, storing, analysing, and disseminating information relevant to the prevention, detection, investigation, or prosecution of offences or the reduction of crime in other ways, or the mitigation of its consequences (Serious Organized Crime and Police Act 2005, s 3). SOCA has assumed responsibility for receiving Suspicious Activity Reports (see this chapter, section 2.4.2 below); however, the NCIS intelligence database on cheque and plastic card was passed not to SOCA but to the Economic Crime Department of the City of London Police that now acts as a national point of contact for fraud intelligence (paragraph 4.46). This blurring of fraud intelligence responsibilities between the City of London Police and SOCA seems to create the potential for missed opportunities through the failure to recognize intelligence links.

The review recommended that 'SOCA should be one of the main beneficiaries of improved intelligence products and reporting of fraud, but that the reporting and intelligence processing of fraud information should be performed by another law enforcement agency' (paragraph 4.45).

Overall the review identified five key failings in respect of fraud intelligence:

- Raw information is not being collected because fraud at force level is rarely a priority.

- There is no standard mechanism for being able to allocate fraud cases to the most appropriate organization to deal with them.
- Intelligence is not being effectively shared across police forces, let alone with other concerned parties.
- Very few police forces are engaged in developing a strategic response to fraud with partners.
- There is no law enforcement agency tasked with developing strategic assessments of level two and three fraud or contributing to a national antifraud strategy. (paragraph 4.47)

The options for increasing overall knowledge about fraud were identified as:

- changing the Home Office Crime Counting Rules;
- reporting more fraud through existing systems;
- creating a National Fraud Reporting Centre. (paragraph 4.48)

Further information and reading

HM Government *Fraud Review: Final Report* (The Stationery Office, London, 2006)

2.4.2 The Lander Review of Suspicious Activity Reporting 2006

Suspicious Activity reporting (the SARs regime) is the vehicle through which financial institutions and other organizations report to the authorities suspicious transactions that might constitute money laundering or terrorist financing. Entered into a database the use of which can potentially benefit investigation into all forms of acquisitive crime, the intelligence harvested through SARs is intended to be used by law enforcement agencies, regulatory bodies, and policy-makers at both national and local levels. As identified in HMG's *Fraud Review: Final Report* (information panel between paragraphs 4.46 and 4.47), the SARs regime is intended to:

- reduce the harm caused by crime through intervention opportunities created or aided by the intelligence gained; and
- increase knowledge and understanding of acquisitive crime, gleaned from the points at which criminal and legitimate activity interact.

The SARS Review was jointly commissioned in July 2005 by the then Home Secretary, Charles Clarke, and the then Chancellor of the Exchequer, Gordon Brown, and was reported in March 2006, just prior to the establishment of SOCA (April 2006). Set within the context of the restructuring of the police service into larger 'strategic' forces (*SARs Review*, Foreword), initiated by Clarke and abandoned by his successor John Reid, this review was charged with examining the opportunities for enhancing the SARs regime presented by the creation of SOCA, and the assumption of SOCA of former NCIS responsibilities for the Financial Intelligence Unit (FIU) and the ELMER database which underpinned the regime.

The weaknesses of the regime as administered by NCIS were identified as:

- an absence of any single organizational focus for the work;
- an absence of supporting regime-wide governance arrangements;
- inconsistent training;
- poor performance;
- poor dialogue between reporting sectors and intelligence users;
- limited database functionality and access for end-users;
- uneven law enforcement utilization of the database.

(SARs Review, paragraphs 2; 35)

In the wider arena, it was recognized that financial intelligence was not being used to its full potential in securing asset recovery under the Proceeds of Crime Act 2002 (paragraph 9).

In recommending that SOCA assume responsibility for the FIU (and that significant extra investment be made to improve the operation of the unit), the review's author, Sir Stephen Lander (chair of the SOCA board), confirmed that SOCA would 'have no power to direct either the SARs reporting sectors or the regime's end-users' but that its role would be to 'encourage, exhort, influence, advise, support, measure and report' (paragraph 39).

The end-users of the regime were identified as:

- SOCA;
- other national law enforcement agencies, (HMRC, the Assets Recovery Agency, the Serious Fraud Office, the Department for Work and Pensions);
- the UK intelligence community;
- the police service;
- statutory regulators;
- departmental users; and
- the reporting sectors themselves (banks, building societies, solicitors, financial advisers).

All of these users had different needs and interests in relation to the SAR regime and the Review considers these individually. For the purposes of the discussion here it is sufficient to note the broad church of contributors and users encompassed within the concept of financial intelligence. It begs the question whether the concept of intelligence-led policing is in fact self-constraining and whether the concept of intelligence-led partnership might not be a better framework. This is reinforced when the equally broad church of community intelligence is contemplated.

> **Further information and reading**
>
> Lander S *Review of the Suspicious Activity Reports Regime (The SARS Review)* (SOCA, London, 2006). Also available online at <http://www.soca.gov.uk/downloads/SOCAtheSARsReview_FINAL_Web.pdf>.

2.4.3 Intelligence leading up to the invasion of Iraq

The decision to go to war in Iraq in 2003 in order to achieve regime change is still subject to controversy and debate. Much attention has been focused on the role and use of intelligence in the build-up to military deployment. Three separate independent inquiries have examined the issues: the Intelligence and Security Committee (ISC) also reviewed WMD intelligence; Lord Hutton investigated the circumstances surrounding the death of a government WMD inspector, Dr David Kelly, coincidentally assessing the government's published assertion in 2002 that Iraq had the capability to deploy WMD within 45 minutes of a decision to do so; and Lord Butler reviewed the intelligence on WMD available to the government. All three inquiries were undertaken before it became fully apparent that there were no functioning or potential WMD available for use by the Iraqi regime in 2003. The reports highlight the key difference between intelligence (in the sense of raw information) its assessment, and its use by decision-makers (the difficulties surrounding the multiple definitions and perceptions of intelligence are discussed in Chapter 3 below).

The ISC review of WMD intelligence

In its 'Conclusions and Recommendations', the ISC found that 'there was convincing intelligence that Iraq had active chemical, biological and nuclear programmes and the capability to produce chemical and biological weapons' (paragraph D). It found that the Joint Intelligence Committee (JIC) assessed that Iraq had up to 20 missiles and had retained chemical and biological weapons agents from the war in 1991. Even though the status of these weapons was not known to JIC, it was assessed that engineering expertise was available within Iraq to render such weapons viable (paragraph E). Iraq had a history of rapid deployment of such weapons in previous conflicts. The JIC assessment 'did not precisely reflect the intelligence provided by the SIS [Secret Intelligence Service, MI6]' (paragraph F). The now notorious government dossier of 24 September 2002, was intended for public consumption and not for experienced readers of intelligence material. The fact that the assessment of WMD readiness in 45 minutes (asserted four times in the dossier) related to battlefield deployment rather than any other form of attack was omitted in the final draft having been included in earlier drafts, which was 'unhelpful' in understanding the full issues. Also omitted from the final draft was the clarification that the government did not believe Iraq capable of attacking mainland Britain (paragraphs O and P). Although subsequently proved to be entirely false and fraudulent, the SIS assessment that Iraq was negotiating with Niger to acquire uranium was considered reasonable under the circumstances (paragraph Q).

Key here is the distinction between information being gathered by the various intelligence agencies, their overall assessment of all the available information, and how that information was publicly presented. Errors of judgment in presentation do not mean that there were errors in assessments (often best guesses) based on available information.

The Hutton review of Dr Kelly's death

Of relevance here are Lord Hutton's findings recorded at paragraph 467 of his report. Specifically he found that the assertion that WMD could be deployed within 45 minutes was based on a source 'regarded as reliable' at the time of the original assessment and at the time of the inquiry. He noted that concerns raised by one expert, Dr Brian James, about some of the intelligence were considered at a senior level and 'were not acted upon'. The government wanted the September 2002 dossier to make 'as strong a case as possible'. Importantly, Hutton reminded readers that he dossier was a political document written for political ends and 'was not an intelligence assessment'.

This reinforces the conclusions above based on the ISC report. The information itself is separate from the assessed intelligence, which itself is separate from the use to which it is put by decision-makers. These distinctions are important to recall when analysing why a desired outcome has not been achieved. Was the original information wrong? Was an erroneous assessment and interpretation made? Was the use to which the assessment was put an error of judgment? If mistakes occurred in the third of these phases, it is important that responsibility is not foisted on those responsible for working in the first two phases. That way intelligence working is discredited not because of its own lack of professionalism but because an error of judgment was made in acting upon the earlier work.

The Butler review of WMD intelligence

Perhaps the most useful general lesson to emerge from the Butler report is one of context which helps define limitations. It is worth quoting some key paragraphs at length.

47. Intelligence merely provides techniques for improving the basis of knowledge. **As with other techniques, it can be a dangerous tool if its limitations are not recognised by those who seek to use it.**

48. The intelligence processes . . . (validation, analysis, assessment) are designed to transform the raw material of intelligence so that it can be assimilated in the same way as other information provided to decision-makers at all levels of government. Validation should remove information which is unreliable (including reporting which has been deliberately inserted to mislead). Analysis should assemble fragmentary intelligence into coherent meaningful accounts.

Assessment should put intelligence into a sensible real-world context and iden-tify how it can affect policy-making. But **there are limitations, some inherent and some practical on the scope of intelligence, which have to be recog-nised by its ultimate recipients if it is to be used wisely.**

49. **The most important limitation on intelligence is its incompleteness.** Much ingenuity and effort is spent on making secret information difficult to acquire and hard to analyse. Although the intelligence process may overcome such barriers, intelligence seldom acquires the full story. In fact, it is often, when first acquired, sporadic and patchy, and even after analysis may still be at best inferential.

50. **The very way that intelligence is presented can contribute to this mis-perception.** The necessary protective security procedures with which intelli-gence is handled can reinforce a mystique of omniscience. Intelligence is not only–like many other sources–incomplete, it can be incomplete in undetecta-ble ways. There is always pressure, at the assessment stage if not before, to create an internally consistent and intellectually satisfying picture. When intelligence becomes the dominant, or even the only, source of government information, it can become very difficult for the assessment process to establish a context and to recognise that there may be gaps in that picture.

51. [. . .] Judgement must still be informed by the best available information, which often means a contribution from intelligence. But **it cannot import certainty.**

52. These limitations are best offset by ensuring that the ultimate users of in-telligence, the decision-makers at all levels, properly understand its strengths and limitations and have the opportunity to acquire experience in handling it. It is not easy to do this while preserving the security of sensitive sources and methods. But **unless intelligence is properly handled at this final stage, all preceding effort and expenditure is wasted.** (emphasis added)

Subsequently Butler makes the point that often the assessment of a source, partic-ularly a source that has to be protected, is undertaken by those staff who manage or have access to that source and so have a vested interest in promoting the value of the source. Sometimes this vested interest can obscure the more important function of assessing the information provided by the source (paragraph 599).

A recurring theme for Butler, not unconnected with the last point, is the extent to which assessments are written in a manner that enables decision-makers to identify where uncertainty lies within the information or its assessment (paragraph 602).

All of these points are as relevant to agencies working in community safety and criminal investigation as they are in the context of military action and national security.

The overall lesson for public and professional alike from these three enquiries is the reminder to decision-makers and users that intelligence work is not a precise science. It is vulnerable to volatile variables and must be viewed in context, which includes recognition (as far as possible) of what is not known. The inherent limitations are no reason to ignore or downplay intelligence, nor a justification for inaction if partial intelligence justifiably presents certain working hypotheses. Intelligence and its assessment will always be a work in progress, always in need of corroboration and review. Active intervention is sometimes the only means of checking or corroborating intelligence.

Further information and reading

Intelligence and Security Committee *Iraqi Weapons of Mass Destruction–Intelligence and Assessments* Cm5972, (The Stationery Office, London, 2003) Available online at <http://www.cabinetoffice.gov.uk/intelligence/>

Hutton, Lord *Report of the Inquiry into the Circumstances Surrounding the Death of Dr David Kelly CMG* HC247, (The Stationery Office, London, 2004) Available online at <http://www.the-hutton-inquiry.org.uk/>

Butler, Lord *Review of Intelligence on Weapons of Mass Destruction: Report of a Committee of Privy Counsellors* HC898 (The Stationery Office, London, 2004). Available online at <http://www.butlerreview.org.uk/>

2.5 **Key Learning**

The table below (Table 2.3) captures the key learning from this literature review. It is evident that certain themes recur. These provide a context for the more detailed and specific thematic discussions that follow. The case study that follows illustrates that similar lessons are to be learnt in other countries.

Table 2.3 Key lessons emerging from recent intelligence reviews

Issue	Examples
Need for a national intelligence database; need to co-ordinate different databases—in order to access information already in the possession of police and other agencies	Bichard, paras 41, 66–7 (pp 5–6), 3.61, 4.15–4.19 Laming, 1.47 Macpherson, ss 20.14, 35.7, 35.13, 42.35

Table 2.3 Key lessons emerging from recent intelligence reviews *(cont.)*

Issue	Examples
Need for national standards (Codes of Practice) on creation, retention, review, deletion, and information sharing With the corresponding need not to dilute such national guidance as does exist through 43 different local re-interpretations; danger of 'local accountability' being used to defend inappropriate parochialism where national solutions would enhance local provision	Bichard, paras 41, 68–69 (pp 5–6), 3.63, 3.66, 3.81, 4.11
Failure to use existing intelligence systems properly or to their full potential, leading to a specific intelligence gap: agencies not knowing what they already know	Bichard, s 2.5 MacPherson 14.4, 20.14, 35.7, 35.12–35.14 Rice 10.1.1
Lack of staff familiarity with intelligence processes and systems, particularly amongst lead investigators and senior officers Dictating a corresponding need for staff training in intelligence and decision-maker competence in using intelligence	Bichard 2.13, 2.21, 2.24, 2.30, 2.91 Butler ch 1 MacPherson 14.4
Failure to recognise pattern of allegations/behaviour over time that would significantly alter the context within which any current circumstances are understood	Bichard 2.73–2.75, 2.80 Laming 5.34. 9.57 MacPherson 7.10, 7.13, 29.54 Rice 10.1.1, 10.3.4,
Intelligence and intelligence systems are tools that are only as good as the practitioners using them	Butler para 49 Rice 11.12
Recognizing that the intelligence picture needs to be not only an assessment and analysis of what is known BUT ALSO a recognition of what is not known	ISC WMD report ISC 7 July, 111–12. Butler para 50
Decisions made on insufficient intelligence / evidence—failure to recognize that information available was insufficient	Rice 10.1.5
Dangers of misunderstanding what intelligence is and the possible misuse of intelligence—a political dossier is not an intelligence assessment	Hutton para 467
Failure to share key intelligence with partner agencies sharing responsibility for outcome	Laming 1.43–1.47 Rice 10.3.2

Case study from another jurisdiction—the sinking of the SIEV X

In October 2001 353 asylum seekers (mostly women and children) drowned when the Suspected Illegal Entry Vessel (SIEV) on which over 400 were being transported from Indonesia to Australia, sank at an undisclosed location en route. Whether this was a tragedy that could have been prevented given available intelligence prior to the sinking, is still hotly disputed. A Senate Committee inquiring into the incident highlighted a number of issues about the sharing of gathering, collation, and sharing of intelligence between different partner agencies including the police and the military, although not all the government, agency and departmental witnesses to the inquiry revealed all they must have known, itself a matter of further controversy. The official report of the inquiry can be compared with the investigative account of a retired civil servant who had previously worked for the Australian Department of Foreign Affairs and Trade.

Australian Parliament Senate Select Committee on a Certain Maritime Incident (2002) *A Certain Maritime Incident* (Commonwealth of Australia: Canberra). Accessible at <http://www.aph.gov.au/senate/Committee/maritime_incident_ctte/index.htm>.

Kevin T *A Certain Maritime Incident: the Sinking of the SIEV X* (Scribe Publications, Melbourne, 2004)

3

What is Intelligence?

3.1 **Introduction**

On the face of it this question should not be as hard to answer as it is. After all, within the context of criminal investigation and policing, the UK had a National Criminal Intelligence Service, either as part of the Home Office or as a Non-Departmental Public Body, for over a decade, and for very nearly the same length of time the concept of intelligence-led policing has been with us. Since 2004, in theory, all police forces in England and Wales have been adhering to a business process called the National Intelligence Model. Superficially all of this implies a consensus about what 'intelligence' is in relation to policing and crime control. But there remains a significant variety in interpretation of 'intelligence' and the implementation of intelligence-led policing (see Chapter 5 below). This chapter seeks to deconstruct the label in order to identify the different conceptual under-standings that currently prevail. It presents different ways of thinking about con-cepts of intelligence.

3.2 **Intelligence—Information, Knowledge, or Evidence?**

Intelligence, information, or evidence: valid distinctions, interchangeable mean-ings, or sterile semantics? It is an issue that Sir Stephen Lander, whilst acknowl-edging that a debate prevailed, deliberately avoided in the *SARs Review* when declining to reflect upon whether SARs were 'information' or 'intelligence', or in what circumstances they became 'intelligence' (*SARs Review*, p 3, fn 1). Lander chose to use 'information' in a purely descriptive sense and not to imbue the term with specific value or utility. Within the intelligence community 'informa-tion' and 'intelligence' do have different meanings signifying different values and assessments. This illustrates the importance of understanding issues raised by definitions and perceptions.

Part of the answer to this question is to be found in statute. The Criminal Procedure and Investigations Act 1996 prescribes the handling of material gath-ered during a criminal investigation, whilst the Data Protection Act 1998 and the Freedom of Information Act 2000 define the duties and obligations of investiga-tors in respect of information they hold (see Chapter 7 below).

But statutory process is only part of the answer in developing a concept of in-telligence. A rehearsal of the various definitions and interpretations to be found in the literature is unavoidable. To begin, some dictionary definitions:

Definitions of Evidence, Information, Intelligence, and Knowledge

Evidence
1. Ground for belief or disbelief; data on which to base proof or to establish truth or falsehood; information indicating whether a belief or proposition is true or valid;

2. Matter produced before a court of law in an attempt to prove or disprove a point at issue.

Information

1. Knowledge acquired through experience or study;
2. Facts or knowledge provided or learned;
3. Knowledge of specific and timely events or situations, news;
4. A charge or complaint laid before justices of the peace usually on oath, to institute summary criminal proceedings.

Intelligence

1. The capacity for understanding; ability to perceive and comprehend meaning; the ability to acquire and apply knowledge and skills;
2. News, information;
3. The gathering of information of military or political value (about enemies, spies etc); information gathered in this way.

Knowledge

1. The facts, feelings or experiences known by a person of a group of people;
2. Awareness, consciousness, familiarity, information, and skills acquired through experience, education, and learning;
3. Specific information about a subject.

Compiled from the *Collins English Dictionary* (HarperCollins, Glasgow, 2006) and the *Concise Oxford English Dictionary* (11th edition, Oxford University Press, Oxford).

Clearly even the application of lexicographical forensics cannot entirely distinguish the three concepts of intelligence, information, and evidence. There is overlap between all three. Within the context of the emerging debate about the concept of *knowledge-based policing*, seen as an enhancement of intelligence-led policing as currently implemented, if intelligence-led policing is, de facto, about targeting specific problems or offenders in order to meet certain performance indicators, then knowledge-based policing is seen as providing the context within which to understand criminality, the community, and organizational/partnership capacity and capability and so act on intelligence in a meaningful way.

The issue goes beyond sterile semantics in that practical implications ensue. In written evidence to the Home Affairs Committee (report on *Terrorism and Community Relations*, 2005, vol 2, Ev2, paragraph 2.2), ACPO noted that overcoming alert-fatigue and widespread scepticism about the nature of the threat of terrorism to the UK post-9/11 was difficult because:

a) there was a need to manage intelligence about terrorism in order to protect sources; and

b) good information that might illustrate the reality of the threat was often subjudice.

This perception distinguishes and identifies a tension between intelligence and evidence by recognizing that intelligence falls short of proof of fact (evidence), but that proof of fact or other knowledge is often needed in order to assess the value of intelligence.

Dean and Gottschalk, in discussing the architecture of knowledge management within law enforcement, offer a different perspective with definitional variations. They view knowledge as a continuum, with *data* (raw material), *information* (data and perceived facts organized through relevance and purpose), *intelligence* (information subject to analytical interpretation), and *knowledge*: the latter operating at a higher level of abstraction than intelligence, incorporating intelligence and prior learning within the context of judgments, assessments, beliefs, truths, and expectations (2007: 5–6; 80–83)

To this permutation of definition must be added the prism of interpretation. How then, in relation to policing, has 'intelligence' been interpreted in different conceptual contexts? There are three such arena to consider: the representation of 'intelligence' in official guidelines; the academic perspective; and the frontline practitioners' perspective.

Further information and reading

Dean G and Gottschalk P *Knowledge Management in Policing and Law Enforcement: Foundations, Structures, Applications* (Oxford University Press, Oxford, 2007)

3.2.1 'Intelligence' as defined in official sources

HMIC, quoting the 1999 Metropolitan Police Intelligence Manual, envisages intelligence as: '**the product of information which has been taken from its raw state, processed, refined and evaluated**' (*Under the Microscope: Thematic Inspection Report on Scientific and Technical Support* Home Office, London, 2002, p 46).

The ACPO *Guidance on the National Intelligence Model* (2005, p 196) echoes this thinking, describing intelligence as '**information that has been subject to a defined evaluation and risk assessment process in order to assist with police decision making.**'

This theme, that intelligence is information that has been processed, is recognized in other jurisdictions. In 2000 the Australian Customs Service defined intelligence as '**a value-added product, derived from the collection and processing of all relevant information relating to client needs, which is immediately or potentially significant to client decision-making**' (quoted in J Ratcliffe *Intelligence-led policing* Australian Institute of Criminology, Paper 248, 2003, p 3).

Police management theory, then, would appear to view intelligence as a three-stage activity:

a) raw information
b) which is processed
c) to inform decision-making.

This mechanistic perspective is subject-type neutral. It is equally applicable to intelligence about crime, community issues, roads policing, and/or the routine business and management information needed to run a large organization such as a police force. It tells us nothing about what sort of raw information might be gathered in order to be processed to the point where it can inform decision-making.

The material that might comprise such raw information is defined in the multi-agency Code of Practice on *The Recording and Dissemination of Intelligence Material* (ACPO, ACPO(S) and HMCE, 2005, paragraph 1.8.1).

> Intelligence material includes: personal information of value to national security, the prevention or detection of crime or disorder, the maintenance of community safety and the assessment or collection of any tax or duty or of any imposition of a similar nature, other than that required to be held for legal or administrative purposes, which has been assessed for accuracy and relevance, or similar non-personal information which has been assessed for accuracy and relevance and in respect of which it is necessary to protect the identity of the source.

This perspective sees intelligence material not so much as raw information but as having value for a specific purpose. Thus the three-stage activity continuum identified above can be refined as follows:

a) information of value in relation to specific purposes
b) which is processed
c) to inform decision-making.

In relation to one specific type of intelligence, community intelligence, HMIC and ACPO have gone further and prescribed a type definition.

Community intelligence is '**local information, direct or indirect, that when assessed provides intelligence on the quality of life experienced by individuals and groups, that informs both the strategic and operational perspectives of local communities**' (HMIC *Policing with Intelligence* Home Office, London, 1999, paragraph 7.13.2).

ACPO elaborated upon this. '**Community intelligence is local information which, when assessed, provides intelligence on issues that affect neighbourhoods and informs both the strategic and operational perspectives in the policing of local communities. Information may be direct and indirect and come from a diverse range of sources including the community and partner agencies**' *Practice Advice on Professionalizing the Business of Neighbourhood Policing* Centrex, Wyboston, 2005, 12).

Community is itself a term open to variable interpretation and means different things in different context and the definitions cited above are police-specific, although they might also be useful for local authorities. Other agencies interact with different communities. HMRC, for instance, enjoys a form of self-generating community intelligence in the form of VAT returns and import/export returns that other agencies do not derive from their communities.

Even in this type of definition, intelligence is seen in terms of output that informs decision-making, presumably to achieve a defined outcome. It is process.

If purpose is any guide in achieving a definition, then ACPO's written evidence to the Home Affairs Committee (report on *Terrorism and Community Relations* 2005, vol 2, Ev2, paragraph 6) defines an intended outcome: '**Our intelligence must help identify all criminality, including terrorism criminality, but it must also guide police activity in addressing anxieties and concerns within communities that can lead to tension, disorder, alienation or non-co-operation**'. The ACPO Memorandum does not couch it in these terms but this is beginning to look beyond the performance-focused implementation of intelligence-led policing towards the wider context of citizen-focused, knowledge-based policing.

3.2.2 **'Intelligence' as conceptualized in academic sources**

Academic studies differ on how intelligence might be defined. Opting for a description of process, Whittaker, presaging the thinking of Ratcliffe (see section 3.3 below) defined intelligence as '**the systematic and purposeful acquisition, sorting, retrieval, analysis, interpretation and protection of information**' (*The End of Privacy: How Total Surveillance is becoming a Reality* (New Press, New York, 1999), 5). Others, however, have opted to describe intelligence in terms of information rather than process.

Nina Cope, a senior Metropolitan Police analyst, perhaps not surprisingly offers a précis of the ACPO definition: '**intelligence can be understood as information developed to direct police action**' ('Intelligence-led policing or policing led intelligence' *British Journal of Criminology* 44 190 (2004)). Together with criminologists Innes and Fielding, a year later she expressed the same notion using rather more academic terminology: '. . . **intelligence can be defined as a mode of information. It is information that has been interpreted and analysed in order to inform future actions of social control against an identified target**' ('The appliance of science?' *British Journal of Criminology* 45 42 (2005)). It is a theme with which Innes and Sheptycki concur and upon which they elaborate (see box below).

Definition of intelligence

M Innes and J Sheptycki 'From detection to disruption: intelligence and the changing logic of police crime control in the United Kingdom' *International Criminal Justice Review* **14 1–24 (2004)**
[*bold emphasis added, italicized emphasis original*]

'intelligence is an informational construct . . . information that is organizationally **encoded in such a way** as to make evident the need for, or **to enable** the conduct of, **acts of social control** at some point in the future' (p 5)

'The distinction between *information* and *intelligence* is well established, but it can be difficult to grasp. Information consists of bits of data that, when combined and viewed together with relevant background knowledge, may be used to produce intelligence, which informs the actions and decisions of policing organizations . . . It

---

is not uncommon to refer to any information that comes into police hands by covert means as intelligence. In this context, there is a distinction between covert intelligence (information obtained by covert means) and intelligence product, which is intelligence in the classis sense that Willmer described. **This elasticity of terminology should serve as a warning**.' (p 6)

'Although there are differences in the terminology employed across the police sector, there is some general agreement that tactical intelligence refers to the use of data to inform specific, bounded, and targeted interventions against a nominated problem, whereas strategic intelligence consists of data providing a longer-term vision of the contexts and problems relevant to police practice.' (p 8)

'. . . the concept of intelligence is fluid, and different definitions prevail in different parts of the police sector. . . . [we] define intelligence as information that has been **subjected to some form of analysis and evaluation with the intention of informing future acts of social control**.' (p 10)

'. . . bits of intelligence can concurrently function as crime and criminal intelligence or as community and contextual intelligence. The point is that **the meaning of intelligence does not inhere in the information itself but is dependent upon how it is interpreted and defined by its users**, who are themselves situated in an organizational context.' (p 10)

So for academic commentators, also, the distinction between information and intelligence is one of process. Intelligence is processed information. The purpose of this process is to inform decision-making.

3.2.3 'Intelligence' as understood by frontline practitioners

---

Further information and reading—John Grieve on 'intelligence'

J Grieve 'Developments in UK criminal intelligence' in J Ratcliffe (ed) *Strategic Thinking in Criminal Intelligence* (The Federation Press, Sydney, 2004) 25–36

Intelligence is 'information designed for action. (p 25)

Once again, a précis of the ACPO position. But Grieve goes further in describing how the processed information informs decision-making and in particular, decisions about prioritization.

'. . . intelligence is about making sense of ambiguities or contradiction and recognizing the relative importance of different elements.' (p 35)

To what extent do frontline practitioners view intelligence in the same way as former Deputy Assistant Commissioner John Grieve, one of the architects of intelligence-led policing? Research into the perspectives of UK police intelligence staff undertaken by Norwegian Police Superintendent Maren Eline Kleiven offers some insight.

Case study—Examples of practitioner responses to Kleiven survey question: how would you define 'intelligence'?

'Information that has been given some added value after being collated and assessed.'

'It is anything we can use which allows us to take action.'

'It is the classic question between intelligence and evidence. These days there is very little difference. Some would say action, some would say evidential. Intelligence is evidence.'

'You as investigation officer should be at the scene looking for nothing—it should be all there.'

'Without exceptions what the customers want is evidence to arrest and charge. The detectives want the intelligence unit to do the investigation for them.'

M Kleiven *Where's the Intelligence in the National Intelligence Model?* unpublished Masters Dissertation, University of Portsmouth 2005.

See also M Kleiven 'Where is the "intelligence" in the National Intelligence Model', *Journal of International Police Science and Management*, 9(3) 257–73.

The first two responses above view intelligence in a manner consistent with the ACPO definition. The third perspective—that intelligence is evidence—is one with which some intelligence professionals both within and without the police service might disagree. Indeed, the Security Service has operated for almost 100 years on the basis that intelligence is not evidence but can give rise to evidential opportunities. This is not unconnected with the Cold War logic that discreet disruption of foreign espionage was preferable to vulnerability exposure through criminal prosecution when viewed within the context of international diplomacy and national security. This insight highlights that the three-stage activity considered above is in need of yet further refinement. The final element is organization-specific. The decisions to be informed with the processed information define what intelligence material is required and how it is to be used. Intelligence necessary to achieve disruption may look very different from intelligence needed to secure problem-solving or detections leading to convictions. Thus the three-stage activity must be viewed within the context of desired outcome which will vary according to organizational purpose:

a) information of value in relation to specific purposes
b) which is processed
c) to inform decision-making within the context of organizational function.

With each refinement of this model, so the potential for variation in intelligence perception and use increases with a consequential decrease in standardization and consensus on what intelligence is and is for.

The concept that intelligence should remain apart from the evidential chain was adopted by NCIS in its own work. It was part of the rationale behind having intelligence processed in an organization separate from those with a remit to gather evidence for the purposes of prosecution. The sterile corridor was physical as well as conceptual. There were many who argued that this impeded the flow of intelligence to investigators, particularly in relation to organized crime. The creation of SOCA seems to justify this point of view but SOCA's remit is far less focused on detection and prosecution than was that of the NCS, and disruption figures as prominently in SOCA's strategy as it did in the MI5 Cold War strategy (Harfield 2006).

The 'intelligence is evidence' argument leads on to the final two perceptions in which the work of police intelligence units is seen as being to identify the evidence with which detectives can then arrest and charge suspects. This view seems mired in the complex organizational culture and sub-cultures of the police service, an area that has attracted some popular literature but almost no serious anthropological study. In brief, a key reason that Sir David Phillips (former Chief Constable of Kent County Constabulary) pioneered intelligence-led policing in Kent was the desire to restore the status and pre-eminence of criminal detection, and with it the status of the CID, within the police service as a counter-weight to the political emphasis (in response to focus groups and vox pop surveys) on visible neighbourhood reassurance policing. In a sense this crusade backfired because the codification of intelligence-led policing into the NIM business process highlighted the intelligence unit rather than the CID office as the epicentre of crime fighting. In the same way that many forces have some form of specialist file preparation or prisoner processing units for minor crimes, the theory being that patrol officers should merely arrest and render the suspect into custody before resuming visible patrol rather than end up in the police station dealing with prisoners for a whole shift so, too, in the experience of the authors, some CID officers have come to view their role as prisoner processing for more serious crimes. From this perspective, to which performance indicators focused on detections and convictions (and therefore biased towards reactive investigation) offer some unwitting reinforcement, the ideal intelligence package is one that provides evidence, rather than evidential opportunities for proactive investigation. Kleiven's survey certainly confirms that the experience of the authors is neither unique nor confined to the various forces in which they have served.

Kleiven went on to explore practitioner perceptions of community intelligence.

Case study—examples of practitioner responses to Kleiven's survey question: how would you define community intelligence?

'It is intelligence we receive from a wide range of sources, not only agencies but special members of the community like imams in the Muslim communities.'

'It is actionable intelligence provided by individuals or bodies of individuals or members of a group who have interest in directing the police to encounter crime that is affecting their lives.'

'Intelligence which informs us what actually is happening in the neighbourhood.'

'Open source material like things on the web, local newspapers and such.'

> M Kleiven *Where's the Intelligence in the National Intelligence Model?* unpublished Masters Dissertation, University of Portsmouth 2005.

See also M Kleiven 'Where is the "intelligence" in the National Intelligence Model', *Journal of International Police Science and Management,* Vol 9 No 3 (pp 257–73).

These responses reveal a greater diversity of understanding. For some respondents, community intelligence is information derived from community sources. Others understand community intelligence to be processed information about communities. If the purpose of crime fighting is merely to render up to the courts those accused of crimes, then an intelligence process focused on criminals only needs to understand the community to the extent necessary to identify crime victims willing to testify. If, however, the purpose of crime fighting includes prevention and problem-solving in order to reduce crime and create safer neighbourhoods, then intelligence that focuses only on criminals is of little relevance unless it is viewed within the wider context of community intelligence. HMIC observed (*Diversity Matters*, 2003) that some forces were developing capability in criminal intelligence but were ignoring community intelligence. Kleiven's subsequent research demonstrates that, as currently implemented (local variations of interpretation notwithstanding), the use to which the NIM is being put obscures or even ignores community intelligence. In the context of neighbourhood policing and problem-solving, focusing on intelligence about criminals is rather like looking through the keyhole instead of opening the door. Criminals do not operate in a vacuum. They live off different communities, whether their criminal focus is residential burglary or commercial fraud or fundamentalist political violence. Trying to understand the criminal without understanding the context of the community and the criminality is to limit the options for successful intervention. Theorists would argue, of course, that the NIM does not exclude community intelligence and that it is the role of analysts to provide the contextual link between criminal intelligence and community intelligence. Kleiven's research suggests that reality falls some way short of rhetoric, not least because practitioners providing raw material to be processed into intelligence are not necessarily thinking in terms of community intelligence.

3.2.4 **The limitations of 'Intelligence'**

Whilst on the subject of definitions, it is worthwhile calling upon some well-respected figures outside the policing arena who have defined the limitations of intelligence, the parameters of the possible being a useful alternative approach to defining a concept.

Definitions of the limitations of intelligence

In the midst of a continuing political furore about the use or misuse of intelligence in relation to national security, Lord Butler observed:

Intelligence merely provides techniques for improving the basis of knowledge. As with other techniques, it can be a dangerous tool if its limitations are not recognised by those who seek to use it.

Review of Intelligence on Weapons of Mass Destruction HC898, 2004 p 14.

Speaking of intelligence evaluation, Dame Eliza Manningham-Buller, then Director-General of the Security Service (MI5), said:

. . . some is gold, some dross and all of it requires validation, analysis and assessment. When it is gold it shines and illuminates, saves lives, protects nations and informs policy. When identified as dross it needs to be rejected: that may take some confidence. At the end of the day it requires people of integrity not only to collect it but also to prioritize, sift, judge and use it.

Speech to Dutch Security Service, 1 September 2005, <http://www.mi5.gov.uk/output/Page375.html> (accessed 12 September 2005)

In its examination of the London bombings of 7 July 2005, the Parliamentary Intelligence and Security Committee defined a Security Service intelligence operation as:

. . . the process by which intelligence collection resources and analysis are directed to develop these fragmentary pieces of information into a picture of activity, identity, intentions and location. The picture that emerges is rarely complete and the investigative process then involves seeking further information and analysis, to make the picture clearer.

Report in the London Terrorist Attacks on 7 July 2005 Cm 6785 (The Stationery Office, London, 2006, paragraph 20)

Butler, using the term 'intelligence' in the sense of processed information, draws attention to the fact that processed information is merely a tool, not an end in and of itself. Tools are only as useful as the skill with which they are used. Manningham-Buller, using 'intelligence' in the sense of raw information, not only illustrates the different usages to which 'intelligence' is put but also explains why processing (validation, analysis, and assessment) is necessary before intelligence (in the output sense of processed information) can be used. The Intelligence and Security Committee, following the logic that sees intelligence as a process, drew attention to the fact that process cannot overcome the fragmentary nature of the raw material being processed.

3.3 Process, Product, or Structure?

The thrust of most of the definitions considered above has been on intelligence as process, but as Ratcliffe has observed, 'a broader view of intelligence could incorporate the view that intelligence is a structure, a process and product' (2003, 3). This gives rise to what might be termed a triptych conceptualization of intelligence, incorporating three definitions.

Table 3.1 A triptych conceptualization of intelligence based on Ratcliffe 2003

Intelligence as . . .	Defining characteristics
Structure	The existence of an intelligence unit or department as an individual entity within an organizational framework, equipped with people, skills, methods, and organizational structure.
Process	A continuous cycle of tasking, information collecting, analysis, evaluation, dissemination leading to intervention action or the identification of an intelligence gap requiring further tasking.
Product	The output of the intelligence process, the processed information, such as a Subject Profile or a Tactical Assessment, intended to inform decision-makers.

As will be seen in Chapter 5 below, this conceptualization is manifest in the NIM, which envisages the existence of an intelligence structure in order to process raw material and information into defined products for the benefit of decision-makers. This conceptualization highlights the fact that even within a single theoretical model, intelligence can have more than one conceptual (as well as literal) meaning and that it is important, when debating issues and considering strategy and tactics, to be certain that all parities understand which meaning is under consideration at any given moment.

Further information and reading

J Ratcliffe 'Intelligence-led policing and the problem of turning rhetoric into practice' *Policing and Society* 12(1) 53–66 (2002)

J Ratcliffe *Intelligence-led Policing* Australian Institute of Criminology: Trends and Issues, Paper 248, (2003)

3.4 **Encoding Frames and Modes of Intelligence**

An alternative approach to understanding intelligence is to examine how it is used. It is an approach that has been adopted by academics and involves categorizing intelligence (encoding) into usages (modes of intelligence).

Arguing that the distinction between strategic and tactical intelligence, as in the NIM for instance, does not actually offer any insight into how intelligence is used in modern policing, Innes and Sheptycki devised four encoding frames, the better to understand how investigators invest meaning and significance into the information being processed into intelligence. Such an approach sub-divides the definition and understanding of intelligence as a product. The four encoding frames, identifying individual modes of intelligence, are set out in Table 3.2.

Table 3.2 Innes & Sheptycki's four encoding frames for intelligence (2004, 10)

Criminal intelligence	'Data that provides some understanding about the identity and activities of a particular nominated individual or group of individuals.'
Crime intelligence	'Insight in relation to particular types of crime, crime hot spots, or crime series.'
Community intelligence	'Information provided by ordinary members of the public . . . tends to refer to the local problems they view as significant.'
Contextual intelligence	'Concerned with the meso- and macro-structures of social organization . . . predicting how changes at this level shape the environment for policing.'

In furthering the understanding of what intelligence is, the important point here is that intelligence, the output derived from the processing of information, has no inherent meaning. It acquires meaning through the interpretation of those using the intelligence, and from the purposes to which they put the processed information. From this perspective it is the tasking process that is the key determinant in distinguishing intelligence from information.

The encoding (a form of triage prior to processing) of raw material information into the four intelligence modes above is achieved through utilization of the nine analytical techniques defined by the NIM (see Chapter 5 below).

This encoding frame is an academic construct devised by non-practitioners in order to make sense of what practitioners are doing with processed information defined as intelligence. These sub-categories of intelligence as product should not be viewed as exclusive. Information provided by an ordinary member of the public in connection with a perceived local problem (Innes and Sheptycki's definition of community intelligence) may well constitute data that could also equally be used, and therefore classified, as criminal intelligence or crime intelligence. Equally, criminal, crime, and community intelligence as defined by Innes and Sheptycki, could inform their construction of contextual intelligence.

In terms of understanding what intelligence is, this illustrates that any one piece of information may be amenable to more than one use as a piece of intelligence but that the manner of its processing may unwittingly confine it to just one interpretation thus running the risk of missing connections or restricting a wider understanding of any given issue or individual.

Extrapolating this concern to the NIM intelligence products—strategic assessments, tactical assessments, subject profiles, and problem profiles (which might be termed an alternative classification of modes of intelligence—if analysts and intelligence officers only ever think of their output as these four prescribed products, there is a danger that they will process information to service the product rather than apply an open mind and free thinking when analysing and evaluating information raw material. Equally there is a danger that tasking based on intelligence products will become a self-fulfilling prophecy that services the NIM intelligence products thus ignoring or constraining opportunities to identify information peripheral to the tasking which nevertheless harbingers emerging issues.

From a practitioner's perspective in respect of community intelligence, Lancashire Constabulary has devised an encoding frame to enhance data gathering in order to monitor changes and trigger signals in community cohesion and tension. The encoding frame is intended to facilitate environmental scanning rather than analyse the use to which intelligence is put: it is an intelligence tool rather than an academic device. The broad headings of issues that might have beneficial or adverse impact on community relations are *economic, political, racial,* and *criminal* (Burnley Borough Council and Lancashire Constabulary, written evidence to the Home Affairs Committee, 2005, vol 2, Ev10, paragraph 2). For the purposes of understanding what intelligence is, this theoretical framework illustrates the types of information being sought in order to be processed into intelligence about the community. It is another way of thinking about intelligence.

Encoding raw material into modes of intelligence is also a feature of competitive intelligence in the commercial world. West (2001) suggests one possible framework based on the following categories of information:

- Financial
- Technical
- Sales and marketing
- Pricing and discount
- People
- Operational

This a framework that a police analyst might adopt when constructing a market or criminal business profile.

Finally, as counter-terrorism demands drive the blurring of different agency roles and functions across the policing, security and military arena, a coding framework used by the military is also worth noting. In this framework intelligence is characterized by collection methodology. The definitions are outlined in Table 3.5 below and in typical military fashion, abbreviations have been constructed (Butler 2004, ch 1.2).

Table 3.5 Coding framework based on collection methodology

Sigint—signals intelligence	Information obtained by intercepting communications
Humint—human intelligence	Information from human sources
Imint—imagery intelligence	Information from photography (conventional, satellite, infra-red etc)
Masint—measurement and signature intelligence	Information from techniques designed to identify traces emitted from substances or as a result of processes (eg use or dumping of radio-active material)

Coding by collection methodologies can be a helpful approach when planning multi-agency joint operations in relation, for instance, to investigating suspected terrorist activity or the trafficking of illicit commodities across national borders. Different agencies will have access to different technologies and resources and therefore will have different methodological capabilities. This in turn will influence considerations about necessity, proportionality, risk assessments, creating evidential opportunities, and subsequent disclosure at trial.

Further information and reading

The Rt Hon Lord Butler *Review of Intelligence on Weapons of Mass Destruction* report of a Committee of Privy Counsellors, HC 898 (The Stationery Office, London, 2004)

Home Affairs Committee *Terrorism and Community Relations* 6th Report of Session 2004–05, HC 165 (3 vols) (The Stationery Office, London, 2005)

M Innes and J Sheptycki 'From detection to disruption: intelligence and the changing logic of police crime control in the United Kingdom' *International Criminal Justice Review* 14 1–24 (2004)

M Innes, N Fielding, and N Cope 'The appliance of science? The theory and practice of criminal intelligence analysis' *British Journal of Criminology* 45 39–57 (2005)

C West *Competitive Intelligence* (Palgrave, Basingstoke, 2001)

3.5 The Intelligence Cycle

What, then, does intelligence as process look like in more detail? Figure 3.1 presents what is termed 'the intelligence cycle', a sequence of activities intended to take information from the status of raw material to the point of intelligence fed into decision-makers in order to define policy or intervention.

The **Direction** phase describes the decision-making process about what raw material information needs to be collected. For police investigators direction will be determined from a number of sources depending upon context. The force Control Strategy, derived from the strategic tasking and coordination group, identifies the priorities for intervention across the force. These priorities are implemented at BCU level with direction about specific interventions being given from the tactical tasking and coordination group. At BCU level direction will also come from the local CDRP (or CSP in Wales) which, following amendments to the Crime and Disorder Act 1998 enacted in the Police and Justice Act 2006, is now subject to the scrutiny of the local authority crime and disorder committee. Local ward councillors are now under a duty to respond to a 'community call for action' on issues perceived within a community to be a crime and disorder problem. One possible response, within this mechanism intended to make local authorities and the police more responsive to community needs, is for the ward councillor to refer an issue to the local authority crime and disorder committee and for that committee to make recommendations which can be passed to the local CDRP/CSP or to other cooperating bodies. The recipient partnership or agencies are then under a duty to consider and respond to the recommendations. Through this mechanism, it is possible that direction for an intelligence operation at BCU level might come ultimately from individual citizens or the local authority as well as from the force Control Strategy.

The direction phase having identified the intelligence requirement, the next phase of the cycle is the **Collection** of raw material information relevant to the task at hand. Sources of information are considered in more detail in Chapter 4. Collection can be undertaken by intelligence unit staff, including dedicated field intelligence officers. It can also be tasked to patrolling officers and PCSOs. Collection plans provide direction and guidance about the required information.

Information gathered during the collection phase is then subject to **Evaluation**, during which phase consideration will be made of the reliability and operational value of each item of information. There follows the **Analysis** phase upon which hypothesis, inferences, and decisions will be founded. The intelligence is presented in a form prescribed by the NIM and doctrine within the police service or in such format as is required within other agencies, and then **Dissemination** of the product takes place. Dissemination will inform either intervention action or the decision to commission a further intelligence operation in recognition of new intelligence gaps and requirements identified during the analysis phase. Analysis is considered in more detail in Chapter 9.

An alternative view of the information processing functions is the 'Filter—Focus—Task—Target' model. In this description **filtering** distinguishes from the overall picture of crime and disorder those issues on which it is feasible to take action, which will then identify priorities upon which to **focus**. From this are derived specific information-gathering or intelligence-processing **tasks** in order to develop intervention options for individual **targets** (people, organizations, problems).

Figure 3.1 The intelligence cycle

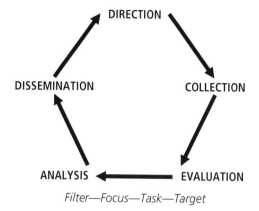

Filter—Focus—Task—Target

> There are a number of representations of this cycle. This figure represents an amalgam of such representations. Cross-reference this simple schematic with ACPO (2005) *Guidance on the National Intelligence Model*, p 14 for the relationship between the cycle and the NIM.

3.6 **Validation of Intelligence**

The intelligence cycle is a defined process from identified need to informed decision. Within the overall process come necessary sub-processes that must be undertaken if decision-makers are to have any confidence in what they are being told. Two phases of the cycle are particularly important: evaluation and analysis which together comprise validation of the intelligence.

Evaluation asks simply, to what extent can we believe each different piece of information before us? The faith invested in each individual item of information determines the influence it exerts in the overall interpretation of all the information available. See the case study below.

Case study—Evaluation

Information comes to the attention of investigators that known suspects intend to meet together. The basic questions, as always, are:

— who (will be at the meeting),
— when (will the meeting take place),
— where (will the meeting take place),
— why (are they meeting, as opposed to communicating by other means),

— what (is the purpose of the meeting), and

— how (will it be conducted: methods of travel to and from venue, in open sight or behind closed doors, in a public place or in private).

Any one of these pieces of information might individually be significant— mere proof of association between individuals or between individuals and premises for instance—whilst taken together the assemblage could provide the opportunity to deploy resources in order to gather evidence of an ongoing conspiracy.

If the attendees are known but the date or venue is not known, then round-the-clock surveillance of the individuals may be appropriate and proportional (depending on the circumstances) until the meeting takes place. If the only certain pieces of information are the venue and the time, then surveillance of the meeting premises for the relevant hours over a period of days may be the appropriate and proportionate tactic.

If it is known the meeting will be for a non-criminal purpose, then any further investigative action may be inappropriate and disproportionate.

In some circumstances, it may be necessary and proportionate to conduct surveillance to test the reliability of the source.

In all cases, authorizing officers and lead investigators will require an understanding of the value and reliability of each piece of information forming the overall intelligence in order to discharge their duties of care to staff, the public and in avoiding a violation of the suspect's rights that may result in a procedural acquittal.

The issue in relation to all the questions in the case study above is how reliable is the information?

Evaluation tests each piece of information.

- What is the provenance of the information? Where does it originate?
- How does the source providing the information come to be in possession of the information (eg directly or indirectly)?
- Has that source provided reliable information in the past?
- If the source provides information in relation to only some of the questions above, why does the source not know the remaining pieces?
- Can any of the above information be corroborated by a second source?
- And if a second source does have access to the same information, is the second source providing truly independent direct knowledge of the information concerned or is the second source merely confirming that the first source had indirect access? (In which case the second source would not be confirming the information provided by the first source.)

- Is there any likelihood that the information, even if it can be corroborated, is being planted in order to confuse and mislead the investigators (and the power of deception will of course be reinforced if misleading information can be corroborated)?

And in the subsequent results analysis,

- If anticipated events did not occur, what information can be obtained to ascertain why the anticipated actions did not occur?

Further information and reading

'The validation of a reporting chain requires both care and time, and can generally only be conducted by the agency responsible for collection. The process is informed by the operational side of the agency, but must include a separate auditing element, which can consider cases objectively and quite apart from their apparent intelligence value.'

Review of Intelligence on Weapons of Mass Destruction, report of a Committee of Privy Counsellors chaired by The Rt Hon The Lord Butler of Brockwell, HC 898 (The Stationery Office, London, 2004) paragraph 29.

Validation then progresses from evaluation to analysis. Once the coherence and consistency of the information gathered from the source(s) has been evaluated, in the following analysis stage 'the factual material inside the intelligence report is examined in its own right' (*Review of Intelligence on Weapons of Mass Destruction* paragraph 30). The sub-process of analysis assembles individual information reports into intelligence that derives meaning from context and being part of a strand of separate reports relating to the same issue. In some cases it will be necessary to convert complex and fragmentary information into intelligence material that a decision-maker can use. Within the context of neighbourhood policing or regulation of the night-time economy this might require analysis to be conducted by or in association with experts from different agencies (eg trading standards or the local authority licensing department). At the level of protective services it might require linguists or individuals familiar with the jargon and verbal codes adopted by certain organized crime groups, or by skilled accountants. If the intelligence is to be used for decision-making about strategic intervention or community safety policies, then analysis by relevant policy or academic experts might be required.

Evaluation and analysis ideally should be conducted independently of the decision-makers and intelligence-users. Lack of rigour in evaluation and lack of appropriate expertise or independence in the analysis phase may result in investigators misleading themselves through erroneous or prejudiced interpretation. Evaluation and analysis are considered in greater detail in Chapter 9 below. It is sufficient here to note that these two processes are crucial in the transformation of raw material into intelligence, and should therefore be viewed as defining characteristics when considering what is intelligence.

3.7 Conclusion—So What is Intelligence?

So what, then, is intelligence? Although for some practitioners it is each individual item of information gleaned from sources outside the organization (this is one of the senses in which the word is used in the Butler report for instance, at paragraphs 27 and 28), the majority of practitioner and academic sources consulted for this book view intelligence as being created from raw material information that has been evaluated and analysed. Part of the importance of validation involves assessment of provenance. Appropriate duty of care obligations cannot be assessed without knowledge of provenance. The original recipient should probe provenance in order to apply the 5x5x5 initial risk assessment properly.

Ratcliffe, as has been shown in Table 3.1 above, offers a multi-faceted, triptych perspective in which intelligence is, simultaneously, a *structure* that serves to *process* information into *products* that inform decision-makers. This business analysis overview, arguably made manifest through the implementation of the NIM (see Chapter 5) does not and cannot, however, encapsulate the influence of organizational culture, practice, and 'conventional wisdom' (an antithesis of intelligence if ever there was one). These influences help determine structure (is there a willingness to provide appropriate resources and training within the structure?), characterize the processes (is the role of the analyst little more than that of collation?), and so dictate the value of the product (if a profile fails to identify possible intervention options through inadequate analysis, can a decision based on the profile be considered to be informed?).

Intelligence, because it is a label with such a variety of meanings, is widely used but not necessarily commonly understood. There is scope for misunderstanding, particularly in partnership or joint agency working. If nothing else, the considerations above have highlighted the need for practitioners to be sure that when talking about intelligence, they are all talking about the same thing before the conversation progresses too far. Like conventional wisdom, assumption is almost the opposite of intelligence and can seriously derail outcome. Above all, as this chapter has illustrated, intelligence is about different ways of thinking: thinking that can illuminate all aspects of an issue or, through the constraints of organizational culture, confine what would otherwise be key understanding to the shadows.

Because intelligence, in the sense of processed information, can both inform or misinform decision-making (depending upon the resources invested and the quality of evaluation and analysis), intelligence-led policing, no matter how well-intentioned, could head in the wrong direction.

4

Sources of Information

4.1 **Introduction**

Potential sources of information, which can then be processed into intelligence, are limited only by the imagination of the investigator and certain legal constraints on accessing legally privileged, confidential, and journalistic material. Similarly the manner of information acquisition is regulated according to circumstance (see the PACE Codes of Practice, the Police Act 1997 Part III, and RIPA; also Harfield and Harfield 2005). This chapter considers, in turn, various generic sources of information starting with internal and partner agency sources, then the community and suspects within the community before introducing the wider intelligence community and considering criminal use of intelligence.

In terms of intelligence theory, sources can be divided into primary and secondary, internal and external. The key skills for intelligence officers and analysts alike are the 'ability to identify the sources that are likely to have the data that are required and the ability to extract them' (West 2001: 50). Sources that are publicly available are not necessarily readily available. Just because a lot of information is available from any given source, does not mean that all the available information will be relevant. Focused intelligence collection is required, concentrating on what is needed to achieve the particular tactical, operational, or strategic analysis, but always mindful of gaps that cannot be filled and the absence of information influences interpretation of the information that is available.

Figure 4.1 Source matrix based on West 2001, 51

External Secondary Sources eg partner agencies	External Primary Sources eg CHIS
Internal Secondary Sources eg databases, staff knowledge	Internal Primary Sources eg staff engaged on surveillance

4.2 **Frontline Staff**

Further information and reading

'. . .the evidence and intelligence gathering trail commences with the initial contact between the person reporting an offence and the police.'

ACPO *Investigation of Volume Crime* (NCPE Centrex, Wyboston, 2001), p 9

When a patient is delivered by ambulance to a hospital accident and emergency department the subsequent diagnosis (analysis of the raw information) and treatment crucially is informed by basic information about injury and circumstance gleaned by the paramedic crew when recovering the patient. In every agency and organization it is the frontline staff interacting with the public who have the largest number of opportunities and the greatest potential to gather information necessary to the functioning of the organization. Frontline staff can be directed to seek out and gather specific information pursuant to an intelligence collection plan. This directed information gathering is supplemented by spontaneous information collection through the normal course of work. If, as was argued in the previous chapter, intelligence for policing, regulation, and investigation is as much a way of thinking as it is a procedure or business process model, then how frontline staff derive their understanding of intelligence issues is a crucial success factor in any organization purporting to be intelligence-led.

Neighbourhood policing teams and PCSOs, together with colleagues from local authority partner agencies, are the frontline information-gatherers whose daily conversational interaction with the public is the most effective means of gauging community tensions and identifying emerging issues. The relationships thus fostered promote the goodwill to provide specific information when needed to assist individual crime enquiries.

Frontline staff do not always recognize their potential intelligence contribution. HMIC identified the untapped intelligence potential in crime scene investigation and forensic analysis (*Under the Microscope*, 2002; see also s 2.2.2 above). The HMIC thematic inspection discovered that scenes of crime investigators were not always aware of how they could invest the intelligence process with relevant information when interacting with victims and examining crime scenes and that they did not necessarily regard themselves as being within the intelligence loop. As the Macpherson Inquiry established, there can be a tendency for information to be retained in unit-specific databases (in this case the card index system of the Racial Incident Unit at Plumstead police station, MacPherson 1999, paragraphs 35.12–35.14) in which case it may elude intelligence-collection operations and subsequent analysis. Other specialist yet frontline units would include (but exclusively) those established to investigate domestic violence, licensing compliance, vice, drugs, street robberies, and roads policing including ANPR units. These all generate information that provides intelligence for the specialist function of the specific unit which may also be of use to colleagues outside the unit provided it is fed into a database which is accessible outside the relevant unit.

Stop-and-search, detention, and arrest all provide opportunities for intelligence-gathering. In particular, arrest should lead to a number of cross-referencing intelligence checks:

- Check against the PNC for previous convictions, pending cases and outstanding warrants: the arrested person may not be resident in the force area and for that reason may not feature on local databases.
- Check against the force intelligence database to ascertain if previously known within the force area.
- Check modus operandi on databases to identify possible further offences.
- Cross-check against other known information such as home address.

In support of the information-gathering of frontline staff, the NIM envisages certain key intelligence roles within police forces and by extrapolation, to other organizations using the NIM as an intelligence business process. At the executive level within an organization, ACPO level within a police force, the designation of an **executive lead on NIM implementation** is recommended in the ACPO *Guidance on the NIM* (2005). The guidance refers specifically to an organizational lead for the NIM, the management of the business process, rather than for intelligence itself as a professional skill. ACPO envisages that the lead on professional intelligence skills should come from a **Head of Profession**, also termed a Director of Intelligence, 'normally of Superintendent rank with a credible track record in the field of intelligence and/or proactive investigations', whose responsibility it would be to have 'ownership of the intelligence function, its development, strategic direction, production of the intelligence products, control strategy and intelligence requirements for the force tasking and co-ordination group' (ACPO *Guidance on the NIM*, p 39).

At NIM level 1, the BCU or its equivalent, ACPO recommends that the local intelligence unit should be headed by an **intelligence manager** with the following responsibilities (ACPO *Guidance on the NIM*, p 39):

- *Strategic and tactical assessment*—reporting and advising on what is important to the BCU, including issues of risk to the public and policing;
- *Understanding intelligence gaps*—reporting and advising on setting intelligence requirements;
- *Identifying criminal profiles*—understanding how criminals operate in order to identify weaknesses in their systems, who is involved in their criminal networks, and who their associates are;
- *Infiltration and penetration*—establishing tactical opportunities from collected intelligence and analytical products to secure infiltration or understanding of the criminal/organization;
- *Operational review*—determining what worked or did not work and why;
- *Management representation*—ensuring that intelligence as a discipline is adequately represented in management discussions on resources;
- *Tactical direction*—engaging with managers of the command unit/force on behalf of the T&CG to ensure that specialists are consulted to provide options under the tactical menu which are realistic and clear;
- *Understanding covert tactics*—ensuring that the intelligence unit is equipped to handle information that is already known or acquired during reactive investigation, and gathering information through proactive or covert means.

Equally, these may be regarded as appropriate generic duties for the intelligence manager heading the force intelligence bureau (FIB) at level 2, although this individual will also have regional liaison duties on behalf of the organization. Specialist training is available for intelligence managers.

Within both the FIB and local intelligence departments there reside certain key functions although their labels may vary from organization to organization. The key staff, in terms of processing information into intelligence, are the **analysts**. Their status within a police organization varies considerably and they may not always enjoy a positive perception (Cope 2004). There will be staff whose role it is to **gather information 'in the field'**, ie actively seek out information pursuant to directed tasking. There will probably be staff whose role it is to **collate raw information submitted by colleagues** and staff whose role it is to **disseminate relevant intelligence and information-collection plans** to frontline staff, sometimes referred to as briefing officers. Possibly at force level rather than BCU level within police forces there will be a prison intelligence officer. Ideally there should be sufficient administrative support for this team of specialists.

Often alongside the intelligence department and apparently quite frequently under the same manager although this is contrary to stipulated good practice (ACPO *Guidance on the NIM*, p 41 and ACPO/HMCE *Manual of Standards for Covert Human Intelligence Sources* 2004), will be a dedicated source unit (DSU) whose task it is to manage covert human intelligence sources (CHIS). CHIS handling and management require specialist training and the DSU should operate strictly within defined professional parameters and in deliverance of the organizational Control Strategy (see Chapter 5). Regulation of CHIS is set out in RIPA and guidance is provided in a Code of Practice (see Harfield and Harfield 2005, Chapter 9 and Appendix E). Particular attention should be paid to the code in relation to using vulnerable persons and juveniles as CHISs.

4.3 **Partner Agencies**

With particular reference to neighbourhood policing and community safety, information held by partner agencies may be of particular significance. The key local community safety partnership is the Crime and Disorder Partnership, established under section 5 of the Crime and Disorder Act 1998, which now comes under the scrutiny and review of the local authority crime and disorder committee (Police and Justice Act 2006, s 19). The crime reduction strategies required of CDRPs can only realistically be drafted on the basis of shared intelligence between the partners about perceived problems and potential solutions. It could be argued that the NIM strategic assessment will inform the crime audit process for the CDRP. Equally, intelligence from partner agencies that informs the crime audit could also inform the strategic assessment. Partner agencies within a CDRP have a statutory duty 'to disclose to all other CDRP relevant authorities any information held by the authority which is of a prescribed description, at such intervals and in such form as may be prescribed' by the Secretary of State (Crime and Disorder Act 1998, s 17A, as amended).

Consideration should also be given to how information and intelligence can be acquired from and shared with Local Criminal Justice Boards and Local Strategic Partners. Outside the immediate statutory composition of a CDRP will be agencies whose own work can significantly inform community intelligence analysis: local authority housing departments, trading standards, and social services, for example. Welfare organizations, subject to confidentiality protocols regarding individual clients, may be a source for information about quality of life issues that might not otherwise come to official attention. Within an intelligence unit, ownership of partner agency liaison must be clearly defined and assigned. Relationships with external partners have to be attentively managed. The Victoria Climbié Inquiry illustrates why. Even when partnership arrangements enjoy positive mutual support and collaboration, working practices should still be challenged to ensure the work is intelligence-led rather than assumption-led. The Anthony Rice review illustrates why. (See Chapter 2 above.)

Amongst the issues relevant in the Rice case is that of the information and intelligence about Rice made available to the parole board that considered his release. Prison intelligence and how, if at all, partner agencies can access information within prisons is a complex arena which, at time of writing (2007), is currently under review nationally (for the progress of this project see <http://www.npia. police.uk>). Of particular relevance to police/CDRP tasking and coordination are prisoner release dates. The re-emergence into society of prolific burglars or prisoners convicted of domestic or community-based violence can have a significant adverse impact on local crime and community or, in the case of prisoners seeking revenge upon their victims for their conviction, individual safety. The release of serious sexual and violent offenders is generally brought to the attention of agency staff responsible for MAPPA. Notification of the release of prisoners who fall outside these categories is, in the experience of a number of police forces, more haphazard, partly due to the complexities of managing the prison population. It is in the interest of several local agencies, not just the police service, to be alerted to the release of a potential reoffender before that individual arrives in the locality so that appropriate planning can take place.

4.4 **Databases**

There are a number of databases operated by the police service nationally and different national partner agencies. Key databases, intelligence tools, information services, and their acronyms are outlined in the table below. The list is not exhaustive.

Table 4.1 Some key databases and information services for investigators

ANI	Access NI. Northern Ireland equivalent of the CRB, being established during 2007.
ANPR	Automatic number plate recognition. A system used in temporary roadside equipment or via CCTV to identify vehicle registration plates and so trace suspect vehicles or vehicles believed to be being driven untaxed, uninsured or without MOT. Linked to the PNC.

BCS	British Crime Survey, undertaken biannually on behalf of the Home Office, in which victimization is studied rather than reported crime. Usually indicates that much more crime is committed than is reported to the police.
CEDRIC	Customs and Excise Departmental Reference and Information Computer—former intelligence database for HMC, replaced in May 2004 by CENTAUR when HMCE merged with the Inland Revenue to become HMRC.
CENTAUR	HMRC's nominal (names/addresses) and events (activities) intelligence database recording all events of interest to HMRC.
CRB	Criminal Records Bureau. Manages disclosure of previous convictions for pre-employment checks. <http://www.crb.gov.uk>
Crimelink	A PNC-based search tool that be used to identify links and similarities in serious serial crimes investigation.
CRISP	Cross Regional Information Sharing Project. A consortium of local police forces collaborating to share local intelligence, adopted within the IMPACT programme as an interim solution en route to the fully functional PND. Aborted in early 2007 due to Home Office budgetary constraints.
DAF	Disclosure Application Form—standard form used by CRB upon which Registered Bodies may request police information about individuals.
ELMER (SARS)	The database underpinning the Suspicious Activity Reporting regime, which is intended to alert investigators to likely instances of money-laundering.
Equifax	Commercial enterprise supplying credit ratings and histories. <http://www.equifax.com>
FLAC	Faith, Language and Culture database, run and accessible exclusively by ACPO's NCTT, containing details of volunteers prepared to help with cultural interpretation, language skills and advice when required by the police in order better to manage community diversity issues. NCTT is the liaison point for police and external agencies regarding this database.
FLINTS	Forensic Lead Intelligence System. Developed by West Midlands Police and shared access with neighbouring forces. A database to assist in collation of intelligence and evidence in order to link suspects to a scene. Depends upon all crimes being entered as well as hard evidence and intelligence. Also the acronym given by HMIC to their database of good practice and inspection evidence.
IMPACT	Intelligence Management, Prioritisation, Analysis, Co-ordination and Tasking Programme. Programme jointly undertaken by Home Office and police service to improve the management and sharing of information and intelligence between police forces.

75

Table 4.1 Some key databases and information services for investigators *(cont.)*

INI	IMPACT Nominal Index.
List 99	List maintained by Department for Education & Skills of persons statutorily barred from teaching or other employment in the education sector.
NAFIS	National Automated Fingerprint Identification System. First introduced to all English and Welsh police forces to assist in identification and storage of fingerprints. (Not to be confused with the National Association of Foreclosure Industry Specialists.)
NDNAD	National DNA Database, established in 1995 as the first ever national DNA database. Serves England and Wales and shares DNA profiles from Northern Ireland and Scotland which run their own DNA databases.
National Fingerprint Collection	Fingerprints held of all persons convicted of a criminal offence in Scotland.
NIS	National Identification Service—provided by the Metropolitan Police Service.
NOMIS	National Offender Management Information System, the intelligence database of the prison and probation services since their merger into the National Offender Management Service.
OASys	Offender Assessment System. An assessment tool applied to sexual and violent offenders as part of the risk management process informing MAPPA offender management plans.
PLX	Police Local Cross-check. Joint ACPO/CRB/PITO initiative intended to facilitate better Enhanced Disclosure in pre-employment conviction checks.
PNC	Police National Computer. Contains information about wanted and convicted persons. Previously run by PITO and now run by the NPIA, it is the only full-time, operational national police computer system routinely supplied with data from all English, Welsh and Scottish forces and the PSNI. A Code of Practice applies and is accessible at <http://police.homeoffice.gov.uk/news-and-publications/publication/operational-policing/Police_nat_comp.pdf?view=Binary> (accessed 28 August 2007). Other agencies have varying levels of access to the PNC including, amongst others, British Transport Police, the military police forces, the Ministry of Defence Police, SOCA and the National Offender Management Service. See also <http://www.npia.police.uk/en/5977.htm> (accessed 28 August 2007).
PND	Police National Database. At time of writing the planning for this is underway. Recommended by the Bichard Inquiry as a means of ensuring police and partners have access to intelligence about crime and criminals outside their immediate geographical jurisdictions and areas of responsibility. Final architecture and functionality yet to be determined. Key element of the IMPACT programme.

POCA	Protection of Children Act 1999 list—maintained by Department for Education and Skills, recording those considered unsuitable for working with children. <http://www.opsi.gov.uk/acts/acts1999/ukpga_19990014_en_1>
POVA	Protection of Vulnerable Adults List, maintained by the Department for Education and Skills, documenting persons deemed unsuitable to work with vulnerable adults.
PVS	Passport Verification Service.
QUEST	Query Using Enhanced Search Techniques. A PNC search tool enabling search of the nominal database to identify suspects.
Risk Matrix 2000	Complements OASys and is used in drawing up offender management programmes under MAPPA provisions.
SCRO	Scottish Criminal Records Office.
SID	Scottish Intelligence Database.
SIRENE	Supplementary Information Request at the National Entry. A communication network for the exchange of additional data that cannot be stored on the SIS.
SFS	Scottish Fingerprint Service. <http://www.sfs.police.uk>
SIS	Schengen Information System. Established under Article 92 of the Schengen Convention 1990. Records details of wanted persons and certain types of property that are subject to seizure. Currently being upgraded to SIS II. PNC is linked to SIS for the relevant information that may be stored and shared. (Coincidentally SIS is also the abbreviation for Secret Intelligence Service, MI6.)
SSID	Social Services Information Database.
VBS	Vetting and Barring Scheme. Addresses Bichard Recommendation 19 for the registering of those who wish to work with children or vulnerable adults. Registration signifies that there is no known reason to prevent an individual working with these groups. Established under the Safeguarding Vulnerable Groups Act 2006.
ViSOR	Violent and Sex Offenders Register, accessible by police and probation services recording persons required to register with the police in compliance with the Sexual Offences Act 2003; persons imprisoned for more than 12 months for offences of violence; and unconvicted persons considered to present a serious offending risk. Holds nominal details, modus operandi, photographs and is linked to the PNC.
VODS	Vehicle Online Descriptions. A PNC search tool allowing searches to identify suspect vehicles.

At force level various different crime, incident and intelligence-reporting data-bases exist. These are mirrored by the various databases created within partner agencies to assist in administering their work. The variety and lack of connectivity between these databases was subject of criticism during the Bichard Inquiry and prompted the initiation of the IMPACT programme.

Nationally police information is stored on the Police National Computer. It stores details of offenders, convictions, cautions, current court process, whether or not fingerprints and DNA samples have been taken, wanted/missing status, driver disqualification, and firearm certificate details. Details of offences including type and location are also held. It is also used to store details of vehicle registered keepers, lost or stolen vehicles, insurance and (since 2006) MOT information. Details of stolen/found plant machinery, engines, animals, and firearms are also stored on the PNC.

Post conviction, the National Offender Management Information System (NOMIS) is intended to enable prison and probation staff to share information in real time; manage risk; manage sentencing and rehabilitation; and increase efficiency (<http://www.noms.homeoffice.gov.uk>).

The National DNA Database, which holds DNA samples both from convicted and unconvicted persons, is controversial. *R v Chief Constable of South Yorkshire, ex parte S and Marper* [2004] 4 All ER 193 (HL) tested whether retention of DNA samples from unconvicted persons was a breach of Article 8(1) European Convention on Human Rights (ECHR). The House of Lords found that it was a breach but one that was proportionate and justified under Article 8(2). The case has gone for further consideration to the Court of Human Rights at Strasbourg. In 2006 the NDNA held DNA profiles for 5.2 per cent of the total population of the UK.

Further information and reading—the National DNA Database

For further information on the NDNAD see Parliamentary Office of Science & Technology 2006 *Postnote: The National DNA Database* (no 258) accessible via <http://www.parliament.uk/parliamentary_offices/post/pubs2006.cfm>).

As sources of information databases are only as good as the data input in them. This is their inherent weakness. The lack of timely court disposal data is a perceived weakness of PNC data. The revelation that there may be as many as 500,000 false or incorrectly spelt entries on the UK national DNA database made news around the world given the emphasis placed on DNA profiling by investigators (see Independent on Sunday 26 August 2007; Sydney Morning Herald 27 August 2007). Meg Hillier, Home Office Minister, is quoted as saying 'The number of individuals on the database is approximately 13.7 per cent less than the number of subject profiles' (Independent on Sunday 26 August 2007, p 22). Nor is it only when giving biometric samples that criminals give or use false identities. When investigating the extent of identity crimes in Australia, for instance, it was found that in 2003 a total national population of 19 millions had generated 22 million passports and 29 million tax identity numbers (The Australian, 2 June 2003).

An audit of HMRC's CENTAUR database undertaken by HMIC revealed that 82.6 per cent of actionable nominal; reports emanating from the National HumInt Centre (NHC) were not recorded on CENTAUR: a very significant amount of key information from CHISs was not finding its way into the intelligence database. Overall HMIC found that 'over one quarter of actionable intelligence NIU nominal reports are not entered on the Department's intelligence database' (HMIC 2007: 36). This adversely affects not only operational investigations but also the ability to discharge statutory obligations regarding disclosure.

The above are all closed databases—access to which is restricted to trained personnel in specific agencies and in the case of commercially run databases depends upon payment of a fee. The development of the internet has prompted increased public accessibility to a number of other databases and archives.

Open source information is information, howsoever stored or published, that is generally accessible to the public, even if its distribution is limited. Examples include telephone directories, electoral registers, registers of births, marriages and deaths, registers at Companies House (<http://www.companieshouse.gov.uk>), and the broadcast and print media. These sources can be accessed either in hard copy at libraries, local authority offices, or on the internet. In connection with searches on the internet a number of search engines are available either individually crawling the web for the search terms (for instance <http://www.google.com>) or else performing a meta-search function that searches several different search engines simultaneously and merges the results into one (eg <http://clusty.com>).

4.5 **Community**

Case study—a source for community intelligence

In the UK the emergency services can be contacted urgently by telephoning 999. The equivalent number in the USA is 911. In New York City there is also a general number for non-urgent enquiries and problem-reporting—311. The 311 number, which connects citizens to services other than just the police department, has proved to be crucial in accessing hitherto untapped community information about low-level, non-crime, quality of life, and community well-being issues of concern to the public (Johnson 2006, 222–226).

After due consideration, the UK Government has determined that it does not have the money available to support a similar service ('The Today Programme' BBC Radio 4, 11 September 2007).

Information from the community is the life-blood of policing both in terms of developing community safety and in terms of investigating crime. Information will only be forthcoming if the community has confidence in the police service or other agencies seeking community help. Developing and sustaining good links with the community and those who represent it (rather than those who purport to represent it) is a critical success factor in community intelligence. Consultation with every citizen is not feasible but if confidence and trust can be established through representative consultation, such as through **Independent Advisory Groups** (IAGs) for instance then, when enquiries are initiated to discover specific information that might exist within a community, it is to be hoped the information sought will be forthcoming from individuals.

Community information need not be confined to specific items of information passed to police or other agencies and local authorities by individual community members and community leaders or by representative groups and organizations such as **Neighbourhood Watch**. It can also be harvested indirectly through the strategic plans of other local public service deliverers, through census returns and predictions and other government sources, through recorded crime data, and through victimization data. **Partner agencies** will have community profile data to inform their own functional responsibilities and such information may be of particular use in problem-solving approaches. Additional insight is accessible through recognition of signal crimes and disorders and through community impact assessments.

4.5.1 **Signal Crimes**

Further information and reading—the Signal Crimes Perspective

'A **signal crime** is any criminal incident that causes change in the public's behaviour and/or beliefs about their security.

A **signal disorder** is an act that breaches situated conventions of social order and signifies the presence of other risks. They can be social or physical in nature.'

ACPO *Practice Advice on Professionalising the Business of Neighbourhood Policing* (NCPE Centrex, Bramshill, 2005) 24

The concept is drawn from M Innes and N Fielding (2002) 'From community to communicative policing: signal crimes and the problem of public reassurance' *Sociological Research Online* 7/2 at <http://www.socresonline.org.uk/7/2/innes.html>.

The concept of the **Signal Crimes Perspective** (SCP) is derived from and the application of intelligence-led policing to neighbourhood policing. Provision of a flexible policing response dictates the need for good and accurate intelligence in relation to neighbourhood policing in order to understand not only what is happening but also community perceptions about what is happening—which may in turn give rise to new or escalating problems.

The need to understand individual episodes that may trigger significant concerns, in addition to the impact of incident frequency, has only recently been recognized (Innes and Fielding 2002; NCPE 2005). SCP theory suggests that some incidents of crime and disorder may act as signals to people, informing their perceptions about the risk of victimization regardless of whether that perception accords with reality as recorded in crime and victimization statistics. Trigger identification informs the prioritization of resources, in theory achieving a disproportionate increase in the sense of community and individual safety. The consequential reduction in fear of crime means individuals will no longer modify their lifestyles in response to that fear.

Signals comprise three elements which will be identified through consultation with and understanding of the local community (ACPO 2005: 24):

- the **expression**—an incident focusing public concerns;
- the **content**—what the incident means to people and how it is being interpreted/perceived;
- the **effect**—changes caused in peoples thinking and behaviour as a consequence of interpreting/perceiving expressions.

All three elements must be present to constitute a signal. SCP theory views the presence of less than three elements as 'background noise'. The case study below illustrates the concept with an example.

Case study—the Signal Crimes Perspective

In this example EX = the expression, C = the content, and E = the effect.

A member of the public witnesses a drunken fight (EX) taking place in a local shopping precinct. Bottles are smashed and street furniture damaged. Police attend and the member of the public reports being very distressed by the incident (E). Such anti-social behaviour is a regular occurrence in this location. The member of public expresses the concern that if they continue to shop in this area they perceive a significant risk of becoming a victim of crime or disorder (C), which fear will persuade them to shop elsewhere (E).

The SCP 'provides an innovative way of interpreting how the public sees and understands problems of crime and disorder. It suggests a potential for targeting police resources to those incidents that matter most to the public in a particular neighbourhood' (ACPO 2005: 25). It is a context within which to view other information sources such as recorded crime data and victimization surveys.

All of this information, the signals, the recorded crime, and victimization data, is generated by the community and should inform analysts in their understanding of the wider intelligence picture. It may be harvested both through neighbourhood policing teams and crime databases. To be effective in their respective roles, neighbourhood policing teams, analysts, and CDRPs need to understand both the variety of sources of community information and the strategic picture painted by combining these sources.

4.5.2 **Community Impact Assessment**

A **community impact assessment** (CIA) documents the actual or likely impact that a significant incident, investigation, or issue will have or has had on communities. It draws upon analysis of available intelligence and in doing so creates new knowledge and perspective, which in turns become a source of information. The impact of an incident is dependent upon a range of factors including the inter-relationships that may exist between the different strata that make up a community, thus creating a range of potential hubs in which impacts and tensions may develop and emerge.

The assessment is informed through effective community engagement and consultation with independent advisory groups and community representatives, partner agencies, and community policing teams. Thames Valley Police have had particular experience of using this methodology. Following the arrests of a number of terrorist suspects in London and High Wycombe in August 2006, Thames Valley Police used community impact assessments to help understand community issues arising from the counter-terrorist operation. In particular it was realized that the composition of the independent advisory group needed review and restructuring in order to make it more representative and so to engage more closely with the resident communities.

Further information and reading

S Thornton and L Mason 'Community cohesion in High Wycombe: a case study of Operation Overt' *Policing: a Journal of Policy and Practice* 1/1 57–60 (2007).

ACPO has established a National Community Tensions Team (NCTT) that undertakes tension monitoring and community impact assessments, publishing weekly intelligence bulletins on community tension for police forces and partner agencies including government departments. The NCTT has the operational lead for the 'Prevent' strand of the national counter-terrorism strategy.

The CIA process suggested by the National Community Tension Team is as follows:

- consultation (eg IAG, community groups, Gold Groups, Safer Neighbourhood/ Community Policing Teams, partner agencies, NCTT);
- presentation of information upon which assessment is based;
- assessment for legislative compliance;
- risk identification;
- identification of response options;
- implementation plan.

The commercial community, although reluctant to divulge information that is commercially sensitive information can be a useful source of data about crime types, trends, and methods. In particular the financial sector will be a source of information about fraud and money laundering. The mechanism for capturing such information, besides individuals working in the financial sector, is the suspicious activity reporting (SAR) system, which contributes data to the ELMER database now maintained by SOCA (Lander 2006).

Covert human intelligence sources (CHIS), whether they be informants recruited to assist in information-gathering or undercover operatives deployed to seek specific information, depend upon their relationships within the community, no matter the size of their social interaction network, as the basis of their capacity to gather information. Indeed, the statutory definition of a CHIS notes the utilization of relationships for this purpose (RIPA, s 29). A person supplying information and covertly using a personal relationship to acquire information that he or she might not otherwise have had, is undertaking the role of CHIS and requires appropriate authorization, registration, and management (Harfield and Harfield 2005, Chapter 9).

4.6 **Technical**

Information capable of being processed into intelligence can be obtained from a number of **proactive technical sources** such as audio, video and tracking surveillance, and communication interception. The levels of intrusion involved in such activity require authorization under RIPA and the Police Act 1997 (see Harfield and Harfield 2005). The authorization focuses on the level of intrusion rather than the specific technology utilized to achieve the intrusion. Such information acquisition is also highly resource intensive, requiring not only sophisticated equipment but also trained staff capable of deploying it without compromising methods, technology, or the investigation. Such is the sensitivity surrounding some technologies there have been instances in both Australia and the UK (and very probably in other jurisdictions beyond the personal knowledge of the authors) in which technical capability has been developed but not utilized because adducing the product in evidence, for instance, would expose the capability: non-utilization is preferable to revealing that the capability exists. From a different perspective this engages with the issue of proportionality. Just because the capability exists to acquire information in a certain way does not mean that it is proportionate or necessary to do so. And if it is neither proportionate nor necessary, a proposed action will not meet the Article 8(2) tests for a qualified breach of Article 8(1) ECHR.

Further information and reading

J Petersen *Understanding Surveillance Technologies: Spy Devices, Privacy, History and Applications* (2nd edn, Auerbach Publications, Boca Raton NY, 2007) discusses different surveillance technologies from a technical thematic perspective: **acoustic** (audio, infra/ultrasound, sonar); **electromagnetic** (radio, radar, infrared, visual, aerial, ultraviolet, X-rays); **chemical and biological** (chemical and biological, biometrics, animals, genetics); and **miscellaneous** (magnetic, cryptologic, computers).

Less resource-intensive are **passive data generators**, computer systems designed to gather data automatically for business, commercial, and other non-investiga-tivedaily functions. CCTV is a common form of passive data generation. Other examples include subscriber, billing and financial transaction data automatical-ly produced when making a telephone call, sending an email, or using an auto-mated telling machine. Use of a debit or credit card may provide information as to the whereabouts of a missing or wanted person for instance. The London transport system encourages the use of the Oyster card as an automated pay-ment mechanism for train and bus journeys. As a by-product of this payment mechanism, journey details of persons using Oyster cards are recorded. Door security entry systems record who is in or out of a building. Every keystroke on a computer is recorded on the hard drive, a fact which has proved crucial in many investigations involving digital data. Such information will generally only be accessible via a court order or a Data Protection Act notice.

4.7 **Intelligence Agencies**

The Security Service Act 1988 (SSA) (as amended by the Security Service Act 1996) added to the statutory duties of the Security Service (MI5) the function 'to act in support of the activities of police forces and other law enforcement agencies in the prevention and detection of serious crime' (SSA 1988, s 1(4)). Serious crime for this purpose is defined as involving the use of violence, resulting in sub-stantial financial gain or is conduct by a large number of persons in pursuit of a common purpose or, alternatively, is an offence for which a person over 21 could reasonably expect, upon first conviction, to be sentenced to three or more years in prison. Thus MI5 became engaged with the function of law enforcement as required. The reality is that the Security Service is a relatively small organization in terms of staff establishment when compared with the police service as a whole. The intelligence support that MI5 can offer is therefore constrained by resources and the demands arising from its other statutory duties. Historically MI5 has worked with Special Branch and counter-terrorist investigators. Prior to the creation of SOCA (which has recruited former MI5 staff as part of its intelligence enhancement, see Harfield 2006), MI5 also supported the National Crime Squad. Intelligence liaison between MI5 and the police service was generally via the National Criminal Intelligence Service although some parts of the police service had and continue to have direct contact.

Other members of the wider intelligence community, the Secret Intelligence Service (MI6) and Government Communications Headquarters (GCHQ), also have a statutory remit to act 'in support of the prevention or detection of serious crime', although no mention is made in the Act that this necessarily has to be in support of police forces or other law enforcement agencies (Intelligence Services Act 1994 (ISA), ss 1(2)(c) and 3(2)(c)). The extent of the support that can be offered by MI6 and GCHQ is limited by geographical jurisdiction and restrictions that prohibit certain powers from being used in supporting the prevention and detection of serious crime (ISA, s 5).

Realistically, although the definition of serious crime is very broad, the wider intelligence community is only going to be involved in criminal intelligence matters in support of law enforcement at level 3 of the NIM and in relation to counter-terrorism policing. With the radicalization of migrant communities within the UK prompting some individuals to resort to terrorist attacks such as those committed in London (July 2005 and 2007) and in Glasgow (2007), there is a need for those interacting daily with local communities to pass relevant intelligence via force intelligence bureaux and local Special Branches to the wider intelligence community.

Further information and reading—The UK Intelligence Community

In response to calls for greater transparency the UK intelligence community now has a web presence from which sufficient information is available to obtain a general understanding of the intelligence community's framework and activities.

The main government intelligence web page is located at: <http://www.intelligence.gov.uk/>.

It contains a number of information sub-pages and links to most of the intelligence community web sites.

A general information booklet can be downloaded from: <http://www.intelligence.gov.uk/upload/assets/www.intelligence.gov.uk/national_intelligence_booklet.pdf>.

Information about the threat assessment system can be downloaded from: <http://www.intelligence.gov.uk/upload/assets/www.intelligence.gov.uk/threatlevels.pdf>.

The main intelligence agency web pages are to be found at:

MI5 Security Service   <http://www.mi5.gov.uk/>

MI6 Secret Intelligence Service   <http://www.sis.gov.uk/output/Page79.html>

GCHQ   <http://www.gchq.gov.uk/>

JTAC   <http://www.mi5.gov.uk/output/Page63.html>

The police intelligence community comprises the force intelligence bureaux and area intelligence units within individual forces. Prior to 1 April 2006 the National Criminal Intelligence Service, the National Crime Squad and the National Hi-Tech Crime Unit all had individual websites from which could be accessed general information of use and interest to law enforcement and to the public. However, since their merger into the Serious Organized Crime Agency, the individual websites of these precursor agencies have been taken down and replaced by SOCA's website at <http://www.soca.gov.uk/>.

This website does not contain as much information as the previous sites but the current UK threat assessment for serious organized crime can be downloaded from this site. For instance <http://www.soca.gov.uk/assessPublications/downloads/threat_assess_unclass_250706.pdf>.

The government's counter terrorism strategy is accessible at <http://www.intelligence.gov.uk/publications/documents/countering.pdf>.

4.8 Competitive Intelligence

Intelligence is not just a national security or community safety tool, it is also a commercial tool. There is a competitive intelligence industry together with a counter-intelligence industry to guard against activity that constitutes industrial espionage. West (2001, ch 4) identifies six modes of competitive intelligence detailed in Table 4.2 below. Competitive intelligence as an industry services business organizations operating in market economies seeking to maintain or expand their commercial activity. It is information of relevance to regulatory bodies such as the FSA, trading standards, and HMRC. It may also be of relevance to financial investigators and asset recovery investigators. From a rather different perspective, the modes outlined below provide a framework for intelligence collection, mapping and analysing profit-motivated, organized crime groups, and the illicit markets within which they operate. This perspective can offer alternative options for intervention other than prosecution-focused law enforcement.

Table 4.2 Modes of competitive intelligence

Mode	Utility
Financial	Account information, some of which will be publicly accessible in audited accounts, the remainder of which will be commercially sensitive and retained within internal business records.
Technical	Information about products, manufacturing technology and processes, research and development, and technical support. In service industries technical intelligence focuses on the methods by which services are delivered.
Sales and marketing	Sales records, market share, marketing activity all illuminate commercial health and business aspiration.
Pricing and discount	In the commercial arena pricing is considered either very easy or very difficult to monitor. Discounting for retail or wholesale suppliers may be a device utilized in fraud and money laundering.
People	Knowledge of the staff /skills profile and motivations within a commercial competitor can be crucial in understanding opportunities for market advantage.
Operational	The organization, culture, decision-making processes, staffing levels, and efficiency of an organization.

Knowledge products that help inform competitive intelligence analysis include business and professional journals, trade media, academic publications, industry newsletters, conference proceedings, marketing material, contract listings, planning applications, and information registered with Companies House. The object of competitive intelligence is to draw deductions about future intentions, not merely describe current commercial profiles. In this respect, it has great similarity with the intelligence profession in the community safety and policing arena.

Further information and reading—Competitive intelligence

C West *Competitive Intelligence* (Palgrave, Basingstoke, 2001).

The Society of Competitive Intelligence Professionals has issued a code of practice for the industry available via its website (<http://www.scip.org>).

4.9 **Criminals' Use of Intelligence**

Case study—criminal use of intelligence

'Research by West Yorkshire Police with offenders, suggests that offenders sometimes gather considerable intelligence prior to committing an offence. Offenders work in teams, some posing as semi-legitimate door-to-door sales in order to identify the homes of vulnerable people. House-to-house enquiries should be as wide as possible and focus on possible precursors to the offence as well as details of the day in question.'

ACPO *Investigation of Volume Crime* (NCPE Centrex, Wyboston, 2001) 77

Just as investigators use intelligence to inform operations against criminals, so criminals themselves have uses for intelligence:

- to commit crime;
- to compromise investigators;
- to disrupt investigations and trials.

Journalist accounts of criminal careers usefully highlight the ways in which criminals use intelligence. Barnes et al (2000) and Johnson (2005) both look at the criminal career of Curtis Warren (at the time of writing in prison in the Netherlands convicted of drugs trafficking and killing a fellow prison inmate), albeit from different perspectives, the first focusing on Warren himself whilst the subsequent book examined the role of Paul Grimes, the informant whose information helped the investigation into Warren's drug trafficking.

Meticulous planning in the commission of crime is as important in achieving success as it is ensuring successful investigations (Johnson 2005: 10–11). Intelligence-gathering to identify suitable criminal opportunities includes bribing dockers and warehouse staff in order to identify where goods are being stored (Johnson 2005: 14, 30, 66). It also includes simple surveillance in order to identify vulnerabilities arising from target victim behaviour patterns or target premises security features and practices (Johnson 2005: 67, 70–1). Adopting this approach can offer some insights to investigators and those responsible for community safety in identifying crime vulnerabilities, which can also be seen as prevention opportunities.

Sophisticated criminals not only conduct surveillance in planning their crimes, they are 'well-versed in surveillance techniques' utilized by investigators and adopt appropriate counter-surveillance measures (Barnes et al 2000: 132–3), with their own network of sources to provide warning of investigator activity. This can range from their own form of neighbourhood watch to monitor police patrolling activity (Barnes et al 2000: 140) to being tipped off by bank employees when the authorities seek to investigate a suspect's financial circumstances (Barnes et al 2000: 132–3). Just as investigators will seek to recruit informants against criminals (Johnson 2005), so criminals will seek to recruit corrupt investigators, officials, and commercial employees in order to secure information that can compromise investigations or investigators. In this respect unauthorized disclosure of information held by investigators is possibly the most significant vulnerability facing law enforcement.

Further information and reading—criminals' use of intelligence

J Barnes, R Elias, and P Walsh *Cocky: The Rise and Fall of Curtis Warren, Britain's Biggest Drug Baron* (Milo Books, Bury, 2000)

G Johnson *Powder Wars: The Supergrass who Brought Down Britain's Biggest Drug Dealers* (Mainstream Publishing, Edinburgh, 2005)

4.10 **Strategic and Policy Intelligence**

For the purposes of strategic assessment and policy development there are a number of sources of business intelligence pre-eminent amongst which are the Home Office and HMIC. Political proposals to merge the various inspectorate bodies (for the police, prosecutors, court administration, prisons, and probation) failed to win support when placed before Parliament and this may have been a missed opportunity to coalesce disparate criminal justice system expertise within a single organization. Instead the Police and Justice Act 2006, Part 4, provides a framework for enhanced collaboration not only between the criminal justice Inspectorates themselves but also with the Inspectorate for Education, Children's Services and Skills, the Commission for Healthcare Audit and Inspection, the Commission for Social Care Inspection, and the Audit Commission. Inspection reports are published on the websites of these various bodies.

More general research into policing and community safety issues is undertaken and published by the Research and Statistics Directorate of the Home Office with the research being made available online.

Further information and reading

HMIC reports are accessible via <http://inspectorates.homeoffice.gov.uk/hmic>.

Home Office research into aspects of policing and the criminal system is available at <http://www.homeoffice.gov.uk/rds/>.

For alternative perspectives on the criminal justice system, which will highlight mistakes from which lessons can be learned, organizations with a focus on human rights have an important role to play.

Further information and reading

Monitoring the actions of government and law enforcement agencies either generally or in response to specific complaints are:

- The Legal Action Group <http://www.lag.org.uk>
- Liberty <http://www.liberty-human-rights.org>
- Statewatch (particularly useful for monitoring EU developments) <http://www.statewatch.org>
- The Independent Police Complaints Commission <http://www.ipcc.gov.uk>.

5

The National Intelligence Model

5.1 **Introduction**

'What's in a name? That which we call a rose/By any other name would smell as sweet': thus Shakespeare's Romeo lamented the power of branding. Notwithstanding the common sense underpinning Romeo's vexation, in an age when the Western economy has come to be driven by information rather than by manufactured products branding is as important, if not more so, than actual content. And it has the power seriously to mislead. Thus there are three initial questions to ask about the NIM: is it 'national'; is it a 'model'; and, above all, is it about 'intelligence'?

As a prescription for the way in which certain business should be undertaken in order to manufacture defined products, the NIM can rightly be considered a model. 'National', even writing three years after the National Policing Plan deadline for full implementation, is a qualification still more aspirational than descriptive. Partly this is because the requirement to implement the model was imposed only on ACPO forces, not ACPO(S) forces (although at time of writing the latter are considering its implementation) so it is national only in the sense of some of the geopolitical elements that comprise the United Kingdom. It is aspirational also not least because those forces that did implement the NIM did so with such a variety of interpretation and resourcing that any degree of uniformity or consensus implied by the label 'national' is quite misleading. There are parallels here with the lack of uniform approaches to intelligence IT systems noted with concern by Bichard (2004, para 3.63). Such variety should not be unexpected given that the 43 police forces of England and Wales vary significantly in capacity and capability but the lack of uniformity itself inhibits the potential for shared capacity and capability.

The biggest issue is with the 'intelligence' element of the label. Practitioners and commentators alike are dissatisfied with brand 'NIM'.

Definitions of what the NIM is *not*

'I would have named it differently so it does what it says on the tin: the national policing model.'

'I would NOT have called it NIM—I wouldn't have had intelligence anywhere near it because it defines the outcome.'

(English police interviewees in research undertaken by Superintendent Maren Eline Kleiven, Norwegian Police *Where's the intelligence in the National Intelligence Model?* unpublished MSc Dissertation, University of Portsmouth, 2005)

'NIM isn't about intelligence-led policing. It is a business model. It is a misleading title.' Academic Tim John, interviewed as part of the same research.

Kleiven's recent research into NIM implementation amongst English police forces discovered a disparity of definitions and interpretations concerning both intelligence and the NIM but on the issue of labelling she found a large amount of consensus. Indeed, Kleiven regards it as the 'central irony' of the NIM that it sets out to define a common language of intelligence but did not initially provide a common definition (Kleiven 2005: 19). The confusion arises from the failure to distinguish clearly enough between intelligence as a product (information to be acted upon) and (arguably the more important perspective) intelligence as a process leading to informed decision-making, in which sense intelligence is about managing police business and prioritizing resources. Although NIM is usually presented as the starting point for intelligence, it should perhaps be regarded as the end-point of the output process, immediately preceding the outcomes by which the effectiveness of policing might be judged.

Definitions of what the NIM is (variations on a theme)

'The NIM is a business model for law enforcement'

ACPO *Guidance on the National Intelligence Model* 2005, 8

'The National Intelligence Model provides the police service with a framework which not only delivers a structured approach to problem solving policing but also ensures that value for money is secured in terms of the efficient and directed tasking of resources.'

ACPO *Hate Crime Manual* 2005, 15

'The NIM is a business process which drives policing in the United Kingdom'

ACPO *Core Investigative Doctrine* 2005, 15

'The National Intelligence Model is a business process. . . . It is dependent upon on a clear framework of analysis of information and intelligence allowing a problem solving approach to law enforcement and crime prevention techniques'

NCPE *National Intelligence Model Code of Practice* 2005 para 3.1.1

And because it is a business model, it has come to be driven not by criminal intelligence but by performance indicators upon which individual and organizational success is evaluated, an outcome some distance removed from a framework analysis to inform problem-solving and crime prevention as articulated in the NIM Code of Practice.

A model that theoretically could be used to ensure that intelligence about what is actually happening is acted upon thus becomes skewed only to that intelligence which will deliver monthly performance indicators. In terms of performance-led policing directed from the centre this makes perfect sense. In terms of intelligence-led policing responding to community need this is at worst anathema, at best systemic myopia.

5.2 **Managing the Model within an Organization**

The NIM is the outcome of philosophical and paradigm development that took place during the 1990s as a response to the demand gap between recorded crime and available resources. 'The attempts to introduce intelligence-led policing effectively acknowledged . . . that the emphasis in police work had shifted from a doomed effort to detect all the perpetrators of greatly increased volumes of committed crime to a direct attempt to reduce the crime rate and incidences of disorder' (Flood, 2004: 41). The National Criminal Intelligence Service began, in 1999, to draw together lessons learned about intelligence management in order to produce the single doctrine that was published as the NIM in May 2000, the implementation of which by April 2004 was required as part of the National Policing Plan 2003–2006.

Definition—the NIM architect's vision

'The NIM . . . describes methods for identifying priorities, methods for managerial decision-making at strategic, tactical and operational levels, standards in intelligence activity and the range of assets and intelligence products that enable all these things to be done.'

B Flood 'Strategic aspects of the UK National Intelligence Model' in J Ratcliffe (ed) *Strategic Thinking in Criminal Intelligence* (The Federation Press, Sydney, 2004) 37–52, 48

In terms of NIM implementation by an organization, ACPO identifies 11 thematic areas, subdivided into 135 individual minimum standards subject to HMIC inspection, that are used to assess whether any given organization has the capacity and capability to utilize the NIM. The ACPO *Guidance on the National Intelligence Model* (2005) is structured around these 11 areas and the assessment criteria are discussed in detail in Appendix B of the *Guidance*. In summary, these areas are outlined in Table 5.1.

Table 5.1 ACPO's 11 areas of assessment criteria for NIM implementation

1. Knowledge assets	For example current legislation; case law; Codes of Practice; Manuals of Standards; ACPO/NCPE guidance and doctrine; force policies relevant to intelligence; NIM knowledge products
2. System assets	For example physical security; security policies (confidentiality, vetting, integrity standards); implementation of sterile corridor concept; authorities processes and documentation management systems in place; effective briefings; effective debriefings; interagency information sharing protocols

3. **Source assets** For example appropriate resources and procedures for dealing with victims and witnesses; prisoners; Crimestoppers; CHIS; undercover/ test purchase officers; forensic data; surveillance product

4. **People assets** Ensuring that appropriately trained and experienced personnel of suitable rank and authority perform the key functions and roles identified within the NIM

5. **Information sources** For example open and closed source data; sanitisation and risk management protocols in place; compliance with DPA; intelligence, crime, custody and command/control records available in searchable form

6. **Intelligence/ information recording** For example 5x5x5 used as standard evaluation; common standards of data input onto force IT systems; protocols re use of intelligence codes/flags to speed collation and retrieval; data management and supervision protocols

7. **Research & development** For example access to technical support/surveillance equipment; standards products; National Technical Support Unit minimum standards; information exchange protocols; field capability; intelligence specialists/researchers/analytical capability; system for development and review of intelligence collection plans; data collection directed and focused on Control Strategy

8. **Intelligence products** For example force policy dictating corporate standards of products; force policy dictating timing and circulation of products; strategic assessments; tactical assessments; subject profiles/ problem profiles; management ownership; pre-circulation and pre-reading of products before Tasking and Coordinating Group meets; profiles commissioned only by Tasking and Coordination Group or SIO on a major enquiry; command training/appreciation programme relative to intelligence products and analysis

9. **Strategic Tasking & Coordination** For example Tasking and Coordination Group policy covering Chairpersons; Inspection; Strategic Assessment; Attendees; Sanction of the Control Strategy; sanction of the intelligence requirement; minimum six-monthly review

10. **Tactical Tasking and Coordination** For example Tasking and Coordination Group policy covering Chairpersons; Inspection; Tactical Assessment; Attendees; briefing policy; daily management meeting (BCU); Level 2 resource allocation criteria

11. **Tactical resolution** For example having the appropriate investigative and tactical capability

12. **Intelligence/ operational review** For example results analysis and review; monitoring and review of RIPA authorities

---

Further information and reading

ACPO, in collaboration with the National Centre for Policing Excellence, has produced a number of doctrinal guidance documents relevant to the operation of the NIM. In relation to the 11 elements listed above these are:

- *Practice Advice on Resources and the People Assets of NIM* (forthcoming) [elements 1–4]
- *Code of Practice on the Management of Police Information* (2005) [elements 1–4]
- *Guidance on the Management of Police Information* (2006) [elements 5–6]
- *Manual of Standards for Covert Human Intelligence Sources* (2004, in conjunction with HMCE) [elements 5–6]
- *Practice Advice on Tasking and Co-ordination* (2006) [elements 7–11]
- *Practice Advice on Professionalising the Business of Neighbourhood Policing* (2005) [elements 8–11]
- *Guidance on the National Briefing Model* (2006) [elements 8–11].

The value of thinking in terms of these 11 areas of implementation is that it emphasizes for any organization that successful utilization of the NIM is not just about the manufacture of products per se but about having the necessary trained personnel, properly equipped in place to *gather* and *analyse* the intelligence that will inform the products. Products are only outputs. Capacity and capability create outcomes, which is the purpose of effective intelligence.

5.3 Managing Police Partnership using the Model

The NIM is not only a business process model for managing intelligence and interventions within an organization, it is intended to manage intelligence and intervention between organizations and on a collaborative basis. The fact that the model has originated within the police service does not preclude its adoption by non-police agencies. It is a process model for converting information into intervention. To that end, any organization with similar generic functions could adopt the model. With the increasing pluralization of policing, and an ever greater number of non-police actors and agencies undertaking policing functions as a consequence of workforce modernization and police reform, it is highly desirable that, notwithstanding the varied definitions of intelligence considered in Chapter 3, the common language of intelligence identified by Kleiven as a strength of the model, should be adopted by all those undertaking policing and regulatory functions.

Police force boundaries are a geopolitical construct the purpose of which is fiscal rather than functional. They serve to provide a funding and financial accountability structure but otherwise do not advance the business of problem-solving and intervention. It is axiomatic that crime and criminals do not confine their activities to police force areas and therefore for policing to be effective, it cannot solely be conducted on the basis of police organization as it is currently structured. The hiatus since 1974 notwithstanding, that fact alone has driven an almost continuous history of police force creation and amalgamation since the first modern public police force was established in 1800 to police the River Thames in London.

It is part of the purpose of the NIM to overcome the impediment to policing created by police force boundaries. To this end a three-tier hierarchy of criminality has been created to facilitate allocation of investigation responsibility.

Table 5.2 The NIM three-level hierarchy of criminality

Level 1	Crime and disorder contained within police force areas, amenable to local intervention and resolution with the key unit of service delivery being the BCU rather than the force. Scope for partnership intervention within the context of CDRPs.
Level 2	Criminality and disorder that transcends BCU and/or force boundaries, requiring additional resources and partnership collaboration in order to effect an intervention and resolution. (A common misperception is that Level 2 refers only to criminality that transcends force boundaries and not BCU boundaries as well. It could also include criminality that a BCU lacks the capacity and capability to address.)
Level 3	Serious and organized crime at a national or international scale. The basic intervention options (intelligence, prevention, enforcement) remain the same as for Levels 1 and 2 but given that organized crime is an economic activity operating at global market levels, the additional intervention option of disruption (possibly through use of civil or fiscal laws rather than criminal laws) is also considered politically acceptable. Heavy reliance on resource-intensive covert investigation demanding capability and capacity beyond the resources of most local police forces, hence the creation of first the National Crime Squad and subsequently the Serious Organized Crime Agency.

Intelligence that relates to criminality at Level 2 or Level 3 must have a channel by which it can be communicated to the appropriate forum for responsibility and resources to be allocated. This depends upon the communication framework described in section 5.4 below being mirrored at a regional and national level. The NIM has been designed with such broad functionality in mind.

Just as partnership between police forces has to be managed so, too, there is a need to manage partnership between the police and other agencies. Once again, the NIM is sufficiently generic to allow this to happen at and between all three levels of criminality, although problems of organization representation and command responsibility may arise if one organization's Level 2 is another's Level 1.

Equally important is the issue of common understanding about the terms and tools employed within the model. The strength of the NIM lies in the potential it creates for different police forces and partner agencies to have a common basis and language for collaboration. Failure to adopt standard interpretations and definitions is the Achilles Heel of the NIM.

Case study—adverse consequences of a lack of common intelligence language

In reviewing the approaches towards intelligence of HMCE (as it then was), the NCS, the NCIS, MI5, the Benefits Agency, and the Financial Services Authority, academic researchers found that:

'Each of these agencies employs a slightly different intelligence nomenclature. Although it is certainly not impossible for agents to think outside their own institutional terminology, such differences are symptomatic of different ways of doing business. Further, because different terminology implies different expectations of intelligence analysis, these differences may also be symptomatic of interagency tension.'

M Innes and J Sheptycki 'From detection to disruption: intelligence and the changing logic of police crime control in the United Kingdom' *International Criminal Justice Review* 14 1–24, 8 (2004).

Such issues are not irresolvable but require political will and a willingness to accept and adopt common practice—easier said than done with 43 different police forces and 43 different police authorities in England and Wales even before the other jurisdictions and partner agencies are taken into consideration. The NIM provides a framework that can make partnership work between different agencies and departments within a single level of criminality or between different agencies across the different levels of criminality. It offers the potential for a common and comprehensive strategy based on as full an understanding as possible of the crime and disorder environment. But such commonality of approach is dependent upon consensus and concurrence and these supposed strengths of team-working are in fact the inherent weaknesses of NIM implementation.

The NIM hierarchy has one more inherent weakness—the Level 2 gap. With significant performance management focus on Level 1 service delivery at BCU level there is, in effect, a systemic disincentive to intervene at Level 2. If an organization needs to devote resources to Level 1 activity in order to meet certain performance targets, any diversion of resources to Level 2 activity (which may ultimately improve the performance of another BCU or force at the expense of one's own) is always going to be a low priority. Even the creation of Level 2 performance targets for individual forces will not override the primacy of Level 1 targets in a performance framework focused on BCUs and in the absence of identified and dedicated responsibility for overall regional performance. Level 3 criminality generally is dealt with by a single dedicated national agency (SOCA), although depending upon circumstance, larger metropolitan police forces may have the capacity and capability to investigate at Level 3.

5.4 **Using the Model**

The NIM is founded upon a framework of communication within which there are two key design elements: the meeting cycle and the products that articulate information for consideration at the meetings. As with any communication framework, methods of communication generate bureaucracy in the form of documented information upon which decisions are made, records of decisions taken at meetings, and the monitoring of actions decided upon to ensure objectives are achieved. All of which will fit within a wider, organization-specific context of performance management with its own bureaucratic recording mechanisms.

There is a not insignificant danger, therefore, that process and products can come to be seen as ends—the desired outcome—in and of themselves. It is argued here that robust and effective results analysis (see 5.4.2 below) will assist in maintaining a focus on outcomes and so contribute to avoiding the danger of the NIM becoming a self-fulfilling procedural prophecy or merely an accounting tool for performance management.

5.4.1 **The meeting cycle**

The NIM process exists to convey information to decision-makers. The process as defined prescribes certain points at which it is necessary for various parties to come together in order to exchange information, to be consulted and to collaborate on determining priorities and intervention options. The formal meeting cycle creates a hierarchy of information flow, managed through the sluice gates of formal rules governing the creation and exchange of intelligence (Sheptycki 2004, 309).

For a typical shire force, the meeting cycle might appear in the fashion outlined in Figure 1. The prescription of such a cycle presents an impression of rigid and to some extent self-serving bureaucracy. The key in this process being a vital and meaningful information exchange and intervention setting depends on leadership at the Tasking and Coordinating meetings. The chairperson at such meetings will have a significant influence over the success or otherwise of the NIM application in any given force or BCU.

A further moot point is the extent to which CDRP partners are involved in this process or else participate in a parallel process in determining and monitoring crime reduction strategies.

Figure 5.1 Representation of the NIM meeting cycle from a shire force perspective (with acknowledgement to Warwickshire Police)

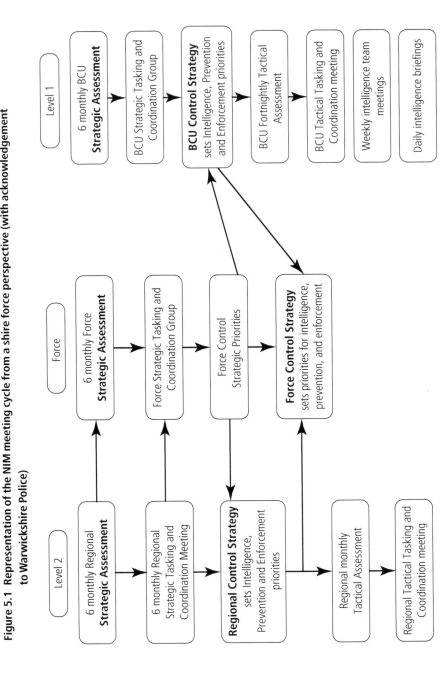

5.4.2 **The products**

There are four broad categories of 'product' defined within the NIM. They will each be considered in turn.

- Analytical products and techniques (for example results analysis, demographic analysis).
- Intelligence products (for example, strategic and tactical assessments; subject and problem profiles).
- Knowledge products (for example data-sharing protocols).
- System products (for example appropriate information technology support).

NIM analytical products and techniques

The NIM identifies nine techniques used in the creation of analytical products.

Table 5.3 The NIM analytical tools and techniques

Tool	Purpose
Results analysis	To evaluate effectiveness of law enforcement activities, in particular of intelligence, prevention, and enforcement operations undertaken
Crime pattern analysis	To identify the nature and scale of emerging and current crime trends and patterns, linked crimes or incidents, and hotspots of activity
Market profiles	To analyse the criminal market around a given commodity or service in a specified geographical area
Criminal business profiles	To detail how criminal operations/business and techniques work at a micro (individual) or macro (thematic) level in the same way that legitimate businesses may be explained
Network analysis	To understand the nature and significance of the links between people who form criminal networks, or organisations that interrelate, together with the strengths and weaknesses of criminal groups or organizations
Target profile analysis	To provide sufficient detailed analysis to initiate a target operation or support an ongoing operation against an individual or networked group of individuals by identifying options for intervention or disruption
Demographic/social trends analysis	To examine the nature of demographic changes and their impact on criminality, as well as the analysis of social factors that might underlie changes or trends in crime or offending behaviour To describe statistically the constitution of the population of a given area and the associated economic/social/environmental indicators with reference to law enforcement requirements

Table 5.3 The NIM analytical tools and techniques *(cont.)*

Tool	Purpose
Risk analysis	To support assessment of the scale of risk posed by individual offenders, organizations or crime types to potential victims, the public generally, the law enforcement agencies or the criminal justice system
Operational intelligence assessment	To ensure that ongoing investigations remain focused and are not side-tracked by new and unanticipated intelligence that may require a separate operational response

Which techniques should be used in any given situation will be determined by the circumstances and the desired outcome. Demographic and social trends analysis, for example, is more likely to be employed when constructing a strategic assessment or when working with partner agencies in longer-term problem-solving. Target profile analysis may be more appropriate within the context of a specific individual operation. However, circumstances should not be thought of as exclusive.

The more analytical techniques applied to any given issue, the greater number of perspectives will be brought to bear in informing possible resolutions. An intelligence 'package' delivered for tasking and coordination group consideration should not be judged merely on the number of different analytical products and techniques evident within it but upon the contribution these make to providing the widest possible optional menu for prevention, the requirement for further intelligence, enforcement, and/or partnership resolution.

Perhaps the least used technique, although in the view of these former intelligence managers arguably the most important, is that of results analysis; the detailed consideration of whether or not a chosen resolution achieved the desired outcome and confirmation of how it did or why it did not. Of the nine analytical techniques and products it is the one most likely to be viewed as a desirable luxury rather than an operational necessity when the time management of under-resourced analysts is dictated by the fortnightly cycle of tasking and coordination group meetings. But if time is never devoted to evaluating what works and what does not, then outcomes characterized by mistakes and the waste of resources are destined to be perpetuated without correction. Conventional wisdoms will remain unchallenged, good (and poor) practice unrecognized. If the effective use of intelligence is best judged from the perspective of outcomes rather than outputs, then the use of results analysis is non-negotiable in any organization that purports to be a learning organization.

Intelligence products

Decision-makers, whether at force or BCU level, whether within the context of strategic determination or deciding operational tactics, require information and analysis upon which to base their decisions. The vehicles for presenting such information are prescribed in the form of the NIM intelligence products.

Within the operational experience of the authors, considerable effort has been made within different forces to achieve standardized formats for these products in the face of sometimes entrenched opinions on how the products should be structured. But such effort once again is in peril of confusing output with outcome. The danger to be guarded against in any formulaic approach is that it can become merely a tick-box process for analyst, investigator, manager, and partner agency alike. The ACPO *Practice Guidance on Tasking and Co-ordination* (2006) identifies appropriate contents structures for each of these documents.

There are subtle variations in the way in which the four intelligence products are defined in the *NIM Code of Practice* (2005), in the ACPO *Guidance on the National Intelligence Model* (2006) and in the ACPO *Practice Advice on Tasking and Co-ordination* (2006). This may well represent an evolution of doctrine rather than merely inconsistent writing. For example, Target Profiles, which were always intended to apply to victims and third parties as well as offenders, had, by 2006, been renamed Subject Profiles, a more value-neutral label which overcame the inappropriate impression that victims were viewed as police targets. Table 5.4 below represents a conglomeration of these different sources together with author interpretation.

Table 5.4 Intelligence products, their purpose, and anticipated outcomes

Product	Purpose	Outcome
Strategic Assessment (reviewed every six months)	1. Identifies at organizational and partnership level the apparent and emerging medium to long-term issues likely to influence intervention priorities and resource allocation 2. Informs the business of the Strategic Tasking and Coordination Group	• Informed decisions at command level about intervention priorities, articulated in the 'Control Strategy' • Revised intelligence requirement • Policing and partnership engagement and collaboration that is responsive to local community needs (NB—performance targets prescribed by central government may not reflect local community needs but will have to be incorporated in the Control Strategy)

Table 5.4 Intelligence products, their purpose, and anticipated outcomes *(cont.)*

Product	Purpose	Outcome
Tactical Assessment (reviewed every fortnight)	1. Identifies short-term issues requiring prevention/ enforcement intervention or intelligence development, linked to Control Strategy priorities 2. Monitors progress of ongoing interventions 3. Identifies new and emerging issues that fall outside the Control Strategy but which may have to be considered in forthcoming strategic assessments	• Informed decisions at service delivery level about local problem-solving and specific prevention, intelligence or enforcement interventions • Revised intelligence requirement • Policing and partnership engagement and collaboration that is responsive to local community needs (NB—performance targets centrally allocated may not reflect local community needs but will influence local intervention resource allocation)
Subject Profile (previously labelled Target Profiles)	1. Analysis of an individual or community to identify vulnerabilities that will increase risk of victimization 2. Analysis of an individual or network to identify opportunities that will facilitate problem-solving and authority intervention 3. Identification of relevant risks to be managed 4. Identification of partner agency involvement 5. Identification of intelligence gaps	• Informed decisions about the proportionality of a proposed intervention • Informed decisions about intervention priorities and partnership opportunities • Bespoke interventions, responsive to victim or community needs • Informed decisions about operation / investigation management • Revised intelligence requirement
Problem Profile	1. Analysis of individual problems or an identified series of problems to understand scope and context 2. Identification of intervention and prevention opportunities 3. Identification of relevant risks to be managed 4. Identification of partner agency involvement 5. Identification of intelligence gaps	• Greater understanding of individual & community needs • Enhanced problem-solving capability • Informed decisions about the proportionality of a proposed intervention • Informed decisions about intervention priorities and partnership opportunities • Bespoke interventions, responsive to partner agency, victim, or community needs • Informed decisions about intervention management • Revised intelligence requirement

104

Knowledge products

Intelligence work is supported by tools and resources that are termed knowledge products within the NIM. These comprise documented learning and practice that can inform the acquisition, analysis, and application of intelligence. As a business process model, the NIM is itself a knowledge product. Other examples of knowledge products are:

- intelligence training;
- statutory investigation powers;
- case law;
- procedural manuals, standards, doctrine, and guidance documents;
- the Data Protection Act and associated guidelines;
- intelligence-sharing protocols.

System products

In addition to the practitioner learning accumulated in knowledge products, the work of intelligence units is also supported by enabling facilities: systems established to record and process information and intelligence. These include:

- databases (crime recording, intelligence, PNC, Sirene/SIS, custody records);
- information acquisition systems such as NAFIS, ANPR, CCTV;
- DNA;
- surveillance product;
- secure accommodation within which intelligence staff can operate ensuring the proper handling of sensitive material.

Knowledge and systems products underpin capacity and capability and whilst they form part of the original elements of the NIM, are probably better understood in the context of the 135 implementation minimum standards. Without these key cogs, the rest of the machinery does not work.

5.5 External Perspectives on the NIM

There have been a number of external studies of the NIM in operation, some commissioned by the Home Office, others as undertaken as academic research projects. A number of issues have been highlighted and it is worth drawing to the reader's attention three in particular:

- problematic implementation;
- organizational pathologies;
- competing initiatives.

5.5.1 **Problematic implementation**

John and Maguire looked at the initial implementation of the model and found a missed opportunity. Their study of early implementation and initial effectiveness of the NIM in three pilot forces failed to draw any conclusions about the effectiveness of the NIM because none of the three pilot forces had fully implemented the model (John and Maguire 2004a). Two issues underlay the incomplete implementation. Strong organizational cultural resistance was encountered to the concepts of intelligence and the NIM. In particular, managers found it difficult to promote organization-wide and individual ownership of the NIM and concept of intelligence-led policing because the label was interpreted as indicating a specialist and discrete function rather than a philosophical foundation (John and Maguire 2004a: 2). The language of the NIM was disliked by staff because it seemed too academic and the variable quality of intelligence products had led to a loss of respect for and confidence in tasking and coordinating groups, thus reinforcing the cultural resistance (see also Maguire and John 2006: 69).

The second area of failing was found at national rather than force level, in that the NIM Implementation Project (NIMIP) was unable to ensure a consistency of approach in implementing the NIM. 'The national [implementation] team did not acquire sufficient resources to fulfil this role and in the meantime other forces began their own implementation of the model' (John and Maguire 2004a, 1). As a consequence, 'the NIMIP missed an opportunity to encourage standardisation of practices and products at an early stage' which led the reviewers to conclude that 'considerable variation has developed which will be difficult to change, as forces and BCUs have already become accustomed to their own way of doing things, This is a problem which needs attention as standard products are important to the links across and between levels' (John and Maguire 2004a: 55).

In terms of achieving a desired outcome—enhanced community safety and reductions in crime and disorder through the effective use of intelligence within and between police forces and partner agencies—such varied implementation can only be counter-productive.

Further information and reading—NIM implementation perspectives

T John and M Maguire *The National Intelligence Model: Early Implementation Experience in Three Police Force Areas* (Cardiff, University of Cardiff School of Social Sciences Working Paper Series 52, 2004a)

T John and M Maguire *The National Intelligence Model: Key Lessons from Early Research* (London, Home Office RDS On-line Report 30/04, 2004b)

M Kleiven 'Where's the intelligence in the National Intelligence Model?' *International Journal of Police Science and Management* 9(3) forthcoming 2007

M Maguire and T John 'Intelligence-led policing, managerialism and community engagement: competing priorities and the role of the National Intelligence Model in the UK' *Policing and Society* 16 67–85 (2006)

J Sheptycki 'Organizational pathologies in police intelligence systems: some contributions to the lexicon of intelligence-led policing' *European Journal of Criminology* 1 307–32 (2004)

5.5.2 **Organizational pathologies**

'Reading official documents about information flows in crime intelligence systems one is more often confronted with a version of how they *ought* to work than how they do work [original emphasis]' (Sheptycki 2004: 313). Viewing intelligence systems such as the 'intelligence cycle' or the NIM from a slightly different perspective, specifically to examine whether or not they are capable of providing strategic and comprehensive intelligence about serious and organized crime (and he concludes incidentally that they cannot), Sheptycki has identified 11 systemic organizational pathologies militating against effective intelligence exchange. Whilst focusing on the UK, Sheptycki cross-checked and corroborated his findings through examination of Canadian, Dutch and Swedish police intelligence structures thus establishing that these are generic issues and not just applicable to the UK. Given that the NIM exists to facilitate intelligence exchange within and between organizations, it is important here to give these pathologies further consideration.

Table 5.5 Sheptycki's 11 organizational pathologies of intelligence exchange

Pathology type	Problems identified
1. **Digital divide**	Multiple and incompatible intelligence databases and communications systems rendering impossible the timely analysis of intelligence data. SOCA reportedly has inherited 138 different ICT systems with its merger of various different police, intelligence, immigration and customs agencies. This is but one extreme example. The Bichard report drew attention to the multiplicity of ICT systems that prevent police forces exchanging intelligence.
2. **Linkage blindness**	Inadequate or insufficient data hinders effective analysis and prevents the identification of linked series of crimes/incidents. Linkage blindness most likely to occur when a series transgresses organizational boundaries. The fact that information flows have been designed to be vertical rather than horizontal also hinders series identification.

Table 5.5 Sheptycki's 11 organizational pathologies of intelligence exchange *(cont.)*

Pathology type	Problems identified
3. Noise	Since those who process intelligence are often unaware of the circumstances of the original recording decisions, it is difficult to distinguish the inherent value of different pieces of information. Thus there may be significant amounts of low-grade, over-sanitized or overly complicated intelligence in any given system.
	The distance between reporting, recording and interpretation of data may also influence noise levels. There is also a danger that intelligence products are themselves a form on input adding to the noise.
4. Intelligence overload	Arises when analytical capacity and associated administrative support is insufficient (either through inadequate or diverted resources) to interpret existing intelligence.
	'Multiple recording of data on multiple systems at multiple levels is a contributing factor.' (Sheptycki 2004, 316) More data is not necessarily better data.
5. Non-reporting/ non-recording	Given political commitments to reduce the 'burden of paperwork' and the fact that intelligence-reporting in and of itself may not contribute to measured activity upon which individuals or units are assessed, there is little direct incentive to take the time to record intelligence.
6. Intelligence gaps	A consequence of non-recording and the hierarchical nature of the information flows.
	Most obviously manifest in the so-called Level 2 gap which refers both to intelligence about Level 2 criminality and the lack of intervention capacity at Level 2—a vicious circle.
7. Duplication	Active criminals of interest to more than one BCU, force or partner agency will always be the subject of duplicated effort.
	One obvious adverse consequence is the waste of resources but duplication can also exacerbate the problems of linkage blindness.
8. Institutional friction	The realization that the prescribed performance regime had created detrimental inter-agency competition rather than collaboration prompted the government to merge different agencies into a single entity, SOCA (Harfield 2006). Such rivalry and competition can nevertheless also exist within a single entity. The necessity of meeting performance targets may tempt the retention of intelligence that could otherwise be shared so that others do not benefit from it.

Pathology type	Problems identified
9. Intelligence-hoarding and information silos	Intelligence-led policing is dependent upon intelligence-sharing but has already been seen above, there are numerous systemic disincentives to share intelligence. The 'need-to-know' principle is also vulnerable to misunderstanding and misuse. Vertical information flows dictate silos, which then preclude the identification of linkages through horizontal exchange. The vision of the post-Bichard IMPACT programme, that there ought to be a single intelligence database accessible to and used by all police forces, has itself encountered ICT practicalities in that in may not be feasible to create a single database, in which case the next best option is a data-mining solution with access to various intelligence category silos.
10. Defensive data concentration	The tendency to concentrate data collection on known problems or certain crime types to the exclusion of analytical development capacity to search for and identify emerging trends. Failure to identify emerging trends constrains intelligence-led policing to yet another mode of reactive policing—exactly the opposite outcome of what was intended for intelligence-led policing.
11. Occupational subcultures	These exist at both inter- and intra-agency levels and are a consequence of the intelligence system being configured as an environment of sometimes competing interests rather than as a single network. Both Sheptycki and also Cope (2004) draw attention to the generally negative experience of analysts working within the police service as a result traditional occupational sub-cultures within the police service. The drive for intelligence-led policing has created sub-culture tension between (the new specialism of) intelligence staff and (the traditional role of) investigators. The latter, measured by detections and afforded peer status by successful prosecutions, are interested only in evidence, not intelligence. There is an ever-present danger that intelligence work will be subverted to an evidential function. Likewise commanders measured by monthly targets can become interested only in data that will enhance performance management and there are examples of intelligence analysts regularly being required to produce products that are effectively about performance data rather than intelligence.

All of the above are current behaviours observed in the British police service that undermine the integrity of intelligence-led policing and therefore the theoretical basis for the NIM. Generic pathologies together with, potentially, other organization-specific pathologies, will exist within partner agencies as well.

Overlaying these organizational pathologies is a key structural pathology inherent in having a policing system comprising a large number of service deliverers (police forces, other policing and regulatory agencies) that vary significantly in remit, capacity, and capability. By definition then, even without the cultural resistance encountered in some quarters, the imposition of the NIM on a foundation of such inconsistency runs the inevitable risk that outcomes will be inconsistent. Whilst it could reasonably be argued that the NIM serves to establish a common language and understanding between police and partners, it cannot overcome the lack of common capacity and capability.

To which may be added, continuing the medical analogy and adapting the work of Ratcliffe (2005), pathologies of understanding. It is possible for decision-makers (BCU commanders for instance) to employ effective strategies without the aid of effective intelligence. There will be a collateral benefit to the community in the short-term success of individual interventions but in the absence of intelligence about the wider criminal environment and results analysis, effective evaluation of the strategies employed is not possible and so the opportunities for long-term benefit through enhanced understanding and organizational learning will be lost. Equally, it is possible for intelligence staff to influence decision-makers without having a complete analysis upon which to offer recommendations and advice. Finally, through cultural resistance or communication failure, intelligence staff can be unsuccessful in conveying an understanding of any given situation to those planning an intervention.

Successful management of intelligence using the NIM processes needs to recognize and counter these pathologies if the desired outcome of a citizen-focused, responsive police service achieving through partnership a safer community and reductions in crime and disorder is to be achieved.

Further information and reading

J Ratcliffe 'The effectiveness of police intelligence management: a New Zealand case study' *Police Practice and Research* 6(5) 435–45 (2005)

J Sheptycki 'Organizational pathologies in police intelligence systems: some contributions to the lexicon of intelligence-led policing' *European Journal of Criminology* 1 307–32 (2004)

5.5.3 Competing initiatives

The final group of issues that will influence application and outcome of the NIM comes in the form of competing initiatives. Maguire and John, in particular, query whether intelligence-led policing, managerialism and community engagement—all paradigms recently espoused for policing—are compatible (2006).

Further information and reading

'During the same period as the NIM has been promoted and 'rolled out' across the country, a number of other major policing philosophies and initiatives have been promoted at national level and urged upon local forces. Some local forces, too, have adopted or adapted other policing models from elsewhere. In some cases, implementation of the NIM has dovetailed fairly comfortably with existing approaches, and the more far-sighted and strategically aware police managers have been able to "add value" by blending them together. . . . [some] initiatives have not only competed for attention and funding with the NIM, but appear at first sight to reflect fundamentally different or even conflicting principles and approaches to policing.'

M Maguire and T John 'Intelligence-led policing, managerialism and community engagement: competing priorities and the role of the National Intelligence Model in the UK' *Policing and Society* 16 67–85 (2006), 74.

See also T John and M Maguire 'Rolling out the National Intelligence Model: key challenges' in K Bullock and N Tilley (eds) *Crime Reduction and Problem Oriented Policing* (Willan, Cullompton, 2003).

H Goldstein *Problem-Oriented Policing* (McGraw Hill, New York, 1990).

Maguire and John identified a number of areas in which alternative policing models might be incompatible with intelligence-led policing as articulated through the NIM. These are summarized in Table 5.6 (Maguire and John 2006: 78–81).

Table 5.6 Tensions and congruence between NIM and other models (based on Maguire and John 2006)

Policing paradigms	Tensions and congruence
Neighbourhood/ Reassurance Policing	Customer-led or consumerist approach (driven by perceptions as much as reality) lack the objectivity of NIM tasking properly informed by analysis. Danger of tasking being driven by populist whim.
	BUT
	Reassurance policing draws upon signal crime theory and NIM processes properly applied would assist in the identification of signal crimes
	If successful neighbourhood and reassurance policing generates increased public confidence, potentially there will be greater public willingness to share information with police and partner agencies. Such willingness can be fostered with feedback about how information has been used.

**Table 5.6 Tensions and congruence between NIM and other models
(based on Maguire and John 2006) *(cont.)***

Policing paradigms	Tensions and congruence
Volume crime management [VCM] and performance targets	Focus on individual detections to meet targets and increased emphasis on quantity rather than quality is directly at odds with intelligence-led policing principle of focusing on the criminal not the crime. National performance indicators unduly influence local intervention priorities. BUT VCM and NIM share a holistic approach to the management of crime based on business processes.
Partnership and CDRPs	Research indicates little evidence of direct engagement between Tasking & Co-ordinating Groups and CDRP partners as well as a tendency for Tasking and Co-ordinating Group chairpersons to focus only on those aspects of the Strategic Assessment and Control Strategy that address central police performance indicators. BUT Analysis, the identification of intervention options and tasking are all aspects of the NIM process around which CDRP work could be structured.

Not all other paradigms necessarily involve tensions. Problem-oriented policing, developed in the USA, and the NIM share common ground in the theoretical emphasis placed on the role of analysis. Both have the potential to inform partnership approaches in order to prevent and address the causes of disorder and crime. Lancashire Constabulary provides an example of both theories successfully being applied in conjunction (John and Maguire 2003).

Also from the USA comes the concept of zero-tolerance policing supported by Compstat, a policing model that depends on up-to-date computerized crime and performance data with which local police commanders are held to account on a weekly basis. It is data-led rather than intelligence-led. Extolled by advocates of crime control, it has attracted criticism for driving police solely in pursuit of performance indicators in a manner perceived to be unjust by the community and so alienating the police from the community they were seeking to serve and undermining the legitimacy of the police.

Further information and reading

M Moore 'Sizing up Compstat: an important administrative innovation in polic-ing' *Criminology and Public Policy* 2(3) 469–94 (2003)

D Weisburd, S Mastrofski, A McNally, R Greenspan, and J Willis 'Reforming to preserve: Compstat and strategic problem solving in American policing' *Criminology and Public Policy* 2(3) 421–56 (2003)

Both papers reproduced in T Newburn (ed) *Policing: Key Readings* (Willan, Cullompton, 2005)

5.6 **The NIM: Theory, Practice, and Police Reform**

For all the confusion about whether intelligence is a process or a product, the answer to which influences perceptions and application of the NIM, an obvi-ous value of the NIM lies in the practical focus it has given to the concept of intelligence-led policing. The NIM is an attempt to impose a solid framework in circumstances which are otherwise very varied (police force and partner agency capability and capacity, community needs, crime environment). It provides a common language although this can become distorted through local translation. Its application now faces further challenges through police reform—both what has happened and what has not happened.

Although in theory the NIM provides a framework for addressing Level 2 crimi-nality and disorder, in practice the lack of consistent or coherent Level 2 inter-vention capability detracts from effective policing at the domestic cross-border level (be that across force borders or across BCU borders). The polarization of policing function into *neighbourhood policing* and *protective services* (Home Office 2004, HMIC 2005) draws attention to the same issue in a different way by high-lighting and defining the areas of policing most likely to make demands of and benefit from Level 2 capability. Regional collaboration projects exist but are beset with problems of ambiguous command responsibility, uncertain oversight, and varied force contributions which tend to mean the biggest contributors gain all the benefits of collaboration. Increasing focus on neighbourhood policing and performance management at BCU level merely draws further attention to the capacity gap at Level 2.

There is a danger that the existing gap in capability will generate an additional gap in communication as the SOCA relies on the NIM hierarchy of communica-tion for a link into community-level intelligence. A communication gap under-mines the whole intelligence process.

In terms of counter-terrorism work, this communication gap has been recognized and alternative policing structure with inbuilt Level 2 and Level 3 capability is being constructed (F Gregory 'The police and the intelligence services' in C Harfield et al (eds) *The Handbook of Intelligent Policing* (Oxford University Press, Oxford, 2008). This experience suggests that far from asking whether the NIM is 'fit for purpose' to service UK policing, the question should perhaps be reversed—is UK policing fit for purpose to maximise the potential of the NIM?

The issue of turning rhetoric into reality is one examined by Ratcliffe (2005) who identifies that intelligence products within the NIM are outputs and so easy to measure. On a theoretical basis therefore, it is quite possible for the NIM processes to result in tangible products and so be seen to be functioning normally, whilst not necessarily having any significant outcome. The solution to this, argues Ratcliffe, is to focus on intelligence-led crime reduction rather than policing, and so focus—and this is partly a branding issue once more—on outcome rather than agency activity.

Ratcliffe proposes the '3i model'—interpret, influence, impact—as a framework for *evaluating the outcome* of intelligence processes (not just the NIM). Within the 3i model true intelligence-led policing only exists if all three elements are present (Table 5.7).

Table 5.7 Ratcliffe's 3i model with additional commentary (in italics)

Interpret	Analysts and intelligence staff must have the capacity and capability to interpret the wider criminal environment, both as a means of maximizing the options for intervention and as a benchmark for results analysis and evaluation.
	The NIM analytical tools and techniques are the foundation for this, but depend upon intelligence units having adequate levels of trained staff in dedicated roles.
Influence	Intelligence staff must have the capacity and capability of influencing those making decisions about intervention and use of resources.
	The NIM has the communication framework through which influence could be exerted. But this element is also dependent upon the willingness of the decision-makers to listen to the intelligence staff as well as the force performance manager.
Impact	Decision-makers must have the enthusiasm and skills to be able to have a positive impact on the whole criminal environment.
	This is the element that in particular is supposed to focus attention on outcomes. There is a danger, however, that 'outcome' may be defined in any given situation as nothing more sophisticated than performance targets.

Ratcliffe observes (2005: 436) that although globally, many practitioners will profess to pursuing intelligence-led policing, there have been very few attempts to document what intelligence-led policing actually means. The NIM is one such attempt. In the UK it is doctrine, the implementation of which through the

National Policing Plan was given statutory emphasis because the Police Reform Act 2002 imposed a duty to implement the plan. For all the academic commentary on various aspects of intelligence-led policing and the NIM, a thorough evaluation of outcomes is still awaited. Ironically, the NIM contains its own evaluation tool—results analysis—which could greatly contribute to our understanding of the model and its potential, if only the tool were taken out of the box and used.

Further information and reading

J Ratcliffe 'Intelligence-led policing' *Australian Institute of Criminology: Trends and Issues* 248 (2003)

J Ratcliffe 'The effectiveness of police intelligence management: a New Zealand case study' *Police Practice and Research* 6(5) 435–45 (2005)

See also J Ratcliffe *Intelligence-Led Policing* (Willan, Cullompton, 2008), and <http://www.jratcliffe.net>.

6

The Law and Intelligence

6.1 **Introduction**

Laws relevant to intelligence management can be broadly divided into two functional groups: the first group provides mechanisms and methods for acquiring intelligence; the second group define rights, obligations, exemptions, and powers relating to data held by public authorities. Overarching these two groups is the presiding obligation imposed by the Human Rights Act 1998.

KEY NOTE—RELEVANT LEGISLATION

'It is unlawful for a public authority to act in a way which is incompatible with a Convention right.', HRA 1998 s 6.

The Human Rights Act 1998 <http://www.opsi.gov.uk/acts/acts1998/19980042.htm>.

See J Wadham, H Mountfield, and A Edmundson *Blackstone's Guide to The Human Rights Act 1998* (3rd edn, Oxford University Press, Oxford, 2003) for the full text of the Act, the ECHR, and commentary.

See also R Stone *Textbook on Civil Liberties and Human Rights* (5th edn, Oxford University Press, Oxford, 2004).

Further information and reading

All legislation is currently published online as originally enacted. The Statutory Publications Office is developing a Statute Law Database which will eventually comprise updated versions of all Acts of the UK Parliament and the Scottish Parliament as amended since enactment In the meantime the Annual Chronological Table of Statutes and the Chronological Tables of Local and Private Acts provide information as to which Acts and Statutory Instrument are currently in force or have been amended.

A comprehensive discussion of all relevant legislation is beyond the scope both of this chapter and this book. The intention of this chapter is briefly to summarize the major legislation that falls into each of these groups and then direct the reader towards sources of further information. The term 'intelligence database' in this chapter is intended to include all databases on which public authorities store information even though the relevant authority might not think of its data as intelligence in the way that crime investigators would perceive such data.

6.2 **Acquisition of Intelligence**

All acquisition of intelligence must conform to the four fundamental principles that enable qualified breaches of the respect for private life enshrined in the HRA. These are encapsulated in the mnemonic PLAN, described in the Key Note below. The note includes references to other sources where the tests are discussed more fully. In essence enactment of these principles prohibits 'fishing trips' and the collection of data for data's sake. The Blair government pushed the boundaries of interpretation in relation to its counter-terrorism measures. It remains to be seen whether the exceptional nature of such measures becomes diluted to the extent that the boundaries of interpretation for conventional policing are similarly expanded.

KEY NOTE—TESTS APPLYING THE FOUR FUNDAMENTAL HRA PRINCIPLES

P   Proportionality

Why is it proportionate to obtain the intended intelligence in the manner proposed? (Harfield and Harfield, 2005, section 1.6.5)

L   Lawfulness/Legitimacy

The proposed action must be lawful: there must be statutory authority to undertake the proposed action. But even if it is lawful, it must also be legitimate. For example, in RIPA the legitimacy tests are: the prevention of disorder or crime; the interests of national security; the interests of public safety; the interests of the economic well-being of the country; the protection of health or morals; or the protection of the rights and freedoms of others. (Harfield and Harfield, 2005, section 1.6.4)

A   Authority to Undertake Proposed Action

What is the lawful foundation and authority for the proposed action? From whom must authorization be sought? (Harfield and Harfield, 2005, section 1.6.3)

N   Necessity of Proposed Action

Why is the proposed action necessary? (Harfield and Harfield, 2005, section 1.6.5)

C Harfield and K Harfield *Covert Investigation* (Oxford University Press, Oxford, 2005)

See also K Starmer *European Rights Law* (Legal Action Group, London, 1999) and A Ashworth *Human Rights, Serious Crime and Criminal Procedure* (Sweet & Maxwell, London, 2002).

Where a public official interacts overtly with a member of the public seeking information (eg a police officer taking a witness statement; a revenue or customs officer seeking information about income or goods; an education welfare officer making enquiries about a child's attendance at school; a trading standards officer interviewing a complainant), then there is no statutory power needed to gather information freely imparted by the member of public. As PACE 1984 Code A, Guidance Note 1, governing police-public encounters, puts it: 'This code does not affect the ability of an officer to speak to or question a person in the ordinary course of the officer's duties . . . It is not the purpose of the code to prohibit such encounters between them police and the community with the co-operation of the person concerned and neither does it affect the principle that all citizens have a [civic rather than legal] duty to help police officers to prevent crime and discover offenders'.

KEY NOTE—RELEVANT LEGISLATION—IN CHRONOLOGICAL ORDER

Police and Criminal Evidence Act 1984 (as amended), and its eight Codes of Practice [not available online]

Police Act 1997, Part III
<http://www.opsi.gov.uk/acts/acts1997/1997050.htm>

Regulation of Investigatory Powers Act 2000
<http://www.opsi.gov.uk/acts/acts2000/20000023.htm>

Proceeds of Crime Act 2002, Part 7
<http://www.opsi.gov.uk/acts/acts2002/20020029.htm>
Explanatory Notes <http://www.opsi.gov.uk/acts/en2002/2002en29.htm>

6.2.1 Police and Criminal Evidence Act 1984 (as amended)

Personal identification data, including biometric data (such as finger-prints and DNA profiles) is, of course, vital to the intelligence and evidential functions in identifying and tracing suspects. The power to acquire such personal data derives from police powers enacted in the much amended PACE and its ever increasing catalogue of accompanying, interpretative Codes of Practice.

Upon conviction, such data is entered onto the PNC and DNA database with original finger-prints and photographs being retained by the force in which the suspect was charged. Retention of DNA samples from persons either not charged or not convicted is a controversial power, opposed by many as a civil liberties intrusion. In theory, DNA profiles are as unique as finger-prints. But whereas the probability of two persons having identical finger-prints can now be assessed against over a century of finger-print data gathering, DNA science is far more recent and still developing. Errors of process, errors of interpretation and misunderstandings about probability still bedevil the evidential use of DNA which is no longer regarded as absolutely certain.

Further information and reading

PACE is not available online, although many of the Acts that have subsequently amended the original 1984 provisions are electronically available.

For simplicity's sake, readers are referred to two key texts.

The definitive legal commentary on PACE is provided by Professor Michael Zander, who participated in the original Royal Commission that gave rise to the legislation. His book is entitled *The Police and Criminal Evidence Act 1984* (Thomson/Sweet & Maxwell, London); however the latest edition (5th) predates amendments to police and PCSO powers in SOCAP 2005 and the Police and Justice Act 2006. At time of writing a sixth edition is awaited.

P Ozin H Norton, and P Spivey *PACE: A Practical Guide to the Police and Criminal Evidence Act 1984* (Oxford University Press, Oxford, 2006) is a companion volume to this present work in the Blackstone's Practical Policing Series and includes all relevant amendments up to 1 August 2006. Therefore it, too, omits amendments to bail and charging procedures enacted in the Police and Justice Act 2006.

On the evidential and intelligence value of DNA see D Chalmers (ed) *Genetic Testing and the Criminal Law* (UCL Press, London, 2005); also D Lucy *Introduction to Statistics for Forensic Scientists* (John Wiley & Sons, Chichester, 2005) particularly chs 11 and 13.

6.2.2 Police Act 1997, Part III

Part III of the Police Act 1997 makes provision for specific public authorities to trespass on and interfere with private property in order to facilitate certain restricted forms of covert surveillance. This may include operations intended to gather intelligence through reconnaissance as part of a longer-term strategy to inform eventual enforcement action.

Further information and reading

Police Act 1997, Part III
<http://www.opsi.gov.uk/acts/acts1997/1997050.htm>

For discussion of the covert investigation powers provided by Part III of the Police Act 1997, see the companion Blackstone's Practical Policing volume: C Harfield and K Harfield *Covert Investigation* (Oxford University Press, Oxford, 2005).

6.2.3 Regulation of Investigatory Powers Act 2000

Whereas the Police Act 1997 facilitates certain covert surveillance *tactics*, the statutory authority to undertake covert surveillance is enacted in RIPA. Different surveillance powers are available to different agencies in different circumstances. These are specified in various statutory instruments. It is interesting to note that powers granted to SOCA to conduct surveillance are not as extensive as those to ordinary police agencies. Whilst intrusive surveillance powers are restricted to law enforcement agencies and intelligence services, directed surveillance powers, and the deployment of covert human intelligence sources are intervention options available to a far wider selection of public authorities, including local councils.

It is a widely-held view that intelligence or evidence gathered covertly outside the surveillance regime will have been gathered unlawfully. Exposure of unlawful acquisition may undermine subsequent intervention founded upon such intelligence.

This view has recently been challenged by the case of *C v Police and Secretary of State*, heard before the Investigatory Powers Tribunal, and deemed of such significance that the tribunal took the extraordinary measures of sitting as a bench of five instead of three, holding the hearing in public and publishing their judgment. In a dispute over a claim relating to an occupational ill-health pension C, a former police officer, was covertly videoed by inquiry agents employed for the purpose by the police force. C argued that because the surveillance of him had been conducted covertly, it should have been conducted within the regime laid out in RIPA and that, as it was an employment issue rather than a criminal matter that was being investigated, there was no lawful avenue under RIPA to authorise such surveillance.

The Investigatory Powers Tribunal disagreed relying in part on RIPA, s 80, which provides that nothing that is not otherwise unlawful under RIPA shall not be deemed unlawful simply because a warrant, authorization or notice pursuant to the Act was not in place. Additionally the tribunal took the view that RIPA does not restrict surveillance only to criminal investigations but provides that where a crime or serious crime is being investigated, then such surveillance must be authorized. The tribunal went on to draw a subtle distinction between the 'core' functions of a public authority (in the case of the police, the investigation of crime for instance) and the 'ordinary' functions common to all public authorities such as employment. This fine but fundamental distinction is reinforced by the extent to which statutory instruments define which public authorities can avail themselves of which legitimate authorities under RIPA.

In short the tribunal held that, because the covert surveillance had been conducted pursuant to an investigation outside the RIPA regime, so the authorization regime set out by RIPA did not apply, and so the matter lay outside the competence of the tribunal.

It remains to be seen whether this line of reasoning is adopted or disapproved in subsequent judgments.

What does this mean for the conducting of covert surveillance for intelligence purposes? Clearly the test set out by the tribunal rests on RIPA, sections 28(3) and 32(3) supplemented by relevant interpretative statutory instruments (for example SI 2003/3171 and SI 2003/3174).

Hence an authorization for directed surveillance will be necessary if the intended intelligence operation is supporting an investigation that is necessary (RIPA, s 28(3)):

(a) in the interests of national security;
(b) for the purpose of preventing or detecting crime or preventing disorder;
(c) in the interests of the economic well-being of the United Kingdom;
(d) in the interests of public safety;
(e) for the purpose of protecting public health;
(f) for the purpose of assessing or collecting any tax, duty, levy or other imposition, contribution or charge payable to a government department; or
(g) for any purpose (not falling within paragraphs (a) to (f) which is specified for the purpose of this subsection by an order made by the Secretary of State.

Thus the police service core functions in relation to directed surveillance are held to be (a) to (e) inclusive (SI 2003/3171). SOCA's core functions are confined to (b) (SI 2006/594 which amends SI 2003/3171). Local authorities are restricted to function (b) above.

An authorization for intrusive surveillance will be necessary if the intelligence operation is supporting an investigation that is necessary (RIPA, s 32(3)):

(a) in the interests of national security;
(b) for the purpose of preventing or detecting serious crime; or
(c) in the interests of the economic well-being of the United Kingdom.

The number of agencies that may use intrusive surveillance is significantly smaller than the number of agencies that may use directed surveillance and includes both the public police forces and SOCA.

Further information and reading

Regulation of Investigatory Powers Act 2000
<http://www.opsi.gov.uk/acts/acts2000/20000023.htm>

For a full discussion of the covert investigation powers provided by RIPA 2000, see the companion Blackstone's Practical Policing volume: C Harfield and K Harfield *Covert Investigation* (Oxford University Press, Oxford, 2005).

On the various powers to employ covert surveillance, see SI 2003/3171 as amended by SI 2006/594.

On *C v Police and Secretary of State* IPT/03/32/H, 14 November 2006, the judgment is available at <http://www.ipt-uk.com/docs/IPT_03_32_H.pdf>.

6.2.4 **Proceeds of Crime Act 2002, Part 7**

POCA repeals or amends a significant amount of previous legislation in relation to reporting suspicious financial transactions that might constitute intelligence and/or evidence of money laundering. Part 7 of POCA imposes obligations to report suspicious financial transactions in order to combat money laundering. The obligations fall upon businesses in the 'regulated sector' (as defined by POCA, sch 9). Originally suspicious activity reports (SARs) were made to the Director General of NCIS in his role as head of the Financial Intelligence Unit (FIU). As successor agency to NCIS, the FIU role (which includes managing the ELMER database of SARs) is now undertaken by SOCA. A review of the future of the SAR function, and whether the creation of SOCA provided opportunities to enhance the SAR regime, was commissioned in 2005 jointly by the Chancellor of the Exchequer and the Home Secretary and undertaken by Sir Stephen Lander, chair of the board of SOCA.

Further information and reading

Sir Stephen Lander *Review of the Suspicious Activity Reports Regime (The SARS Review)* (Serious Organised Crime Agency, London, 2006). Available online at <http://www.soca.gov.uk/downloads/SOCAtheSARsReview_FINAL_Web.pdf>.

For legal commentary on money laundering disclosure, see chs 26 and 27 in T Millington and M Sutherland Williams *The Proceeds of Crime: Law and Practice of Restraint, Confiscation and Forfeiture* (Oxford University Press, Oxford, 2003).

6.2.5 **Security and Intelligence Services Acts**

Although not their primary function, the legislation that establishes the statutory authority for the security and intelligence services makes provision, in certain circumstances, for these agencies to assist law enforcement in the investigation of crime. Such engagement with the police was formerly managed, depending upon the nature of the liaison, primarily through Special Branch and NCIS, and is now managed through Special Branch and SOCA.

KEY NOTE—RELEVANT LEGISLATION

Security Service Act 1989 (amended by the SSA 1996)
<http://www.opsi.gov.uk/acts/acts1989/Ukpga_19890005_en_1.htm>

Intelligence Services Act 1994
<http://www.opsi.gov.uk/acts/acts1994/Ukpga_19940013_en_1.htm>

Security Service Act 1996
<http://www.opsi.gov.uk/acts/acts1996/1996035.htm>

The provisions are that the Security Service (MI5) may 'act in support of the activities of police forces and other law enforcement agencies in the prevention and detection of serious crime' (Security Service Act 1989, s 1(4) as amended by Security Service Act 1996, s 1); the Secret Intelligence Service (MI6) may use its functions 'in support of the prevention or detection of serious crime' (Intelligence Services Act 1994, s 1 (2) (c)); and the Government Communications Headquarters (GCHQ) may use its functions 'in support of the prevention or detection of serious crime' (Intelligence Services Act 1994, s 3 (2) (c)). MI5 may only provide such assistance within the UK and if the matter under investigation comprises serious crime as defined (the same criteria as for RIPA). MI6 and GCHQ may only provide such assistance outside the UK.

Police liaison with the Security Service and the intelligence agencies was previously coordinated through the National Criminal Intelligence Service, and following its replacement by the Serious Organised Crime Agency (SOCA), is now coordinated through that agency. The line of communication for police forces with SOCA is via the Force Intelligence Bureau.

6.3 **Management of Intelligence**

Since intelligence is comprised of information and data, when it is held by public authorities it is subject to the various laws on data protection and information disclosure that apply to public authorities—to which certain exceptions apply. Whilst it is interesting to see the chronological relationship of the various statutes, which illustrates the development of policy on these issues, the discussion below is structured on a functional basis around:

- the statutory *duty* to disclose information;
- the statutory *duty* to protect data; and
- the discretionary *power* to disclose (share) information.

KEY NOTE—RELEVANT LEGISLATION—CHRONOLOGICALLY LISTED

Criminal Procedure and Investigations Act 1996 & Code of Practice
<http://www.opsi.gov.uk/acts/acts1996/1996025.htm>

Police Act 1997, ss 112–27 & Code of Practice
<http://www.opsi.gov.uk/acts/acts1997/1997050.htm>

Data Protection Act 1998
<http://www.opsi.gov.uk/acts/acts1998/19980029.htm>

Crime and Disorder Act 1998
<http://www.opsi.gov.uk/acts/acts1998/19980037.htm>

Freedom of Information Act 2000
<http://www.opsi.gov.uk/acts/acts2000/20000036.htm>

Explanatory Notes <http://www.opsi.gov.uk/acts/en2000/2000en20.htm>

Serious Organised Crime and Police Act 2005
<http://www.opsi.gov.uk/acts/acts2005/20050015.htm>
Explanatory Notes <http://www.opsi.gov.uk/acts/en2005/2005en15.htm>

6.3.1 **The duty to disclose information**

Disclosure duties fall into three categories: the general duty to disclose created by the Freedom of Information Act 2000, the more specific duties in relation to prosecutions and pre-employment criminal records checks, and the duty imposed on CDRP partner agencies to disclose information to each other.

Freedom of Information Act 2000

The prevailing basic premise from which all else flows is a citizen's 'right to know'. Hence Freedom of Information Act FIA 2000, s 1:

KEY NOTE—RELEVANT LEGISLATION

FIA 2000, s 1.

(1) Any person making a request for information to a public authority is entitled—
 (a) to be informed in writing by the public authority whether it holds information of the description specified in the request, and
 (b) if that is the case, to have that information communicated to him.

'Public authority' is defined in FIA, sch 1 and the full list runs to several pages making it too lengthy to reproduce here. It includes police forces, local authorities, and all partner agencies involved in crime investigation, crime reduction, and community safety; allowing unfettered access to all public authority intelligence and information databases would, of course, frustrate efforts to investigate crime and to enhance community safety. So to the general premise above, there are exceptions defined.

The first generic area of exemption arises from investigations and proceedings, including criminal proceedings, conducted by public authorities. Section 30(1) of the FIA provides that information held by a public authority is deemed to be exempt from the prevailing basic principle if it has been held at any time for the purposes of:

 (a) any investigation which the public authority has a duty to conduct with a view to it being ascertained—

    (i) whether a person should be charged with an offence, or

    (ii) whether a person charged with an offence is guilty of it,

(b) any investigation which is conducted by the authority and in the circumstances may lead to a decision by the authority to institute criminal proceedings which the authority has power to conduct, or

(c) any criminal proceedings which the authority has power to conduct.

Section 30(2) of the FIA provides that information will also be exempt if:

(a) it was obtained or recorded by the authority for the purposes of its functions relating to—

    (i) investigations falling within subsection (1)(a) or (b),

    (ii) criminal proceedings which the authority has power to conduct,

    (iii) investigations (other than investigations falling within subsection (1)(a) or (b)) which are conducted by the authority for any of the purposes specified in section 31(2) and either by virtue of Her Majesty's prerogative or by virtue of powers conferred by or under any enactment, or

    (iv) civil proceedings which are brought by or on behalf of the authority and arise out of such investigations, and

(b) it relates to the obtaining of information from confidential sources.

The next generic area of exemption is in relation to law enforcement.

Section 31(1) of the FIA provides that information which is not already exempt under section 30, shall be exempt information if its disclosure under the FOI would, or would be likely to, prejudice:

(a) the prevention or detection of crime,

(b) the apprehension or prosecution of offenders,

(c) the administration of justice,

(d) the assessment or collection of any tax or duty or of any imposition of a similar nature,

(e) the operation of the immigration controls,

(f) the maintenance of security and good order in prisons or in other institutions where persons are lawfully detained,

(g) the exercise by any public authority of its functions for any of the purposes specified in subsection (2),

(h) any civil proceedings which are brought by or on behalf of a public authority and arise out of an investigation conducted, for any of the purposes specified in subsection (2), by or on behalf of the authority by virtue of Her Majesty's prerogative or by virtue of powers conferred by or under an enactment, or

    (i) any inquiry held under the Fatal Accidents and Sudden Deaths Inquiries (Scotland) Act 1976 to the extent that the inquiry arises out of an investigation conducted, for any of the purposes specified in subsection (2), by or on behalf of the authority by virtue of Her Majesty's prerogative or by virtue of powers conferred by or under an enactment.

The purposes referred to in (g) to (i) include (s 31(2)):

- ascertaining whether any person has failed to comply with the law;
- ascertaining whether any person is responsible for any conduct which is improper;
- ascertaining whether circumstances which would justify regulatory action in pursuance of any enactment exist or may arise;
- ascertaining the cause of an accident;
- securing the health, safety, and welfare of persons at work; and
- protecting persons other than persons at work against risk to health or safety arising out of or in connection with the actions of persons at work.

In relation to the third generic area, the records of any court, tribunal, or body exercising a judicial power of the state (FIA, s 32), information held by a public authority is exempt information if it is held only by virtue of being contained in:

(a) any document filed with, or otherwise placed in the custody of, a court for the purposes of proceedings in a particular cause or matter,
(b) any document served upon, or by, a public authority for the purposes of proceedings in a particular cause or matter, or
(c) any document created by—
   (i) a court, or
   (ii) a member of the administrative staff of a court,

   for the purposes of proceedings in a particular cause or matter.

Exemption also applies to:

(a) any document placed in the custody of a person conducting an inquiry or arbitration, for the purposes of the inquiry or arbitration; or
(b) any document created by a person conducting an inquiry or arbitration, for the purposes of the inquiry or arbitration.

In the case of all these categories of exemption, there is no duty to confirm or deny possession of any information which is (or if it were held by the public authority would be) exempt information.

What does this mean for those who gather, collate, process, and use intelligence? Essentially, intelligence in relation to criminal activities, investigations, and proceedings is exempt from the general principle of disclosure enshrined in the FIA. Where such intelligence is shared with partner agencies, it may be prudent to annotate the relevant documentation to the effect that the information is so protected in order to ensure that it is not inadvertently disclosed by a third party with whom it has been shared.

Criminal Procedure and Investigations Act 1996

A succession of miscarriages of justice exposed during the 1980s and 1990s highlighted the fact that some prosecutions had proceeded even though the investigation had discovered exculpatory evidence indicating the innocence of the accused, thus rendering convictions unsafe. As a result the CPIA was enacted imposing upon investigators a general obligation to *reveal* to the prosecutor all unused material that did not form part of the prosecution file. The Act imposed upon prosecutors the consequential duty, in light of investigator revelations, to *disclose* to the defence all unused material that tended to support the defence case or undermine the prosecution case.

What does this mean for those who gather, collate, process, and use intelligence? First, there is a need for liaison between the senior investigating officer, whose responsibility it is to present the file to the Crown Prosecution Service, and the intelligence department. Intelligence forming part of an investigation file is likely to be sensitive, unused material. The prosecutor should not disclose such material unless it weakens the prosecution case or supports the defence case. Intelligence which is neutral in its effect or which is damaging to the defence case but is not being used in evidence, need not be disclosed.

Further information and reading

C Ryan, S Savla, and G Scanlan *A Guide to the Criminal Procedure and Investigations Act 1996* (Butterworths, London, 1996).

See also *R v H and C* [2004] 2 AC 134.

The defence will, not unnaturally, seek to expose sensitive intelligence that it believes may exist, such as the identity of a CHIS for instance, as a disruption tactic to force the prosecution to consider abandoning a case rather than compromise the intelligence. The prosecution can apply for public interest immunity (PII) to protect sensitive information that might otherwise be exposed.

In relation to intelligence derived from the interception of communications section 17 of the RIPA prohibits any reference to interception in criminal proceedings. Section 15(3) of the RIPA requires the prompt destruction of the intercepted communication once intelligence has been derived from it. This runs counter to the general principle of the CPIA and special provisions within the CPIA (ss 3(7), 8(6), 9(9), and 23(6), as amended by the RIPA), accommodate this exception. Nevertheless, there is still a duty imposed upon the prosecutor to consider material that may undermine the prosecution or assist the defence. If the intercepted communication has been destroyed, this is difficult to do. *R v Preston* [1994] 2 AC 130, 166–8 provides a solution based on similar prohibitions under the now repealed Interception of Communications Act 1984. Where the intercepted communication has been destroyed and so no longer exists to be disclosed to the prosecutor under s 18(7), and where a person relevant to a trial has been arrested as a result of intelligence derived from warranted interception, this must be disclosed to the prosecutor together with the declarations that all the material has been destroyed in accordance with s 15(3); that no one has an accurate recollection of exactly what was said in the intercepted conversations; and that a copy of the warrant is available at SOCA to prove the lawfulness of the interception.

Police Act 1997

Sections 112–27 of the Police Act 1997 provide authority to disclose information held by the Criminal Records Bureau, subject to certain conditions. These disclosures are termed **Basic Disclosures** (s 112—current or unspent convictions), **Standard Disclosures** (s 113—spent and unspent convictions), and **Enhanced Disclosures** (s 115—a standard disclosure with additional non-conviction information derived from a local police force record check).

Such disclosures are made only to authorized recipients, in connection with statutory pre-employment checks required for those who work with children or vulnerable adults. Police forces will have dedicated units (usually at headquarters and associated with force intelligence bureaux) as a single point of contact for such disclosure and all requests must be channelled through such units. Disclosure by other means, or for other types of employer, or for other purposes may be unlawful and contrary to the Police Code of Conduct or Police Staff discipline regulations.

What does this mean for those who gather, collate, process, and use intelligence? Police forces will have dedicated units for liaison with the CRB, usually within or closely associated with the force intelligence bureaux. These are the proper channels for such disclosure requests and any requests for such disclosures should be referred to the dedicated unit.

> ### Further information and reading
>
> P Leigh-Pollitt and J Mullock *Point of Law: The Data Protection Act Explained* (3rd edn, The Stationery Office, London, 2001) particularly pp 115–19.
>
> See also the *Code of Practice for Registered Persons and other Recipients of Disclosure Information* at <http://www.crb.gov.uk>.

Crime and Disorder Act 1998 (as amended)

The statutory powers discussed in Part 1 relate to primary acquisition of intelligence by public authorities. Intelligence management includes disclosure for the purposes of sharing or disseminating intelligence outside the immediate organization. This might be termed secondary acquisition, for which there exists a statutory power.

As originally enacted the statute created a *power* to share not a *duty* to share. Subsequent amendments enacted in Police and Justice Act 2006, sch 9 allow the Secretary of State to specify information that must be shared by relevant authorities participating in a CDRP.

CDA 1998, ss 5–7 required 'responsible authorities' to review levels and patterns of crime in their area, invite the participation of others, analyse the results and publish the review, and formulate a strategy for the reduction of crime and disorder in their area. The principal partners are the local authority and the police. The review is widely referred to as a 'crime audit'.

KEY NOTE—RESPONSIBLE AUTHORITIES

- The local council (both district and county if not a unitary authority).
- Chief police officers whose police area lies within the local government area.
- Police authorities where part of their area lies within the local government area.
- Fire and rescue authorities where part of their area lies within the local government area.
- In Wales, every health authority where the whole or part of their area lies within the local government area.
- In England, every primary care trust where the whole or part of their area lies within the local government area.

To these responsible authorities may be added 'cooperating bodies', which include parish and community councils, NHS Trusts, schools, and further education governing bodies. 'Cooperating bodies should be able to provide data or information to improve the understanding of local crime and disorder problems, and to contribute to the benefit of the local community as well as benefiting the core functions of the respective agencies' (Rogers, 2006: 200).

To facilitate this crime audit, CDA, s 115 provides the power, if such a power is not available under any other legislation, for any person to disclose information to a relevant authority 'where the disclosure is necessary or expedient for the purposes of any provision of' the CDA.

What does this mean for those who gather, collate, process, and use intelligence? The police both contribute to and derive benefit from crime audits. In particular crime audits can inform strategic assessments and so influence the control strategy. But as Rogers points out, 'too much reliance upon police data may result in insufficient attention being given to under-reporting of some types of crime, and that the crime audit may just reflect current police priorities' (Rogers 2006: 230). Thus there is a possibility that police intelligence might subvert the purpose of a multi-agency crime audit thus making the crime audit little more than a rubber stamp justification for a police agenda.

The value of a crime audit depends upon the willingness of the agencies involved to avail themselves of CDA, s 115.

Further information and reading

C Rogers *Crime Reduction Partnerships* (Oxford University Press, Oxford, 2006) particularly ch 8.

6.3.2 **The duty to protect data**

Duties to disclose are balanced by duties to protect.

Data Protection Act 1998

Data held by public authorities are subject to principles and rules of acquisition and retention, which apply to intelligence databases.

The Act establishes key principles of data protection which are defined in Schedule 1.

KEY NOTE—THE DATA PROTECTION PRINCIPLES

These principles are defined in Part 1, Schedule 1, Data Protection Act 1998. Compliance with these principles is a statutory duty.

1. Personal data shall be processed fairly and lawfully and, in particular, shall not be processed unless—
   (a) at least one of the conditions in Schedule 2 is met (these include that the processing is necessary for the administration of justice and the exercise of Crown, statutory and other public functions), and
   (b) in the case of sensitive personal data, at least one of the conditions in Schedule 3 is also met (these include the protection of the vital interests of the data subject or a third party, processing in connection with legal proceedings, and for the administration of justice and the exercise of Crown or statutory functions).
2. Personal data shall be obtained only for one or more specified and lawful purposes, and shall not be further processed in any manner incompatible with that purpose or those purposes.
3. Personal data shall be adequate, relevant and not excessive in relation to the purpose or purposes for which they are processed.
4. Personal data shall be accurate and, where necessary, kept up to date.
5. Personal data processed for any purpose or purposes shall not be kept for longer than is necessary for that purpose or those purposes.
6. Personal data shall be processed in accordance with the rights of data subjects under this Act.

---

7. Appropriate technical and organisational measures shall be taken against unauthorised or unlawful processing of personal data and against accidental loss or destruction of, or damage to, personal data.
8. Personal data shall not be transferred to a country or territory outside the European Economic Area unless that country or territory ensures an adequate level of protection for the rights and freedoms of data subjects in relation to the processing of personal data.

Public authorities have a duty to protect the data they hold. Of particular relevance are DPA 1998, ss 1–3, 7, 13, and Schedule 1.

KEY NOTE—RELEVANT DEFINITIONS DERIVED FROM DPA, SS 1–3

Data means information which:
(a) is being processed by means of equipment operating automatically in response to instructions given for that purpose,
(b) is recorded with the intention that it should be processed by means of such equipment,
(c) is recorded as part of a relevant filing system or with the intention that it should form part of a relevant filing system, or
(d) does not fall within paragraph (a), (b) or (c) but forms part of an accessible record as defined by section 68;

The **data controller** is a person who (either alone or jointly or in common with other persons) determines the purposes for which and the manner in which any personal data are, or are to be, processed;

A **data processor**, in relation to personal data, means any person (other than an employee of the data controller) who processes the data on behalf of the data controller;

The **data subject** is the individual who is the subject of personal data;

Personal data means data which relate to a living individual who can be identified—
(a) from those data, or
(b) from those data and other information which is in the possession of, or is likely to come into the possession of, the data controller,
and includes any expression of opinion about the individual and any indication of the intentions of the data controller or any other person in respect of the individual

---

Sensitive personal data means information about:
(a) the racial or ethnic origin of the data subject,
(b) his political opinions,
(c) his religious beliefs or other beliefs of a similar nature,
(d) whether he is a member of a trade union (within the meaning of the Trade Union and Labour Relations (Consolidation) Act 1992),
(e) his physical or mental health or condition,
(f) his sexual life,
(g) the commission or alleged commission by him of any offence, or
(h) any proceedings for any offence committed or alleged to have been committed by him, the disposal of such proceedings or the sentence of any court in such proceedings.

Relevant filing system means both automated and non-automated filing systems.

Data subjects have a general right to access data held about them (DPA, s 7). They have the right to be informed:

(a) whether personal data of which that individual is the data subject are being processed by or on behalf of that data controller,
(b) if that is the case, to be given by the data controller a description of—
   (i) the personal data of which that individual is the data subject,
   (ii) the purposes for which they are being or are to be processed, and
   (iii) the recipients or classes of recipients to whom they are or may be disclosed,
(c) to have communicated to him in an intelligible form—
   (i) the information constituting any personal data of which that individual is the data subject, and
   (ii) any information available to the data controller as to the source of those data, and
(d) where the processing by automatic means of personal data of which that individual is the data subject for the purpose of evaluating matters relating to him such as, for example, his performance at work, his creditworthiness, his reliability or his conduct, has constituted or is likely to constitute the sole basis for any decision significantly affecting him, to be informed by the data controller of the logic involved in that decision-taking." (s 7(1)).

Remedy for a person damaged by non-compliance with DPA provisions is provided for in section 13.

As with the FIA, there are exceptions that protect the work of law enforcement and partner agencies (DPA, ss 27–35) including:

• national security;
• crime and taxation;
• health, education, and social work.

Personal data are exempt from any of the provisions of the data protection principles, Parts II, III, V, and section 55, if the exemption from that provision is required for the purpose of safeguarding national security (s 28(1)).

Personal data processed for:

- the prevention or detection of crime;
- the apprehension or prosecution of offenders; or
- the assessment or collection of any tax or duty or of any imposition of a similar nature

are exempt from the first data protection principle (except to the extent to which it requires compliance with the conditions in Schedules 2 and 3 of the Act) and from section 7 in any case to the extent to which the application of those provisions to the data would be likely to prejudice any these functions (s 29(1)).

What does this mean for those who gather, collate, process, and use intelligence? It adds statutory emphasis to the business requirement that intelligence should be accurate, timely, proportionate, and relevant.

Further information and reading

P Carey *Blackstone's Guide to the Data Protection Act 1998* (Blackstones, London 1998)

P Leigh-Pollitt and J Mullock *Point of Law: The Data Protection Act Explained* (3rd edn, The Stationery Office, London, 2001)

P Carey *Data Protection: A Practical Guide to UK and EU Law* (Oxford University Press, Oxford, 2004)

6.3.3 The power to disclose (share) information

Not all statutory provisions establish duties. In some cases discretionary powers are made available.

Serious Organized Crime And Police Act 2005

As successor to the former National Criminal Intelligence Service (NCIS, created by Police Act 1997, Part I), SOCA, which became operational on 1 April 2006, assumed many of the roles and responsibilities of NCIS. Specifically in relation to evidence and intelligence, it has statutory obligations to gather, store, and analyse information relevant to the prevention, detection, investigation, or prosecution of offences or to the reduction of crime and its consequential harm. SOCA *may* also disseminate. A list of recipients is specified, although since this includes the discretion to disseminate to 'such persons as it considers appropriate' this is a particularly broad discretionary power (see box below).

KEY NOTE—RELEVANT LEGISLATION

Serious Organised Crime and Police Act 2005
<http://www.opsi.gov.uk/acts/acts2005/20050015.htm>
Explanatory Notes <http://www.opsi.gov.uk/acts/en2005/2005en15.htm>

Section 2

(1) SOCA has the functions of—
   (a) preventing and detecting serious organized crime, and
   (b) contributing to the reduction of such crime in other ways and to the mitigation of its consequences.
      [. . .]

Section 3

(1) SOCA has the function of gathering, storing, analysing and disseminating information relevant to—
   (a) the prevention, detection, investigation or prosecution of offences, or
   (b) the reduction of crime in other ways or the mitigation of its consequences.
(2) SOCA may disseminate such information to—
   (a) police forces within subsection (3),
   (b) special police forces,
   (c) law enforcement agencies, or
   (d) such other persons as it considers appropriate in connection with any of the matters mentioned in subsection (1)(a) or (b).
(3) The police forces within this subsection are—
   (a) police forces in the United Kingdom, and
   (b) the States of Jersey Police Force, the salaried police force of the Island of Guernsey and the Isle of Man Constabulary.
(4) In this section 'law enforcement agency' means—
   (a) the Commissioners or any other government department,
   (b) the Scottish Administration,
   (c) any other person who is charged with the duty of investigating offences or charging offenders, or
   (d) any other person who is engaged outside the United Kingdom in the carrying on of activities similar to any carried on by SOCA or a police force.
(5) In this Chapter 'special police force' means—
   (a) the Ministry of Defence Police,
   (b) the British Transport Police Force,
   (c) the Civil Nuclear Constabulary, or
   (d) the Scottish Drug Enforcement Agency.

What does this mean for those who gather, collate, process, and use intelligence? Force intelligence bureaux provide the channels through which local forces will communicate with SOCA. The NIM provides the template for which intelligence shall be exchanged in both directions.

Further information and reading

SOCA's Statement of Information Management Practice is available online at <http://:www.soca.gov.uk>.

The principle of availability

Not yet in force at the time of writing (2007) but an aspiration for 2008, is the principle of availability defined in the Hague Programme within the EU Justice and Home Affairs *acquis*. It is envisaged there should be a free exchange of information between law enforcement agencies in the EU Member States in which information relevant to ongoing investigations will be provided to authorities requesting it. (There are calls for the principle to be taken further and for interoperability of databases to be established to enable direct access to databases held by foreign law enforcement.) The principle applies to all crimes. There are serious concerns about what this would mean in practice, the lack of governance and oversight, and the lack of control over how the data would be used.

Further information and reading

Statewatch (2006) *The Principle of Availability—Statewatch Analysis* accessible at <http://:www.statewatch.org>.

House of Lords *Schengen Information System II (SIS II)* 9th Report of Session 2006–07, European Union Committee, HL49. London, TSO.

6.4 **Conclusion**

This chapter has confined itself to the key legislation of which those involved in local police intelligence and community safety should be aware. The legislation defines duties to disclose and protect data and provides a discretionary power to share. Disclosure and protection generate a tension of competing interests that it is difficult to balance. Intelligence managers, in particular, need to be aware of this tension and the consequences of mismanagement.

The management of information that could be used for intelligence purposes has been a feature of much recent legislation. The indicative table below summarizes not only the legislation considered in this chapter but other legislation excluded from discussion here by reasons of space.

Table 6.1 Summary index of major legislation in relation to information gathering and access

Statute	Provision
Police and Criminal Evidence Act 1984	Various powers in relation to identification and evidence create intelligence and intelligence opportunities.
Children Act 1989	s 47 imposes *duty* on local authorities to investigate and refer to police instances when children resident or found within the area are known or reasonably suspected to have suffered significant harm.
Criminal Procedures and Investigations Act 1996	Proscribes pre-trial disclosure of material gathered during an investigation by investigators to the prosecutor, and revelation by prosecutors to the defence.
Police Act 1997	Part III makes provision for property interference when required to facilitate certain forms of surveillance.
	Part V provides authority for basic, Standard and Enhanced Disclosures in relation to pre-employment criminal record checks. Amended by SOCAP Act 2005.
Crime and Disorder Act 1998	Initially provided a power (ss 5–7) to share intelligence between public authorities, notably CDRP partners. Amended by s 22 Police and Justice Act 2006 which converted the power to share into a duty to disclose to partner agencies.
Data Protection Act 1998	Defines regime for data retention and provides mechanisms for subject access.
Freedom of Information Act 2000	Creates presumption that information held by public authorities will be released to the public unless specific exemptions apply. Section 30 provides exemption in relation to information held in connection with a criminal investigation.
Terrorist Act 2000	Schedule 6 power of police to require information from a financial institution in relation to a terrorist investigation.
Regulation of Investigatory Powers Act 2000	Makes provision for covert investigation through interception of communications and surveillance and thus provides options for information gathering in intelligence operations.
Police Reform Act 2002	s 17 *Duty* imposed on police authorities and chief officers to supply information to the IPCC.

Statute	Provision
Proceeds of Crime Act 2002	Part 7 *Duties* imposed on the regulated financial sector to disclose information to the authorities of suspected money-laundering. Part 8 provides for disclosure orders, customer information orders and account monitoring orders (together with disclosure of such information).
Serious Organised Crime and Police Act 2005	ss 32–35 Use and disclosure of information by SOCA; s 157 imposes *duty* on police authorities to publish local policing summaries annually; s 163 amends Police Act 1997 in relation to criminal record checks.
Childcare Act 2006	Part 4 enables Secretary of State to make Regulations (secondary legislation) for the requisition and provision of individual child information by prescribed persons or categories of persons.
Identity Cards Act 2006	Establishes National Identity Register and creates various powers to require information for the NIR (s 9), and provide information from the NIR (ss 12–21).
Immigration, Asylum and Nationality Act 2006	ss 27–42 (as amended by s 14 Police and Justice Act 2006) detail provisions in relation to HMRC, immigration officer, and police powers in relation to passenger, crew, freight, and voyage information and imposes a *duty to share* information (s 36) upon and between these agencies and a *power to disclose* (s 39) information to other law enforcement agencies.
Police and Justice Act 2006	s 13—Registrar General for England and Wales (or the RG for Northern Ireland) may supply death registration details to police.
	s 22 amends information-sharing powers under the CDA 1998, creating new duties to disclose to partner agencies.
Safeguarding Vulnerable Groups Act 2006	Creates Independent Barring Board and lists of persons barred from working with children or vulnerable adults and creates various *duties* and *powers* in relation to the provision of information in relation to these purposes (ss 30–51).

7

Risk

7.1 **Introduction**

Of course it can be argued that the whole profession of intelligence is about responding to risk. This is equally true in any of the intelligence theatres: national security; policing and community safety; or the competitive private sector. Risks are everywhere and cannot be avoided. They exist, as will be seen in Table 7-3 below, on perpendicular continuums from low probability/high impact to high probability/low impact. They are inherent in all aspects of policing and community safety and are multi-faceted. There is a growing literature on risk, risk governance, and policing risk: far greater than can be usefully summarized here and for wider reading in the general subject area, the reader is referred to the 'Further Reading' box below which identifies a random sample from the literature.

Further reading

Readers seeking a wider, more theoretical discussion of pertinent issues might usefully look at:

J Barker and D Hodes *The Child in Mind: A Child Protection Handbook* (Routledge, London, 2004).

J Coaffee *Terrorism, Risk and the City: The making of a Contemporary Urban Landscape* (Ashgate, Aldershot, 2003).

Home Office *The MAPPA Guidance* Probation Circular 54/2004, 14 October 2004.

H Kemshall *Understanding Risk in Criminal Justice* (Open University Press/McGraw-Hill, Maidenhead, 2003).

J Langan and V Lindow *Living with Risk: Mental Health Service User Involvement in Risk Assessment and Management* (Policy Press, Bristol, 2004).

L Mazerolle and J Ransley *Third Party Policing* (CUP, Cambridge, 2006).

National Audit Office *Managing Risks to Improve Public Services* HC 1078-I and 1078-II Session 2003–4, (The Stationery Office, London, 2004).

S Webb *Social Work in a Risk Society: Social and Political Perspectives* (Palgrave MacMillan, Basingstoke, 2006).

The purpose of this chapter, however, is to drill down beneath the generic purpose of intelligence in order to consider not how intelligence can be used to manage risk, but how to manage risks inherent in intelligence work.

Risk in relation to intelligence matters should be viewed from three perspectives. First, risk analysis constitutes one of the analytical tools and techniques within the NIM. Secondly, there is the issue of managing risks in relation to the execution of an operation to gather intelligence. Successful acquisition of intelligence then creates a third arena of risk in relation to the storing, utilization, and dissemination of the intelligence. This chapter will consider these different areas in turn.

Perceptions of risk and priorities vary and this undoubtedly complicates partnership working; or even collaboration between different units within a single organization. One organization's opportunity—diversion of risk as an alternative to their own intervention—is another organization's risk—assumption of responsibility for resolving a problem. A large number of chief police officers viewed the proposals to merge smaller forces into larger, more strategic forces (a process that has continued almost uninterrupted from 1800 to 1974), arising from the HMIC report *Closing the Gap* (TSO, London, 2005), as an opportunity to minimize risks of failure in the provision of protective services. With very few exceptions, the chairpersons of police authorities viewed such proposals as a significant risk to the successful execution of their statutory duty under the Police Act 1996 to maintain a efficient and effective police force for their police area: a statutory duty that may well reflect the historical constitution of policing in the UK but which arguably no longer reflects the reality of policing demands. It is not clear whether the Home Office undertook any risk analysis when planning how to handle the merger proposals. For example, officials appear not to have adequately anticipated the problematic issue of equalizing different precepts, an oversight that meant even those forces and police authorities that wanted voluntarily to merge, in fact were prevented from doing so. This episode highlights not only the different perceptions of risk amongst partners but also the importance of risk assessment in strategic policy-making as well as operational interventions.

In partnership working risk analysis either has to be undertaken jointly from the outset, or else should be a two-stage process in which organizations individually assess risks and then collaborate in finding the most appropriate intervention once the matter requiring intervention is raised in a multi-agency forum. The risks of intervention have to be balanced against the risks of non-intervention. The information upon which to base risk management will almost certainly be incomplete, and may be imprecise. There may be no right answer and any given decision may have to be based on a professional judgment taking into consideration any number of factors (eg what is known, what is unknown, professional experience about what can be surmised).

The only certainty is that risk can never be entirely eliminated.

But it can be managed.

7.1.1 **The benefits of good risk assessment**

Some definitions at this stage will be helpful.

Definitions

Risk can be defined as the likelihood of an adverse harm occurring. Risk is not to be confused with a **threat,** which is the source of that harm. **Vulnerability** is the measurement of probability against impact. (The probability of an event occurring may be very low but the adverse impact very significant. Equally, there may be a high probability of occurrence but with relatively little adverse impact.) A **risk assessment** is the means by which the risks involved in an operation can be mitigated once identified and balanced against the benefits.

143

The relevance to policing and community safety is to be found at a number of levels. Some operations involve physical danger to staff. There is always a risk of staff acting unlawfully in the absence of effective management or in cases where enthusiasm exceeds knowledge and competence. Depending on particular community sensitivities, a clumsily managed operation might result in public disorder. The mismanagement of information or intelligence held by any given organization may result in harm to third parties: one obvious example being the disclosure of an informant's identity which, on occasions, has resulted in harm caused to or even the death of informants.

Particularly where an operation or general activity engages Article 8 rights, risk assessment helps validate the thinking of staff and managers alike, producing the following benefits:

- professional, credible risk management/reduction processes;
- reviews of working assumptions taking into account changing risk circumstances;
- a process for real-time decision-making amenable to subsequent review (either in an operational debrief or a subsequent public enquiry);
- reduction in the number of perverse decisions;
- reduction in corporate/personal liability.

Lives have been lost, investigations irretrievably compromised, community relations jeopardized, and careers irrevocably damaged through inadequate risk awareness and assessment.

7.1.2 Risk analysis within the NIM

Risk analysis is a key component amongst the analytical techniques and products of the NIM and underpins *risk management*. Risk analysis—which for the purpose here is synonymous with *risk assessment*—informs the prioritization of the intelligence requirement and intervention options. It helps to identify and define the environment within which any given intervention takes place and can highlight whether prevention, reduction, or diversion are alternatives to enforcement. It supports tactical and strategic tasking and coordination in a number of ways, illustrated in the box below.

Case study—purpose of risk analysis within the NIM

By assessing the scale of the threat posed by individual criminals, criminal groups, specific types of crimes to individual victims, the wider public, or law enforcement agencies and their partners, risk analysis facilitates:

- assessment of whether current problems have the potential to escalate;
- prioritization of intelligence gathering;

- prioritization of resources and potential of a partnership response;
- prioritization of intervention options (prevention, diversion, disruption, enforcement);
- prioritization of intervention subjects (individual offenders, specific problems);
- assessment of the likely impact of any given intervention based on results analysis from previous operations;
- compliance with statutory obligations regarding use of investigative powers and data responsibilities.

The process starts with risk identification for the strategic assessment, which ideally should be undertaken both by the police and by partner agencies. At the same time as identifying intelligence gaps and emerging trends, contributors to the strategic assessment, which will inform the strategic control strategy, have the opportunity to identify those areas, future events, or activities that pose a risk to community safety, to individual organizations within a community safety partnership or to the partnership as a whole.

Further information and reading

See Section 2.2 in ACPO 2006 *Practice Guidance on Tasking and Co-ordination* (NCPE, Wyboston).

NIM risk analysis is thus a significant precursor to all future action arising from tasking and coordination. Having identified through NIM risk analysis options for intervention, and the tasking and coordination process having prioritized and commissioned interventions, individual operations (either to achieve the acquisition of further intelligence or to gather evidence as part of an investigation intended to result in prosecution) require their own risk assessments.

7.2 Intelligence Acquisition

This part of the chapter provides a basic risk assessment framework that can be applied at any level of policing and community safety from ward-based neighbourhood policing teams, through CDRPs and BCUs to force strategy meetings. A framework is not a panacea, merely a facilitation of thinking.

Intelligence operations engage the subject of risk in two ways: first, at the micro level, as with any police or local authority actions, there are the risks to staff, operation subjects, third parties, and to the organization inherent in any given operation that have to be managed; secondly, at the macro level, intelligence is vital in order to inform risk assessments for other policing and community safety activity. To adopt a different hierarchical analogy: at the strategic level intelligence will support general (political) policy-making and the biannual strategic tasking and co-ordination process within police forces, local authorities, and BCUs; at the operational level there may be risks involved in managing successful partnership working amongst staff from different organizations with different skills sets and awareness or simply in managing one's own staff; whilst, at the tactical level, for example when planning covert operations, it is regularly necessary to conduct preliminary reconnaissance operations in order to identify the risks involved in conducting the primary covert operation. It is also equally possible that a period of covert surveillance may be necessary, subject to the relevant crime threshold being reached (RIPA, ss 5, 28, 29, and 32), in order to inform the risk assessment and planning of an overt operation, eg the execution of a search warrant.

Case study—investigation risk review

One police force, conducting a risk review during a problematic long-term investigation, concluded that the biggest risk to achieving a successful outcome came not from any external threat but from the staff involved in the operation (for a variety of reasons including lack of management and investigation skills).

It is helpful to have a framework within which to consider possible threats, the risk of such threats occurring and possible control measures when determining a risk management strategy. This chapter presents some models to use as such a framework.

7.2.1 Positive obligations imposed on managers

The failure to consider risks and apply an appropriate strategy constitutes negligence. In certain circumstances such omission goes beyond mere negligence. Court interpretations of Article 2 ECHR place upon public authorities the positive obligation to protect life. *Osman v UK* [1999] 1 FLR 198 illustrates this point: see also S Karmer 'European Human Rights Law' (Legal Action Group, 1999), pp 89–90, 199–200 for general discussion. A positive obligation was held to exist where 'the authorities knew or ought to have known at the time of the existence of a real and immediate risk to the life of an identified individual or individuals from the criminal acts of a third party and that they failed to take measures within the scope of their powers which, judged reasonably, might have been expected to avoid that risk', *Osman v UK* [1999] 1 FLR 198, n 19 at para 116.

This general principle can be held to apply elsewhere even where positive obligations under ECHR do not apply: investigators, community safety staff, and managers should take reasonable measures to manage foreseeable risks in all pre-planned overt or covert operations. Risks anticipated and how they might be managed will have a bearing on the necessity and proportionality considerations in any enforcement action. Experience has shown that risk assessments for covert investigation applications, for example, are not infrequently omitted altogether on initial submission. Those that are submitted are often inadequate. And even where a risk assessment is included on first submission, for subsequent reviews and renewals the assessment is almost never revised and is very often dispensed with a perfunctory 'no change'.

Case study—identifying risks in an overall crime control strategy

Elements that can inform a strategic assessment and so the strategic control strategy include:

- CDRP/BCU crime audit;
- resource audits;
- community demographic profile;
- neighbourhood profiles;
- vulnerable localities index (see <http://www.jdi.ucl.ac.uk>);
- signal crimes (see <http://www.neighbourhoodpolicing.co.uk>);
- risk assessments conducted by partner agencies.

Case study—identifying risks in covert operations

Surveillance conducted for covert investigation may not produce the intelligence anticipated nor the evidence sought, but the one guaranteed product of covert surveillance will be vital information with which to review the risk assessment.

At initial application risk assessments will be estimation. Staff will identify what they think the risks of an operation might be and how these antici-pated risks could be managed. Managers and authorizing officers will review such assessments from their own perspectives considering any additional risks posed by the operation to the organization as a whole. Once a period of surveillance has been conducted information about risks will have been updated by default in one or more of three ways: new risks may have been identified; previously anticipated risks may now be discounted; or previously anticipated risks will have been confirmed. It is important that this informa-tion is captured and included in subsequent risk assessments on submission of investigation authority reviews and renewal applications.

Where initial surveillance has demonstrated that there are no additional risks to take into consideration, and none that can now be dismissed, and where there has been no compromise of staff or equipment, then this should be incorporated in the risk assessment attached to the review consideration or renewal application. It is not simply a case of stating 'no change'. What was previously an initial estimation is now supported by hard information. An initial estimation has become an informed evaluation. At the very least such a revised risk assessment should say: 'following X hours/days of surveillance, no new risks associated with this operation have been identified. None of the previously identified risks can be discounted. There is no intelligence to indicate that staff or surveillance techniques deployed in this operation have been compromised. Therefore the current risk management plan remains valid'.

Risk management or reduction is as dynamic a process as is the manifestation of the risks themselves. It must be held under constant review. In some operations it will be so dynamic that the commanding officer will have undertaken several revised risk assessments during the course of any given phase of the operation, possibly within a very short space of time and with little or no opportunity to record the rationale at the time, it which case documenting the variation as soon as practicable after the event must suffice.

7.2.2 Identifying risks and how to manage them—the model approach

Structuring thinking around established conceptual models aids precise consideration of risk issues. From the police service come three risk assessment models, outlined here by way of example.

The first, created by Deputy Assistant Commissioner John Grieve whilst serving with the Metropolitan Police Service, is a general model that helps staff and managers begin to identify risks associated with any general threat (*risk analysis* within the NIM process) or given operation (*risk management* once an intervention option has been determined). Having a general applicability and often forming the basis of the risk assessment elements of automated authority-application software widely used across police forces, this is often referred to as the '3Ps L E M' model because of its acronym (PPPLEM). The second, created by another Metropolitan Police officer, Roger Billingsley, is called the PLAICE model and has been designed specifically for managing risk in covert interventions.

Once risks have been identified using either model (or any other method, eg the Probation Service OASys and Risk 2000 ASSET models relating to dangerous offenders) a determination has to be made on how to manage them. For this there is the RARA model, which can be used in conjunction with the vulnerability assessment.

The culmination of this consideration should be a structured risk management plan or risk reduction strategy for those risks, amongst the many identified, which are likely to cause the most harm. The use of models aids thinking for both applicants and authorizing officers and should thus facilitate a more succinct written assessment ensuring that it does not become a bureaucratic nightmare that actually adds nothing of value to the investigation or its management.

Over-arching the risk management plan or reduction strategy must be the assessment of how the identified risk control measures themselves might engage the ECHR rights of staff, investigation subject, and general public.

Although staff and managers have primary responsibility for risk assessment and management, on occasions they will need to draw upon expert advice when encountering specialist fields and techniques. For instance, experts from computer crime units will be best placed to advise on what sort of electronic footprints will be created when computers are used to conduct e-surveillance. Non-experts will not necessarily appreciate that there may risks to be managed in specialist arenas.

The PPPLEM model of risk assessment

The acronym translates as follows:

Table 7.1 The PPPLEM model of risk assessment

P police and community risks	Alternatively, public and organizational risks. In general terms what are the risks to the organization within the community of engaging in this operation? Is there any general risk to/from the community at large? Adverse publicity? Public disorder possible? What are the risks to the organization from the investigation subject/staff/public at large? What are the risks to the community from the organization engaging in this operation? What are the risks to the community from the investigation subject? What are the risks to the community from the organization staff? What are the risks of not doing anything?
P physical risks	What are the physical risks to staff/subject/third parties? Organization premises or premises borrowed for the purpose?
P psychological risks	What are the physical risks to staff/subject/third parties?
L legal risks	What are the legal risks to the organization? Its staff? The subject? Third parties?
E economic risks	What are the economic risks to the organization? Its staff? The subject? Third parties? The community? Cost of operation? Possible litigation claims?
M moral risks	What are the moral risks to the organization? Its staff? The subject? Third parties? Can the operation be justified morally as well as legally? Is there a danger that the very essence of the ECHR will be breached as well as the Article 8 rights in question? What are the risks of not doing anything?

It is helpful to apply the PPPLEM model to all the different facets of risk, otherwise regarded as the different 'at risk' groups: risk to the organization, risk to staff, and other resources engaged in the operation (including for this purpose technical equipment remotely deployed; CHISs and members of the public who allow their premises to be used as observation points), risk to the subject of the operation, and risk to third parties such as members of the public unconnected with the investigation but likely to be present in the surveillance arena.

The PPPLEM model, applied to the four risk groups, will help identify the risks inherent in any given operation. A matrix is a useful aid to complete the assessment with the 'at risk' groups placed on the vertical axis and the PPPLEM elements placed along the horizontal axis.

Table 7.2 PPPLEM matrix

PPPLEM matrix	Police/ community	Physical	Psychological	Legal	Economic	Moral
Organization						
Staff						
Subject						
Third Parties						

It may well be the case that not all the elements of the model apply to all the 'at risk' groups. Indeed, if there was something significant to say in each of the matrix boxes the proposed operation should probably be considered too risky! The advantage of using this model lies not only in helping structured consideration: it demonstrates and records the thought processes of investigators and managers alike and in this way saves the trouble involved in composing lengthy prose to make the same point. More detailed discussion can thus be saved for those risks identified through the vulnerability and RARA models as requiring particular management (7.7).

The PLAICE model of risk assessment

This alternative was produced because Metropolitan Police staff were concerned that the PPPLEM model was too general for covert investigation work, which attracts specific risks and therefore demands, so it is argued, a bespoke risk assessment model. Once again an acronym provides the name.

The PLAICE model of risk assessment

P Physical
L Legal
A Assets
I Information Technology
C Compromise
E Environment

See R Billingsley 'Risk management: is there a model for covert policing?' *Covert Policing Review* 98–109 (2006).

Once again, specific risks within each of the above categories are to be identified and documented, together with the proposed control measures. The importance of documenting and continually reviewing risks and reasoning is emphasized, particularly in relation to defending the service and staff against subsequent litigation. For the purpose of using this model, Billingsley suggests that 'information technology' should sensitive data gathered using technology and the systems used to process, analyse, and document such data. The environment, readers are reminded, should include possibly hostile environments overseas when deploying staff abroad on covert investigations.

Deployment overseas is not a consideration that is going to worry the majority of police and community safety managers delivering local policing. But that does not mean that the PLAICE model is too exotic for local policing and community safety managers to use. The issue here is not which model is used (and besides these two currently being used in the police service, there are other models) but that some model of structured consideration and reasoning is used to identify risks and appropriate control measures. The PPPLEM and PLAICE models are not mutually exclusive—and both rely on good intelligence for any meaningful consideration of risk to be undertaken.

The SPECSS+ model

The third model has been developed over six years specifically in relation to domestic violence which measures aspects of victim vulnerability and offender behaviour in order to enable police (or partner agencies adopting the same measures) to filter the volume of domestic violence reports and prioritize interventions according to clear signals and in line with the RARA risk management strategy model (see below). SPECSS+ is intelligence-led policing through risk identification, assessment, and management. This three-tiered structure is discussed in more detail in Chapter 8 below as a methodology for intelligence-led harm reduction.

Further information and reading

The mnemonic SPECSS+ represents high risk identification markers derived from extensive international research

S Separation (child contact)
P Pregnancy (new birth)
E Escalation
C Community issues and isolation (barriers to reporting)
S Stalking
S Sexual assault
+ +mental health, (suicide-homicide, threats to kill, jealous and controlling behaviour, substance abuse)

L Richards 'Homicide prevention: findings from the multi-agency domestic violence homicide reviews' *The Journal of Homicide and Major Incident Investigation* 2/2 53–72 (2006)

7.2.3 Vulnerability and risk strategy models: RARA and TTTT

Once a risk has been identified, a control strategy must be devised. Models exist to facilitate this. Vulnerability, *probability v impact*, can be measured as two scales of 1 to 10, one for each of probability and impact. Alternatively, it can more simply be expressed in terms of 'high', 'medium', or 'low' set in a matrix with one axis representing probability and the other impact.

Table 7.3 Impact/Probability matrix

High impact			
Medium impact			
Low impact			
Impact/Probability matrix	Low Probability	Medium Probability	High Probability

Greatest vulnerability, and therefore risk, will be inherent where the probability and impact are both high or where one is high and the other medium. These are the risks that require management or a reduction strategy. (Shaded areas in the diagram above.) Where there is vulnerability characterized by low probability but high impact, then contingency plans are required rather than immediate intervention. (Hatched area in the diagram above.)

Risks that are both low in impact and low in probability need not concern the investigator, investigation manager, or authorizing officer too greatly.

Once the vulnerability factor has been identified risk management and reduction prioritization can be undertaken. For this the RARA model can be applied.

There are four strategies that can be adopted in relation to any given risk: **Remove it, Avoid it, Reduce** it, **Accept** it—hence **RARA**. This is a sliding scale of strategies. Preferably operations or crime and disorder control strategies should be planned so as to remove all risks. This ideal world is rarely achievable however. Changing tactics to achieve the same objective may afford a means of avoiding a risk. If the risk cannot be removed or avoided, then there may be measures that can be put in place to reduce the risk. There will be a number of risks that investigators will wish simply to accept. This might be because the risks have a low vulnerability factor: low probability/low impact.

Potential control measures aimed at reducing the likelihood or adverse consequences of any given risk may themselves have risks attached. It may not be possible, for instance, to deploy a full surveillance team to provide protective cover for the deployment of an undercover operative because the surveillance team itself would show out in the deployment arena. In which case alternative means of providing protection and rescue for such operatives must be devised, or else the desired evidence or intelligence must be acquired by other means—a way of avoiding identified risks.

As with the PPPLEM model, Billingsley offers an alternative to RARA—the TTTT model: **Terminate, Treat, Transfer** or **Tolerate**. In essence, albeit with the second and third elements reversed, the TTTT model is intended to achieve exactly the same outcome in the same way as the RARA model. The application of either model in determining a risk management strategy and appropriate control measures illustrates and records the thought processes of the decision-takers based on available information at the time and herein lies its value to investigators, managers and authorizing officers.

7.3 **Intelligence Management**

Once acquired intelligence becomes its own risk (through mismanagement and/ or misuse, witting or unwitting), particularly as its value is cumulative. Individual pieces of information not only have their own intelligence value but also acquire a greater value in combination because the whole is often greater than the sum of the parts.

The potential harms to an organization vary: costly civil litigation; financial penalty; reduced effectiveness (eg through misdirected/compromised operations or initiatives based on faulty intelligence-processing); any of which may also be associated with reputational damage and a loss of public confidence. Individuals working for or with an organization, or third parties, can also be harmed by the mismanagement or misuse of intelligence. The compromised, dead informant is an example of the most extreme consequence: staff rendered vulnerable to criminal intimidation and individuals damaged by erroneous or outdated data are none the less serious for not being fatal.

Once again, partnership working complicates this aspect of intelligence risk management because partners may have different approaches to intelligence, its protection and dissemination. The establishment of solid working relationships based on sound, mutual understanding will go a long way towards reducing the risks inherent in partnership. There is no quick fix.

7.3.1 Risk management through training

Intelligence departments within police forces do not always enjoy the same professional perception that other police specialists acquire. One consequence of this is that intelligence often does not attract the same training investment as, for example, CID, roads policing or firearms units. Yet any of the roles within the police intelligence community requires significant training investment. There are numerous computerised databases for which staff have to be trained, access to which is limited to intelligence department terminals. The uninitiated cannot make effective field intelligence officers. Analysts need to be both trained in systems technology but at the same time capable of free thinking. Intelligence managers need to understand their role to achieve the best from their departments and to be able to manage upwards when encountering BCU and force commanders whose command of the intelligence discipline may not be all that it could be.

Too often intelligence managers find themselves managing a department with a high turnover of staff on temporary postings because higher up the chain of command, the intelligence department is seen as a useful desk-based role that provides opportunities to deploy staff considered not fully fit for 'frontline' duties. Resourcing intelligence departments with a constant turnover of unskilled staff is about as absurd as it gets when aspiring to deliver intelligence-led policing.

The logic that dictates that risk to colleagues and the public must be managed by restricting the driving of fast cars and the carrying of firearms, for instance, only to those staff who are properly trained, should be extended to those charged with collating, analysing, and disseminating intelligence. Training staff reduces risk.

7.3.2 Risk management through procedure

Alongside training, security-vetting reduces organization and staff vulnerability to cultivation and compromise by hostile elements keen to acquire illicit access to police databases. All staff working in intelligence departments should, as a minimum, be vetted to SC (Security Clearance) level. Key roles should require vetting to DV level (Developed Vetting). This, of course, costs money (as does training). Intelligence-led policing is often justified on the basis of increased efficiency and improved performance. Nowhere has it been suggested that that outcome can be achieved on a cost-neutral or negative investment basis.

154

Related to security-vetting of staff is the practice of security classification of documents which has been codified in the **Government Protective Marking Scheme** (GPMS) adopted for the police service by ACPO on 17 January 2001. All documents produced within the police service must be GPMS compliant in order to be provided with the appropriate level of risk management.

GPMS classification is determined by the harmful consequences of compromise (see the Further information and reading box below). The system informs:

- the correct level of protection a document should be afforded;
- the procedures to be followed regarding the production, dispatch, receipt, and destruction of the document;
- the severity or impact of the loss or comprise of the document, and therefore the risk such eventualities pose to the organization.

Further information and reading

There are four levels of protective marking:
Top secret, Secret, Confidential, Restricted
Documents falling outside all of these areas of sensitivity are Unclassified.

Top secret—Compromise would:
—threaten directly the internal stability of the UK or friendly countries;
—lead directly to widespread loss of life;
—cause exceptionally grave damage to the effectiveness or security of UK or allied forces or to the continuing effectiveness of extremely valuable security or intelligence operations;
—cause exceptionally grave damage to relations with friendly governments;
—cause severe long-term damage to the UK economy.

Secret—Compromise would:
—raise international tension;
—seriously damage relations with friendly governments;
—threaten life directly or seriously prejudice public order or individual security or liberty;
—cause serious damage to operational effectiveness or security of UK or allied forces or the continuing effectiveness of highly valuable security or intelligence operations;
—cause substantial material damage to national finances or economic and commercial interests.

Confidential—Compromise would:
—materially damage diplomatic relations, that is, cause formal protest or sanctions;
—prejudice individual security or liberty;
—cause damage to operational effectiveness or security of UK or allied forces or the effectiveness of valuable security or intelligence operations;

—work substantially against national finances or economic and commercial interests;

—substantially undermine the financial viability of major organizations;

—impede the investigation or facilitate the commission of *serious crime*;

—seriously impeded the development or operation of major government policies;

—shut down or otherwise substantially disrupt significant national operations.

Restricted—Compromise would:

—adversely affect diplomatic relations;

—cause substantial distress to individuals;

—make it more difficult to maintain the operational effectiveness or security of UK or allied forces;

—cause financial loss or loss of earning potential to, or facilitate improper gain or advantage for, individuals or companies;

—prejudice the investigation or facilitate the commission of *crime*;

—breach proper undertakings to maintain the confidence of information provided by third parties;

—impede the effective development or operation of government policies;

—breach statutory restrictions on disclosure of information.

For further information and access to supporting papers regarding ACPO's rationale for adopting the GPMS, see <http://www.acpo.police.uk/asp/policies/Data/covering_letter_prot_marking_scheme_16feb01.doc> (accessed 26 February 2007).

Police officers and staff are unlikely to encounter top secret material and indeed, those with access to top secret or secret material will be occupying posts for which developed vetting (DV) is usually mandatory as an additional security measure. The access to such documents that partner agencies or other regulatory bodies have will depend upon their primary functions. It is usually a requirement that inter-agency liaison regarding such sensitive material will only involve DV-cleared staff and officers.

An example of secret information held by police or indeed by any of the other partner agencies and organizations empowered under RIPA, s 29 is the full personal details of a covert human intelligence source (CHIS). Clearly the compromise of such information represents a direct threat to the life of the CHIS.

Any reference to the fact that a CHIS has been deployed will warrant a confidential classification because unauthorized access to such information could indirectly lead to a threat against the life or well-being of the CHIS. Such a leak would also compromise the ongoing operation on which the CHIS had been deployed.

Indeed, information about any ongoing operations focusing on serious crime is likely to be confidential regardless of whether or not a CHIS has been deployed.

Examples of documents for which restricted might be appropriate include documents concerning management issues.

Whilst an individual document might be classified as restricted or confidential on its own, its inclusion together with similarly marked documents might warrant the overall file being classified as secret if the accumulated information taken together would result in the appropriate level of harm in the event of compromise. Hence a single document containing a number of pieces of information that had been provided by a CHIS, even though each original intelligence report would have been confidential, taken together would warrant a secret classification because the unnamed CHIS could be more readily identified the more that his or her information was viewed in combination.

Proper procedure for intelligence work is supported by a statutory framework. The Human Rights Act 1998, the Data Protection Act 1998 and the Freedom of Information Act 2000 provide an overall management context. PACE, RIPA, and the Police Act 1997 provide the framework of powers within which intelligence may be gathered.

The legislation is a foundation for a professional intelligence environment. Failure to maintain a professional intelligence environment undermines all risk management in intelligence. Professionalism within the organization tends to be assumed by its members when it should constantly be under review. Deviation from professionalism can be invidious and go unnoticed to the extent that the deviation becomes the new professionalism. Hence the checklist in the box below is framed in terms of warning signals rather than a good practice tick-box that it would be too easy simply to complete automatically.

Checklist—professional intelligence environment? The danger signals

- Lack of robust ethical standards explicitly set and constantly promoted

- Lack of training in intelligence skills

- Lack of security awareness and policies, including physical security and restricted access to intelligence department offices

- Lack of regular auditing

- Lack of effective management and supervision

- Tolerance of improper procedure

- Tolerance of unauthorized disclosure

- Tolerance of improper relationships with sources or with persons seeking access to intelligence (including colleagues)

- Organizational culture that views procedure as an impediment to performance and something to be got round or overcome

- Organizational culture that does not support or encourage the challenging of inappropriate behaviour

- Organizational culture that fails to observe the proper 'need to know' principle (this can work both ways—a department that fails to disseminate anything useful in assertion of this principle is as unprofessional as a department that leaks)

At time of writing (2007), the NPIA is drafting guidance on the lawful and effective use of covert techniques, which will contain material of relevance to secure intelligence environments.

7.3.3 Risk management through security

Alongside procedural security, physical security is an additional means of risk management. Unauthorized disclosure takes place either when the hostile element accesses the intelligence themselves or when they secure complicity from a member of the intelligence department staff in passing on the intelligence. Assuming that the measures above have been implemented, the risk of the latter scenario, whilst not eradicated, is reduced. Removing the opportunities for self-initiated unauthorized access is a means to reducing the former risk.

Physical security means quality locks on doors (for instance a combination of monitored personal key card and digital lock access would be an example of good security); a clear desk policy; regular password-changing on computers; security filing cabinets in locked offices for classified hard-copy documents; locked offices for those computer terminals networked to sensitive databases. It also means regular review by the organization's security officer.

7.3.4 Risk and partnership

Case study—partnership (not quite) working 1

A specialist police unit negotiated a written agreement with an intelligence agency to share intelligence. After several months the police unit commented that they had not received any intelligence from their partners. The agency retorted that they had not received any from the police unit but a robust audit trail revealed just how much intelligence had actually been formally passed from the police to the agency. In the spirit of reciprocity, a date was set for a formal exchange the other way and representatives from the intelligence agency duly attended the police offices . . . and presented the police unit with a heavily sanitized version of a report that the police had previously submitted to the agency.

Discretion and security dictate that the above case study must be devoid of further detail; suffice it to say that this episode is not apocryphal but is drawn from author personal experience. It highlights the issue of trust in partnership—and the value of dissemination audit trails!

Case study—partnership (not quite) working 2

Five separate investigation teams in two different law enforcement agencies were investigating the same network of transnational organized crime groups, initially unaware of each other's investigations. Each team had intelligence of great value to the other teams. Once the different investigation teams became aware of each other's operations, the pressure of performance indicators acted as a perverse incentive in sharing intelligence, even amongst teams within the same organization. Each investigation team saw the other teams not as partners but as a risk to their own potential success and performance achievement.

Collaboration was instigated only when crown prosecutors realized what was going on and became concerned about the disclosure implications, which posed a different sort of risk: the risk to the trial process and so to achieving a successful prosecution. Recognition of the need to address such perverse incentives was part of the government rationale for creating the Serious Organised Crime Agency.

C Harfield 2005 *Processes and practicalities: mutual legal assistance and the investigation of transnational crime within the EU from a UK perspective, 1990-2004* unpublished PhD thesis, University of Southampton

C Harfield 2006 'SOCA: a paradigm shift in British policing' *British Journal of Criminology* 46(4) 743–71; available online at <http://bjc.oxfordjournals.org/cgi/rapidpdf/az1009v1>

The importance of robust partnership in intelligence exchange cannot be overestimated. Regrettably, it is failures (sometimes fatal in their consequences) that bring the issue into sharp focus.

In fact, at ward and BCU level, information and intelligence exchange between police and other community safety partners is often very good, although not always formalized, and so not always amenable to supervision—which, of course, it should be for risk management purposes. The statutory framework permits intelligence exchange. Of concern to partners will be secondary dissemination—where an agency to which intelligence has been passed, then passes it on to a third party. Within a formal partnership agreement, procedures for secondary dissemination should be clarified so that risk assessments do not become an obstacle to intelligence-sharing: dissemination being assessed as an individual organizational risk rather than as an enhancement to the partnership.

An organization established specifically with a function of sharing intelligence about previous criminal convictions is the *Criminal Records Bureau* (CRB), which assumed responsibility for the management of criminal records from the police service in 2002 and undertakes standard and enhanced pre-employment checks on applicants for certain categories of employment. In its first year of operation, the CRB made 1.5 million disclosures. Its Annual Report for 2005–06 revealed that the annual disclosure figure had, in four years, almost doubled to 2.9 million. One of the generic organizational risks faced by the CRB is a failure to disclose, which might have the consequence of an unsuitable person being appointed to a role involving children for instance. Yet a less obvious risk faced by the CRB is also the failure properly to record by the police or court agencies. This illustrates how one organization's processed information is another's intelligence.

Further information and reading

This aspect of risk intelligence and the role of the police service as information gatherers and providers for third parties is explored more fully in R Ericson and K Haggerty *Policing the Risk Society* (Clarendon Press, Oxford, 1997).

Case study—partnership (not quite) working 3

More of an issue for organizations engaged in transnational investigations, the sharing of intelligence with foreign agencies could be problematic if the UK investigators are not fully conversant with the relevant foreign criminal procedural laws. There are numerous examples of information passed to foreign agencies in good faith, on the basis of 'for intelligence purposes only', only for the British investigators to discover that all information enters the *procés verbale* and will probably be made available to the defence. One British SIO learnt a lesson the hard way when the intelligence was not only disclosed to the defence but the defence disclosed the intelligence to the press, there being no prohibition against doing so in the relevant jurisdiction. This highlights the need for a common understanding of potential risks between partners.

C Harfield 2005 *Processes and practicalities: mutual legal assistance and the investigation of transnational crime within the EU from a UK perspective, 1990–2004*, unpublished PhD thesis, University of Southampton

7.4 **Conclusion**

Risk assessment, be it for strategic planning, partnership working or for individual operations, depends upon having information and intelligence that is as accurate as possible and as up-to-date as possible. If such information has not been recorded and assessments consequently reviewed, then individuals and organizations are vulnerable to a further risk—negligence.

There is always scope for the unforeseen to occur. Use of models or adherence to procedural good practice to aid risk management will not alter that truism. Models cannot accurately predict the future. They will help identify those risks that can reasonably be foreseen. They will help prioritise a risk management strategy according to whether any given risk can be removed, avoided, reduced, or accepted. The models must be utilized in conjunction with the latest available information and intelligence. Procedures must always be up-to-date. In the event of something unforeseen occurring that leads to particularly adverse consequences, the documented use of these models and procedures may well determine whether the investigators and the organizations concerned had done everything that was reasonable in the circumstances or whether they are vulnerable to a civil claim based on negligence. A regularly audited professional intelligence environment is intolerant of negligence and so less vulnerable to harm so caused.

8

Planning Intelligence-Led Intervention

8.1 **Introduction**

The previous chapter focused on the risks to an organization in acquiring, managing, and using intelligence. This chapter moves on to consider the planning of intelligence-led interventions in terms of managing the risk of harm to the community. The strategic context is considered before discussion moves on to specific planning tools.

Policing, in its widest sense, is concerned with the reduction of harm and the enhancement of community safety, and this overarching objective is central to the current thrust in both neighbourhood policing and policing organized crime.

Further information and reading

'The Government wants to see a police service with the capability to deliver the breadth of its role—protecting individuals, securing public safety, preventing and reducing crime, bringing criminals to justice, working with children, young people and families—including *safeguarding them from harm*—reassuring the public and helping to build strong, cohesive communities.' (para 1.25)

'[SOCA] will be a wholly new body, operating in new ways and driven by the intelligence assessment of what will be most effective in terms of *harm reduction*.' (Appendix III, para v.)

Home Office *Building Communities, Beating Crime* (2004)
(emphasis added)

After consideration of how harm reduction planning informs intelligence-led interventions, the following chapter will consider techniques and approaches to the evaluation and analysis of intelligence. In a very real sense, Chapters 8 and 9 of this book have a cyclical relationship, not least because they articulate the mechanics of the intelligence cycle.

In policing terms there are two strategic contexts in such planning. Intelligence-led policing was initially conceived as an enhancement of and aid to **criminal investigation**, the strategic focus of which may be summarized in the familiar six-element interrogative strategy: who, what, where, when, how and why.

The second strategic context is that of **neighbourhood policing** (taken to be synonymous with community policing) articulated in ACPO's principles of neighbourhood policing (see box below).

Both strategic contexts are amenable to intelligence-led intervention through harm reduction.

Further information and reading—The 10 principles of neighbourhood policing

ACPO *Practice Advice on Professionalising the Business of Neighbourhood Policing* NCPE (Centrex,Wyboston, 2006).

1. Police, partners and the community work together to **problem solve** and improve neighbourhood conditions and increase feelings of security;
2. Neighbourhood policing is a mainstream policing activity and is integrated into other policing services;
3. There is **evidence -based deployment** of the Safer Neighbourhood Teams (SNT) against **identified needs**;
4. Each community has a dedicated, identifiable, accessible, knowledgeable and responsive SNT, providing the community with a named point of contact;
5. The SNT **reflects local conditions and is flexible responsive and adaptable**;
6. The SNT works with the community to **identify problems**, thereby giving them influence over priority setting;
7. There is joint **partnership working in a problem solving framework**;
8. **NIM is used as a basis for deployment**;
9. There is an effective framework of **community engagement, communication and feedback**;
10. There is a performance management framework, which includes performance monitoring against local plans.

The bold text identifies the key role of (community) intelligence in delivering neighbourhood policing. Intelligence and knowledge are inherent in seven of the ten principles and offer a framework for planning intelligence-acquisition and intelligence-led operations.
(emphasis added)

8.2 **Understanding Harm in Order to Manage and Mitigate**

Harm reduction can be approached through a three-phase model widely used by various agencies and professions (see further information below): **Identify—Assess—Manage.**

Further information and reading

Identify—Assess—Manage is an approach that has been utilized by, amongst others:

Kent County Constabulary (in relation to domestic violence investigation and information-sharing with partner agencies relevant to domestic violence intervention): <http://www.kent.police.uk/About%20Kent%20Police/Policy/n/n30.html>

Wealden District Council (risk management strategy): <http://www.wealden.gov.uk/moderngov/Published/C00000292/M00001908/AI00011797/$20060427CabinetRiskManagementReport.docA.ps.pdf>

Cornwall County Council (social workers working with children and young persons): <http://db.cornwall.gov.uk/recruitment/docs/3265-Specialist%20Social%20Worker%20Aug%202007%20JDP%20&%20PSP.pdf>

And in the private sector where examples include risk management auditing (Independent Audit Ltd, <http://www.independentaudit.com/audit-governance/enterprise-risk-management-audit.htm>); and paramedic training (Paramedic (ENT) Technology curriculum <http://www.bsc.nodak.edu/faculty/paramedic/paramedic.pdf>)

(All websites accessed 29 September 2007)

It is a generic model suitable for application to community safety, policing, and regulation. This can be linked to a generic stratified quality model that identifies how particular business elements correspond to levels of business, thus facilitating prioritization of effort enhancement at the appropriate level within an organization. Within this model it is argued that ensuring processes, people, and products (including outcomes) are properly resourced and managed within the appropriate context will help to ensure quality within the work of an organization.

Further information and reading

See R Berry, A Sloan, P Reid, R Murray, J Cooke, and K Rogers 'Quality—Making it Happen: Relevance and Realism for the Police Service' *The Police Journal* 72/3 191–203 (1999), particularly pp 198–201 for the Stratified Quality Model.

See above, based on figure 1, p 199—The Generic Stratified Quality Model

Organizational Quality ────────▶

Management responsibility	Processes	People	Product (includes outcomes)
Strategic	X		
Tactical		X	
Operational			X

◀──────── Continuous Improvement

With the onset and imposition of national priorities and targets for policing set by central government (eg the former National Policing Plan which was replaced by the National Community Safety Plan; and the Police Performance Assessment Framework (PPAF)) which has come a focus on outputs and outcomes. Occasionally the language of these two related but separate concepts becomes confused, particularly within the context of the political sound-bite.

Police organizations can have a tendency to base their strategic priorities on achieving the national targets set for them. As suggested earlier (Chapter 5) it can be argued this has redirected intelligence-led policing towards performance-management policing. Performance indicators measuring outputs incline intelligence-led policing towards specific crime types or specific criminals in isolation. Hence, police strategic assessments sometimes include amongst the stated strategic priorities, sanctioned detections. Such detections are a tool leading to an output, not an outcome.

Harm reduction is an outcome. As will be illustrated in the detailed argument below, individual outputs can meet performance indicator targets without actually reducing harm. An alternative approach to seeking a desired outcome through specific outputs would be to start with the desired outcome and work backwards. This requires an understanding of the threats that constitute and give rise to risks of harm to society. It is from this basis that strategic priorities can then be identified.

This is not necessarily something that can be done at national level unless there is a national mechanism for addressing the harm. Although police performance management is increasingly being viewed in terms of comparable BCUs because of the variety in size, capability, and capacity between forces, it is control strategies at the level of the force that direct activity and within which context BCU control strategies are set. Force control strategies which reflect national priorities may have to afford lesser priority to reducing significant local harms.

There is also a conceptual incongruence: although specific crime types, such as burglary, violence, and commodity crimes, may make suitable strategic priority themes, individual criminals do not necessarily confine themselves to specific crime types. Violent crime and commodity-based criminality may be symptoms of organized crime: interventions against individual criminals may not be the most effective solution to the wider problem even if they address specific instances of criminality. It is therefore necessary to understand the wider picture both by crime and target criminal(s). A strategic priority could legitimately be focused on a specific crime theme but, it is argued, there will always be justification in considering organized crime activity which will cross-cut many of the crime theme areas.

Ultimately statements of harm may appear in a variety of forms: local authority crime and disorder committee reports; a CDRP crime audits and crime reduction strategies; a strategic assessment and its consequential control strategy within the NIM methodology; or a threat assessment from SOCA or Europol. Which introduces the harm reduction cycle that begins with the identification phase.

Figure 8.1 The harm management cycle

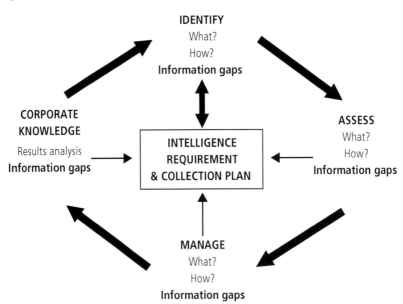

8.2.1 The identification phase

The identification phase is dependent upon understanding all possible sources of information (for example and not exclusively, community, CHIS, databases, partner agencies); how intelligence is gathered in all these areas; and the capacity and capability of the organization to access and process raw information in preparation for assessment. The key organizational questions are:

- Does the organization know where all of its sources are? (the *What* in figure 8.1)
- Can it access them and draw out relevant information? (the *How* in figure 8.1)
- Having answered these preliminary questions, what gaps are left to be filled? (the *Information gaps* in figure 8.1)

This phase is concerned with the identification of information about an established or emerging threat. Identification activity involves gathering and collating the information so that an assessment can be made which indicates whether the threat poses a sufficient level of risk to warrant the management and mitigation of that risk. This is done by identifying and tasking the correct sources of intelligence about the recognized threat (researching, gathering internal and external information, accessing intelligence already documented in databases). This phase should also identify information gaps the filling of which would be useful in informing the assessment phase. An intelligence requirement thus identified requires and appropriate collection plan. This requirement dictates an organization having staff and resources devoted to the broad research necessary to recognize established and emerging threats.

In circumstances in which the anticipated or actual harm impacts on a geographical or functional responsibility beyond the remit of the organization undertaking the harm management cycle, an immediate partnership and intelligence-sharing gap is identified. The nature of the identified threat will identity potential partners. For example, a relocated MAPPA subject will give rise to the need for several police forces, probation areas and social services departments to work together—as was illustrated in the Anthony Rice case (Chapter 2 above). Identification naturally reveals information gaps that generate further work.

8.2.2 **The assessment phase**

The assessment phase which follows requires a methodology to assess the relative importance or relative impact of each of the threats identified in the previous phase, some of which will be priorities contained within the NIM control strategy or emerging threats as yet outside the strategy. The collated data is now analysed and assessed in order to understand the level of risk inherent in each recognized issue. This could take the form, for example, of a subject or problem profile. The assessment phase should provide decision-makers with sufficient facts and inferences from which to understand the wider picture and informs their determination of intervention priorities within that context.

It also provides the opportunity to understand where any gaps might exist. That requires the right processes and the right people in place to carry out the various functions; these may or may not be the same staff involved in the identification phase. It is entirely possible that the assessment phase will identify capability and information gaps that have to be filled before the organization is in a position to work towards achieving a desired outcome (figure 8.1).

Suggested examples are listed below of assessment considerations that will assist decision-takers:

- Is it a strategic assessment priority? (It would be anticipated that threats recognized in the identification phase already to be strategic assessment priorities, and therefore already considered important enough to warrant previous action and activity.)
- Does the assessment demonstrate any impact arising from previous interventions?
- If an already identified strategic priority, does this assessment demonstrate any chance in level of risk already identified?
- If not already an identified strategic assessment priority, does it need to be considered as an emerging issue not previously identified?

An appropriate NIM or other product should be developed to inform operational progression—this should include: an analysis of information collected, inferences drawn on the basis of that analysis, those inferences must assist a decision-maker to decide whether to implement activity in a particular area or not. A summary statement of the intelligence is not sufficient.

The assessment phase should provide inferences (conclusions based on evidence and reasoning) that include predictive analysis of the nature of offending behaviour and/or information about harm escalation as a result of the offending behaviour.

Further information and reading

Possible methodologies to assist in adoption and prioritization are detailed in Appendix 1 of ACPO *Practice Advice on Tasking and Co-ordination* (NCPE Centrex, Wyboston, 2006).

They include a variation on the use of the PPPLEM model, the Metropolitan Police Intelligence Standards Unit Strategic Assessment Matrix and the National Public Order Intelligence Unit Risk Assessment Matrix. These are just three (police-oriented) examples and should not be considered an exhaustive catalogue.

8.2.3 The management phase

Following the identification of threats and assessment of the risk of harm posed by each threat, the management phase is characterized by prioritization. Where capability gaps exist, part of the management decision-making is about whether the gaps are to be filled or not, which will be dependent upon the assessment. The management phase continues with any appropriate action to address perceived capability gaps. Such actions are themselves a strategic priority and should be labelled and resourced as such.Resourcing is then structured around delivering impact against the areas identified as high-risk threats, likely to lead to significant harm.

The cycle then immediately begins again meanwhile, in fulfilment of the organizational learning cycle, comprehensive results analysis is required to understand what activity worked and why, what activity did not work and why, and this then feeds back into the identification phase as enhanced information about the nature of possible threats (including the threat of not being able to address and issue because of insufficient capability or capacity).

Successful identification—assessment—management is a continuous cycle dependent upon having the right processes and people in place which produce the right products which feed back into the correct element of the cycle.

Suggested examples are listed below of management considerations for each identified threat:

- Is the level of harm sufficient for further activity to be actioned?
- Is the emerging issue one that requires immediate action because of the significance of the harm level?
- If so what are the fast-track procedures to ensure such an issue can be adopted and actioned expeditiously or actioned prior to the next T&CG mtg (organizations should have in place fast-time processes to deal with immediate risk of serious and significant harm; decision-maker needs to have responsibility for all prioritization and associated implications and so ideally would be the Tasking and Co-ordinating Group Chair)
- Operational objective agreed and adopted
- Activity to prevent, reduce or neutralise the threat
- Appropriate deployment of resources and assets
- Resources identified to fill intelligence gap, (through CHISs, partner agencies etc)
- Each intelligence activity should have an 'owner' (more than one activity may owned by the same individual depending upon scope of requirement)
- Completion timetable agreed
- Where a threat is sufficient to warrant intervention to mitigate the risk, is there an appropriate range of prevention and enforcement tactical options (including asset recovery measures) to employ?
- Is there a mechanism for documented and auditable decision-making?
- Commission results analysis of all interventions

It is entirely possible that the management phase will identify capability and information gaps that have to be filled before the organization is in a position to work towards achieving a desired outcome.

8.2.4 **Corporate learning**

From the results analysis of all the interventions employed, corporate learning is derived. Each organization needs the capacity and capability to document and access such learning as this will feed back into the harm management cycle.

Further information and reading

On appropriate knowledge management systems, see G Dean and P Gottschalk *Knowledge Management in Policing and Law Enforcement: Foundations, Structures, Applications* (Oxford University Press, Oxford, 2007).

Results analysis is defined as 'a method of evaluating the effectiveness of activity and a means of learning lessons and improving outcomes. As such it should be a genuine assessment of the success and failures of activity' (ACPO *Practice Advice on Tasking and Co-ordination* (NCPE Centrex, Wyboston, 2006) 88). In each of the identification, assessment, and management phases activity is being carried out from which organizational learning may be derived and could be captured. The important element is how that learning changes future activity so that impact is increased and desired outcome success is sustained.

Results analysis is only worthwhile if the learning derived is then utilized in the harm reduction cycle. Fulfilling an operational objective may not achieve the desired outcome, hence the harm management cycle taken together with results analysis must be used to refine intervention aims. The following two hypothetical case studies illustrate this point.

Case study—Manage phase

A

A trading standards intervention results in the prosecution and conviction of a suspected counterfeit goods dealer in a small town. On the face of it this is a successful operation. However, a new supplier immediately fills the void in the supply chain and so the harm to the local community has not been reduced even though a conviction has been secured.

This unsuccessful outcome should be apparent through results analysis.

The organizational learning in this instance is that simply repeating the same intervention is likely to achieve the same outcome. Therefore any future intervention must include, on the basis of this identification, a tactical option to ensure that another dealer does not simply immediately fill the supply void.

B

An intervention on a BCU results in the arrest and conviction of a heroin supplier and action is taken to prevent the void in the supply chain being immediately filled by another dealer. As a consequence of this intervention heroin users in the immediate locality approach the local Primary Care Trust (PCT) in order to access methadone. The local PCT cannot fulfil the demand for methadone and so the heroin users move on to neighbouring police areas to access heroin this increasing associated anti-social behaviour and crime problems in neighbouring BCUs. Harm has not been resolved, merely displaced.

Results analysis in this case will reveal a need to liaise at an early stage of any future planning with partner agencies such as the PCT in order to enable them to plan for the consequences of an enforcement intervention.

Both the above examples also illustrate the need to coordinate level 1 and level 2 activity in the 'manage phase' of the harm management cycle.

8.3 **Possible Planning Tools**

The cycle described above is a framework for planning intelligence led intervention. There is no definitive right or wrong way of informing the harm reduction cycle. Various tools can contribute to the process and some of the key tools are considered below. Organizations will need to determine which tools to employ according to circumstance.

8.3.1 **Intelligence gap tools**

Tools for managing intelligence gaps exist at strategic and operational levels. The intelligence gap matrix portrayed at figure 8.2 below is suitable for use either within the context of a strategic assessment, control strategy, CDRP crime audit, or at the level of an individual investigation.

Figure 8.2 Intelligence gap matrix

1. What we know we know	2. What we know we don't know
3. What we don't know we know	4. What we don't know we don't know

Box 1 comprises information known to analysts, investigators, and intelligence staff, of which they are aware, for instance a person who comes regularly to local police attention is known to have a PNC entry as well as an entry on the local force intelligence database.

Box 2 is that information which practitioners know exists but which is not currently known to them, eg the name of a suspect may be known and the fact that s/he has access to a vehicle but not his or her date of birth or the vehicle identity. Alternatively, it may be known that counterfeit goods are being sold through market stalls in neighbouring towns but it is not known whether the different market tradesmen are all part of a single conspiracy to supply counterfeit goods or whether in fact they are all the local manifestations of different counterfeit supply chains. This box defines immediate, obvious intelligence gaps to be filled. It also begins to highlight, through the process of identification, whether collaboration with other partner agencies would be of particular benefit in any given investigation.

Box 3 essentially defines information that has already been gathered and which is relevant to a current investigation but of which analysts, investigators, and intelligence staff working on the operation remain unaware. An example of this would be the information known to the officers staffing the Racial Incident Unit at Plumstead police station, retained either in their heads or in the card index system they ran and of which officers investigating the murder of Stephen Lawrence were not immediately aware (*The Stephen Lawrence Inquiry*, paragraph 20.14). Such information may be lost in the wealth of data already amassed by an organization, or it may be on the databases of another organization or agency. For example, information about the suspicious behavioural history of Ian Huntley was known to a number of authorities but was not made readily available to those making the decision about whether or not to employ him at Soham School. When the MAPPA management plan for Anthony Rice was drafted, police were unaware that certain information of significant relevance had not been passed on by HM Probation Service (see Chapter 2 above). SOCA, as of February 2007, had 380 incompatible databases which were recognized as a considerable impediment to the effective working of the nascent organization (Sir Stephen Lander, Chairman of SOCA quoted in The Times, 17 February 2007, p 8). In essence, this box is also an intelligence gap, simply because investigators do not know the information and do not know that it is already captured and available.

Box 4 is not as Rumsfeldian as it might at first appear: (<http://www.onthe-media.org/transcripts/2006/11/10/02>, accessed 12 September 2007). It describes that category of information of which investigators are not only unaware, but also the possible existence of which has not yet been considered. For example, investigators may be unaware that the suspects in which they have an interest are also of interest to investigators from another agency. A burglary suspect being investigated by the police might also be under suspicion of smuggling (HMRC) or benefit fraud (Fraud Investigation Service of the Department of Work and Pensions). The nominal flagging system established by NCIS and passed to SOCA is a system intended to overcome that type of intelligence gap. Alternatively, investigators might have identified a criminal gang comprising four co-conspirators, unaware that in fact there were others involved in the conspiracy yet to come to notice. Careful and detailed analysis of the known conspirators and their activities may reveal anomalies from which the hidden presence of other conspirators may be inferred and the intelligence gap recognized. Although at first sight the Box 4 intelligence gap seems impenetrable, in fact it is vulnerable to lateral thinking together with meticulous and imaginative analysis.

At the operational level, ACPO's *Core Investigative Doctrine* outlines one intelligence gap management tool available to investigators, intelligence offices and analysts (2005: 69):

Figure 8.3 Gap analysis matrix—identifying intelligence role and needs

	What is known	What is not known	Conflicts	Consistencies
Who				
What				
Where				
When				
How				
Why				

This tool is particularly useful in identifying information and intelligence that may require further corroboration and cross-checking or re-examination if conflicting interpretations or 'facts' are identified. It follows that this tool is also useful in highlighting and managing required investigative actions.

8.3.2 Collection planning

Having identified the intelligence/evidential gaps to be filled, the tactical options available to acquire the necessary data can be identified by a number of determinants (based on West 2001: 52):

- Characteristics of the information required
- Possible sources for the information (cost-effectiveness being a discriminator in circumstances in which the information may be available from more than one source)
- Depth and detail of information being sought
- Frequency of information collection
- Staffing and skills available for information collection

- Staffing and skills available for intelligence analysis (there is little point in collecting information if there is insufficient analytical capacity and capability)
- Time available to conduct the operation
- Budget available

The desired information may already exist on databases within the organization or one of its partner agencies. There may be a number of ways in which it has been passively collected through automated monitoring systems. It may be that officers or PCSOs can be tasked to note any sightings of individuals or vehicles during the course of their patrols. The identification of persons using a particular vehicle, for instance, will require uniformed officers to exercise their powers under the Road Traffic Act to stop-check the vehicle when it is seen being driven on the road. It may be that intelligence unit field officers must be tasked to develop initial information reports submitted by patrol staff.

Alternatively, information collection may require active surveillance, which is governed by a statutory regime comprising Part III, Police Act 1997 and RIPA 2000. The statutory regime is, in essence, an initial planning tool because it defines surveillance and the circumstances in which it may be utilized.

Further information—definition of surveillance, s 48(2) RIPA

Surveillance includes:

(a) monitoring, observing or listening to persons, their movements, their conversations or their other activities or communications;

(b) recording anything monitored, observed or listened to in the course of surveillance; and

(c) surveillance by or with the assistance of a surveillance device.

Any surveillance required will fall into one of two categories, directed or intrusive. Directed surveillance can be undertaken by a wide range of public authorities and includes the deployment of covert human intelligence sources (CHIS).

Further information and reading

See C Harfield and K Harfield *Covert Investigation* (Oxford University Press, Oxford, 2005).

Definition of Directed Surveillance

Perhaps a little confusingly, directed surveillance is defined (s 26(2) RIPA) both by what it is not as well as what it is. Surveillance will require a directed surveillance authority if:

- It comprises covert observation or monitoring by whatever means.

- It is for the purpose of a specific investigation or specific operation (any crime or any other offence).
- It will or is likely to obtain private information about *any* person, not just the subject of the operation (this is the key element that engages Art 8 ECHR).

But:

- It does not include observations conducted in an immediate response to spontaneous events.

Such surveillance may be authorized as directed surveillance and can take place anywhere except:

- inside any premises at the time being used as a residence, no matter how temporary, including hotel accommodation, tents, caravans, a prison cell or even railway arches;
- in any vehicle which is primarily used as a private vehicle either by the owner or the person having the right to use it, (taxis are specifically excluded from this definition, s 48(7)(a) RIPA);
- or outside such premises or vehicles if conducted by remote technical means (for instance a long-range microphone) which enabled events and conversations inside residential premises and private vehicles to be monitored from outside producing a surveillance product of the same quality as would be obtained by devices or persons inside such premises or vehicles.

Intrusive surveillance can only be undertaken by police, customs, or military agencies as defined in RIPA (see Harfield and Harfield 2005, ch 3).

Definition of Intrusive Surveillance

Intrusive surveillance is (s 26(3) RIPA):

- covert surveillance
- carried out on any residential premises *or* in any private vehicle

and which involves

- the presence of an individual on the premises or in the vehicle

or

- the use of a surveillance device (ie audio or visual probe).

The term CHIS covers informants, under-cover officers, and test-purchase operatives. The tactical option of infiltration by any of these methods has been advocated on the basis of value for money although this argument has been seriously questioned by academic commentators suggesting that advocates have failed to take account of the true costs of running handlers and informants.

Further information and reading—economic argument for infiltration

'Properly cultivated and used, informants can be a most cost-effective means of detection—a study undertaken by one force showed the cost per detection through informants to be as little as £57 per detected crime.' (Audit Commission *Helping with Enquiries* (Audit Commission, London, 1993, paragraph 96).

'The value of informants is well recognized by the police service. Properly managed and controlled, they represent a cost effective means of detecting crime and gathering evidence on criminal activities when contrasted with the cost of more traditional police evidence gathering methods.' (HMIC *Policing with Intelligence* (HMIC, London, paragraph 2.13).

For the alternative interpretation, see C Dunningham and C Norris 'the detective, the snout, and the Audit Commission: the real costs in using informers' *The Howard Journal* 38/1 67–86 (1999).

R Heaton 'The prospects for intelligence-led policing: some historical and quantitative considerations' *Policing and Society* 9 337–55 (2000).

If the deployment of CHISs is under consideration as a means of filling an information gap, the statutory regime must be complied with for both authorization and management. The mnemonic PLAN focuses consideration about whether such a deployment may be authorized. There is also a Code of Practice that must be complied with and which provides specific guidance when contemplation is being directed towards the use of vulnerable persons or juveniles as CHISs (see Harfield and Harfield 2005, Chapter 9 and Appendix E).

Case study—Planning covert investigation actions

Remember to include the PLAN for covert investigation tactics in all investigation policy-book entries relating to covert investigation considerations and decisions.

P Proportionality
   Why is it proportionate to obtain the intended product of this surveillance in the manner proposed? (Harfield and Harfield 2005, section 1.6.5)

L Legitimacy
   What is the legitimate purpose of the proposed action: the prevention of disorder or crime; the interests of national security; the interests of public safety; the interests of the economic well-being of the country; the protection of health or morals; the protection of the rights and freedoms of others? (Harfield and Harfield 2005, section 1.6.4)

A Authority To Undertake Proposed Action
What is the lawful foundation and authority for the proposed action? From whom must authorization be sought? (Harfield and Harfield 2005, section 1.6.3)

N Necessity Of Proposed Action
Why is the proposed action necessary? (Harfield and Harfield 2005, section 1.6.5)

Whether CHIS deployment is the appropriate option can be determined by combining the intelligence gap tools identified above with a CHIS management matrix which plots CHISs against strategic priorities.

Table 8.1 For use by CHIS controllers, an example of a CHIS management matrix showing the strategic priorities with which each individual CHIS can assist

	Strategic Priority 1	Strategic Priority 2	Strategic Priority 3	Strategic Priority n
CHIS 1	YES	YES	–	YES
CHIS 2	–	–	YES	YES
CHIS 3	YES	–	–	YES
CHIS n	YES	–	–	YES

In the example matrix above there is an apparent need to cultivate additional CHISs in relation to strategic priorities 2 and 3 because of the inherent dangers in relying on a single source for which corroboration may not be possible. In the event that no suitable CHIS is available to discover the required information, consideration must be given to recruiting a CHIS that can access the information or else seeking an alternative means of filling the information gap. Good practice and CHIS security dictate that those who require the intelligence gap to be filled will almost certainly not be those involved in the day-to-day management and deployment of the CHIS. Successful deployment in such circumstances depends on secure and clear communication of need from the investigators to the CHIS management team as the CHIS management team (often termed a Dedicated Source Unit in the police service) will have to plan deployment in such a way as to minimize the risk of compromising the CHIS. Planning for a safe and successful deployment may take some time, particularly if recruitment of a new CHIS is necessary. Although a CHIS may be able to provide relevant information quickly if it happens to be information required on persons or activity about which the CHIS is already providing information, this is not always the case. The investigator or analyst needing to fill the information gap will not be aware of whether a suitable CHIS exists and must plan accordingly, taking into consideration the time it may take to acquire information through a CHIS.

A possible intelligence intervention menu can be summarized, in conjunction with NIM features and a tactical menu, as follows (Table 8.2):

Table 8.2 Intelligence intervention menu, (derived from Sir David Philips, personal communication)

1. What to focus on	Strategic assessment; control strategy
2. How criminals operate/ victims behave	Problem profile; business profile; market analysis
3. Who they are	Subject profile; network analysis
4. When to intervene	Lifestyle; surveillance; infiltration
5. Review	Results analysis; strategic assessment

8.3.3 Community impact assessment

A community impact assessment (CIA) documents that actual or anticipated impact on a community of a particular incident or threat (whether established or emerging). It may be used in conjunction with other consultative fora such as an independent advisory group (IAG) or a critical incident gold group (ad hoc group of advisers to the chief executive team, assembled on a case-by-case basis). An example of how a CIA might be used as part of a murder investigation is set out in the ACPO *Murder Investigation Manual* (2005, Section 18.3).

Key to an effective CIA is up-to-date and complete information, kept under continual review. The process should be transparent and accountable. Thames Valley Police have articulated the context within which a CIA operates in a model termed the 'Seven Cs' (see below). It is an ongoing process undertaken by the Community and Diversity Officers and does not necessarily have to be triggered by a particular episode.

> **Further information and reading**
>
> 'Quite often the **catalyst** (which is one aspect of the "seven C's") requires something, in this case, a reaction resulting in an event. The catalyst indicates that a situation has changed and an individual or group may be in **confrontation** with another. The reaction of the police and the community begins with **causality**, an examination of cause and affect. Analysis will be conducted by the Police to examine these three themes, resulting in a **Community Impact Assessment (CIA)**, enabling the police to understand the process of different groups uniting and then coming into conflict with others. We view this as a form of **crystallization**, a process whereby groups of individuals have formed, defining themselves

> as having a common purpose. They share the same resonance and can be easily recognised. Within the Police there is one principle individual charged with the responsibility of identifying the consequences of the catalyst. Within Thames Valley Police the function is performed by the Community and Diversity Officer (CaDO). It is their responsibility to **communicate** the potential or actual impact of a **critical incident**.'
>
> A Bhatti 'The mobiles are out and the hoods are up' in C Harfield, A MacVean, J Grieve, and D Phillips (eds) *The Handbook of Intelligent Policing: Consilience, Crime Control and Community Safety* (Oxford University Press, Oxford, 2008).

The elements of a CIA have been defined by ACPO's National Community Tension Team. They comprise:

- a record of who has been consulted (eg IAG, community groups, Gold Groups, community officers/SNTs, partner agencies, NCTT), what information they have been given and what advice has been received from them in consequence;
- the presentation of information upon which assessment is based;
- a compliance assessment for legislation relevant to the circumstances;
- an identification of risks to community peace and well-being and/or to community/police/partner agency relations and reputations;
- an identification of response options; and
- an implementation plan.

The CIA can inform any and each of the three phases of the harm management cycle. Collectively, CIAs form a history of community tensions and cohesions within the corporate knowledge of an organization. Although initiated within the police service in 1999, there is no reason that this methodology could not similarly inform interventions for other agencies.

A technique familiar from problem-oriented policing lends its framework to the process of conducting a CIA.

Table 8.3 The SARA problem-solving tool as applicable to the CIA (drawn from the ACPO *Murder Investigation Manual* NCPE Centrex, Wyboston, 2006, p 235)

SCAN	Which communities, organizations, groups, and individuals have been or are likely to be affected by what has happened?
ANALYSIS	Which communities, organizations, groups, individuals, documentary sources, and databases should be consulted to inform the analysis?
	What is the potential impact? How might it happen? How serious will it be?

Table 8.3 The SARA problem-solving tool as applicable to the CIA *(cont.)*

RESPOND	Identify response options and potential partners within the community or amongst other agencies.
	How will the community be engaged? What will the media strategy be?
ASSESS	Review the initial CIA and undertake a results analysis on the response implementation.

Response options and the overall structure for constructing an implementation plan and identifying possible partners may be based on another strategic analysis tool, the problem analysis triangle.

Figure 8.4 Problem analysis triangle to assist in identifying possible angles of intervention

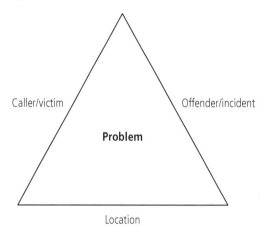

Drawn from fire service theory in which the 'fire triangle' comprises *heat—fuel —oxygen*, the removal of any one of which will extinguish a fire, the problem analysis triangle facilitates problem-solving by focusing on key elements of problems, incidents, crimes (including signal crimes and disorders), which are gateways for intervention. Intelligence-led policing as generally conceived will focus on offenders, but developing knowledge and understanding about the other aspects of the triangle will broaden the tactical menu and increase options for intervention.

Further information and reading

A Leigh, T Read, and N Tilley *Problem-Oriented Policing: Brit Pop* Crime Detection and Prevention Series, Paper 75 (Home Office, London, 1996).

8.4 **Conclusion**

It is relatively simple to view intelligence-led policing in terms of performance indicators. In police or customs terms, for instance, targets for crime types or number of offenders provide a specific focus for intelligence activity. What this chapter has sought to demonstrate is that there is a more holistic approach to planning an intelligence-led intervention that can help make manifest the new political imperative of reducing harm. It is premised on the recognition that meeting enforcement targets will not in and of itself, increase community safety or reduce the risk of harm.

9

Processing Information

9.1 **Introduction**

Further information and reading

'Crime analysis is the process of identifying patterns and relationships between crime data and other relevant data sources to prioritise and target police activity.'

N Cope 'Intelligence-led policing or policing-led intelligence?' *British Journal of Criminology* 44 188–203, (2004) p 188, following:

P Gill *Rounding Up the Usual Suspects? Developments in Contemporary Law Enforcement Intelligence* (Ashgate, Aldershot, 2000).

Processing information to produce intelligence involves evaluation and analysis. This chapter begins with a consideration of the organizational cultural environment within which evaluation and analysis takes place within the police service. The extent to which research findings within the police service are replicated in other organizational cultures would form useful further research. Pending such work, there may be lessons for other organizations from the experience of analysts working within a police environment. The chapter then moves on to discuss elements of the evaluation process including protective marking, the 'need to know' principle and sanitization before reflecting upon interpretation through analysis.

9.2 **The Cultural Context**

Research by Cope (2004), supported by anecdote and informal feedback to the present author (CH) following a paper he delivered to a conference for analysts in 2005, suggests that the British police service has yet to appreciate fully the analyst profession. This is not a universal attitude. In Australia, for instance, within specialist agencies established to investigate serious and organized crime such as the Australian Crime Commission and the New South Wales Crime Commission (Donaghue 2002), the direction of any given operation may be led either by a Commission analyst or a senior investigating officer depending upon prevailing circumstance and need (which may change during the course of any given operation).

Cope discovered significant organizational cultural perceptions within the police service including the following:

- Police officers performing the role of analysts tend to enjoy more credibility amongst police colleagues than civilian staff performing the same role.
- Police officers feel uncomfortable accepting recommendations from analysts who are not police officers.

- Non-police analysts are excluded from and/or intimidated by the organizational culture of the police service, meaning that their expertise is unrecognized or ignored.
- Senior investigators and managers often side-line the role of analysis.
- Analysis is often used retrospectively to justify decisions already taken, rather than to inform strategic and operational decision-making.
- There is often confusion between analysis supporting management decision-making and analysis supporting operational decision-making to the extent that analysts employed to interpret information in order to provide intelligence are often diverted into supporting performance management.

Given the theoretical emphasis on analysis within the NIM, such perceptions indicate both a malaise and lost opportunities in the implementation of intelligence-led policing within the UK. Cope's research reveals the extent to which the organizational culture of the police service has yet to incorporate the rhetoric of intelligence-led policing. Whether or not analysts in other organizations within the wider policing and regulatory family or in partner agencies such as local authorities have similar experiences is an issue warranting further research. There is much anecdotal evidence of police service analysts leaving the service for opportunities in the private sector that are more rewarding in terms of career opportunities, job satisfaction and salary. The majority of analysts within the police service are non-police personnel and if the organizational culture imposes on them a perception of low status, then it is hardly surprising that their work is not valued either.

Why is it that the police service has failed to recognize the potential in analysis? There is a widely-held polemic that the police service is overly bureaucratic and that the proper place for policing is on the streets: it is a view chorused by practitioners, public, press, and politicians alike. This perception inherently promotes the external action of patrolling police officers over internal deskwork, within which latter category analysts would tend to be pigeonholed. Thus an organizational culture that assigns greater value to non-desk work is legitimized by popular, all be it misinformed, mandate. This is consistent with the research responses harvested by Gill (2000) and Cope (2004).

Investigators rely on evidence for the charges and prosecutions that are a measure of their value to the organization and amongst their investigator peers. Intelligence from this perspective is most useful when it leads to evidence of particular offences and therefore an arrest. Analysts paint on a broader canvas. Whilst they may be in a position to support individual criminal investigations, particularly large-scale inquiries, in terms of general policing analysis can particularly support the broader problem-solving activity of neighbourhood policing and CDRP collaboration. Cope takes this further by concluding that police officers and analysts have 'fundamentally different approaches to understanding crime problems' because investigators are looking at the particular whilst analysts are looking at the broader picture (2004: 199). Consequently analytical overviews may not correspond to individual officers' experience of crime within their immediate working environment (Cope 2004: 200).

The broader picture is also the perspective of police management but it is a view very much focused through the lens of performance indicators. Hence the focus on the strategic assessment, the key NIM analytical product that underpins the control strategy that theoretically informs policing in each administrative unit for the next six months. In the experience of the force and BCU intelligence managers writing this book, local analysis for the strategic assessment in reality comes a poor second to the performance priorities handed down by central government. A consequence of this is that the significance of local analysis is undermined with a concomitant diminution of the role of the analyst profession.

Police managers, not unnaturally given political expectations of them, therefore want analysis that delivers performance targets rather than analysis that independently assesses the crime and problem profiles of their area of responsibility. This diversion of analytical effort was recognized in the findings of Cope (2004: 195) and its consequences considered by Sheptycki (2004: 316) who concluded that such diversion reduced capacity for intelligence analysis and so led to information overload, one of the 11 organizational pathologies he argues that bedevil police intelligence systems.

It can be argued that part of the reason this organizational culture prevails and that police officers in all ranks and roles fail to recognize the full potential value of analysis is that analysis as a profession is imperfectly understood (Gill 2000, Chapter 9). This may be equally true of some analysts as well as police officers although it is admittedly difficult for analysts to assert their value in a cultural context that undervalues the profession. Cope identifies the 'paucity of training on analysis' as a reason why police officers do not understand fully how to utilize the profession to best effect (2004: 194). Training is task-oriented; education is comprehension-oriented. Simply being made aware of the analytical products of the NIM will achieve little if there is no wider understanding that analysis is informed by the data available. What data is available depends on what information is gathered by officers, PCSOs, and other staff and fed into the system. Which brings the argument full circle to the control strategy, the intelligence requirement and appropriate intelligence tasking. If management data is more readily available than policing intelligence, which is possible given that much management data is self-generating, then that too can contribute to the diversion of analysts if there is a dearth of relevant intelligence to analyse.

So for a decision-maker, what does good analysis look like? It looks like the consilience of inductions, a concept created by Cambridge philosopher William Wherwell in the 1840s which 'takes place when an Induction obtained from one class of facts, coincides with an induction obtained from another different class. Thus consilience is a test of the Truth of the Theory in which it occurs', (from Whewell's *Philosophy of the Inductive Sciences*, quoted in Johnson 2006: 67). The case study below illuminates the concept.

Case study—consilient thinking

Drawn from S Johnson *The Ghost Map: A Street, an Epidemic and the Two Men who Battled to Save Victorian London* (Allen Lane, London, 2006), a book commended here to every reader and suggested as essential reading for analysts, intelligence officers and their managers.

In August 1854 a cholera epidemic broke out in Soho, London, eventually claiming the lives of 50,000 persons across the country. Out of this destruction came inspirational creative thinking, not that it was recognized as such at the time. Two Soho residents, Dr John Snow (famous for developing the science of anaesthesiology) and Rev Henry Whitehead (the local priest) independently studied the outbreak to identify its cause, approaching the issue from different perspectives, the scientific and the theological. At the time 'conventional wisdom' held that cholera was an air-borne disease. Through methodical research, map-making and thorough local knowledge, and ultimately through their combined effort without which neither would have succeeded, these two researchers identified the water-borne nature of cholera, a challenge to the conventional wisdom that was not readily accepted by the Establishment. Indeed, when confronted with evidence that cholera was water-borne, the authorities indulged themselves in *confirmation bias* by refusing to accept that water could be the infecting agent and arguing instead that in fact the air must be so contagious that it had infected the water supply as well.

Snow and Whitehead's combined success depended upon reconciling seemingly contradictory facts; recognising the significance of both particulars and patterns; recognising when correlation had been mistaken for causation; and above all drawing together different knowledge from a variety of contexts in order to look at a conventional wisdom from a different perspective. One of the key analytical tools was the map drawn by Snow, not to show the mere distribution of instances of cholera within the district but showing the travel of human traffic between the instances of cholera. As a distribution map it would have achieved nothing. As a map of time as it related to space, it helped to inform truly creative thinking. But only because it was itself a piece of creative thinking arising from the juxtaposition of both a bird's eye view of the issue and intimate local knowledge of the community. Snow's scientific analysis identified a street water-pump the likely location of the outbreak, thus pointing towards the cause but it was Whitehead's knowledge of his congregation and their lives that identified *why* the location was the cause. Each needed the other to prove the case.

In recounting the extraordinary history of this intelligence-led discovery, Johnson offers an eternal warning for the intelligence profession (Johnson 2006: 125):

'It's not just that the authorities of the day were wrong . . . ; it's the tenacious, unquestioning way they went on being wrong'.

What, then, are the lessons here for analysts, intelligence staff, their managers, and decision-makers engaged in policing, regulation, investigation, and preservation of community safety (and associated policy-design)?

The consilient chain of argument can be complex and multi-disciplinary. By definition it will challenge the knowledge context of any intelligence officer or analyst working within a specific agency or organization. Its value lies in intelligence-led partnership (Snow and Whitehead would seem to have much to say to CDRPs and other partnership initiates, for instance). Yet it is vulnerable to the seduction of simplicity and the seemingly obvious, which tend to reinforce rather than confront preconception.

Only the known can be policed (this is perhaps an inherent weakness of crime control). What cracked the case in the cholera epidemic was Whitehead's local knowledge of how the community really worked. Ultimately criminals and, so it would appear, modern terrorists, operate within the context of communities. Community safety and policing interventions will succeed where they are based on a thorough knowledge of the community of which no one agency will be in sole possession. An organization's knowledge of a community will only be as good as their interaction with that community. That interaction will be both defined and constrained by the function of the organization. Others will have different, and equally valid, perceptions.

Correlation does not equal causation. This may necessitate the reconciliation of apparent contradictions. But in considering such contradictions Snow and Whitehead achieved new insights. Links are missing only for want of recognition. Fundamental is the ability to recognize both the particular and the pattern in such a way that the significant is not obscured by the strategic. It is perhaps in understanding the epidemiology of crime and other community safety issues drawing upon multiple perspectives beyond the mere police/public interactive arena that knowledge-based policing is distinguishable from intelligence-led policing.

All of which polemic begs important questions about practicalities. It is tempting to ask how can all relevant information be captured by a single agency? This is perhaps to approach the issue from the wrong direction. Of greater significance, as illustrated by the Bichard Inquiry and HM Inspector of Probation's report into the Rice case (see Chapter 2 above), is the issue of whether individual organizations are efficiently and effectively executing their own functional remits and appropriately sharing the information so gleaned with relevant partners. Once an agency is posed a particular problem requiring resolution, creative partnership provides a framework for consilient thinking. Johnson uses the history of the 1854 cholera outbreak to reflect upon issues of urbanization. The implication of Johnson's study of the growth of urbanization and its influences is that current policing infrastructure and methods, including intelligence-led policing, will be ineffective within two decades. We should probably start planning for that now (Johnson 2006: 216).

Further information and reading

N Cope 'Intelligence-led policing or policing-led intelligence? *British Journal of Criminology* 44 188–203 (2004).

S Donoghue *Royal Commissions and Permanent Commissions of Inquiry* (Butterworths, Chatswood, 2001).

P Gill *Rounding Up the Usual Suspects? Developments in Contemporary Law Enforcement Intelligence* (Ashgate, Aldershot, 2000).

S Johnson *The Ghost Map: A Street, an Epidemic and the Two Men who Battled to Save Victorian London* (Allen Lane, London, 2006).

J Sheptycki 'Organizational pathologies in police intelligence systems' *European Journal of Criminology* 1/3 307–32 (2004).

9.3 The Evaluation Process

Further information and reading

'The value of finished intelligence analysis is not measured solely by its accuracy, but rather by the value it has for decision-makers. This value, however, can change depending on the information needs of the decision-maker. Unfortunately, the intelligence community has—for the most part—failed to incorporate different perspectives and approaches into its standard operating procedures for the creation of intelligence analysis, limiting the potential contributions that intelligence analysis can make to decision-making.'

S Marrin 'Adding value to the intelligence product' in L Johnson (ed) *Handbook of Intelligence Studies* (Routledge, London, 2007) 199–210 at 199.

Marrin's caveat (above) reminds us that the creation of analytical products alone is not the be all and end all of analysis. The issue is one of outcomes, not outputs. Nevertheless, and with this warning that processes and products can sometimes obscure purpose firmly in mind, this chapter moves on to consider the stages of analysis, starting with the initial information report.

9.3.1 The initial information report

The test of a good information report is **whether it answers every question that could have been asked at the time**: who, what, where, when, why, how and a full description of persons and vehicles.

For example, a police officer investigating a burglary committed overnight will want to know who has been stop-checked by colleagues during the period in which the burglary was committed and correlate any such information with possible witness accounts gathered during house-to-house enquiries. For this reason officers conducting stop-checks or stop-and-searches should record not only the information required on the records of stop, which will include details of the location where the encounter took place for instance, but also the direction of travel of the individual concerned before and after the encounter. Any explanation of their movements given by the person checked could subsequently provide information to prioritize subsequent lines of enquiry and may provide information that warrants corroboration and verification at a later date.

Similarly, details about what on the face of it appear to be relatively minor incidents of anti-social behaviour may provide the information necessary to trigger a signal crimes or signal disorder perspective (see Chapter 3 above). For this reason it is necessary for all officers and PCSOs to be aware of behaviours identified as signal behaviours within their BCU and provide appropriate information accordingly. This requires effective communication with staff about what is needed. Daily briefings to staff in organizations using the NIM, for example, could include the intelligence requirement for that day based on the morning tasking meeting.

Intelligence gaps (and possible subsequent misunderstandings) start with initial information submissions.

Information reports (also called intelligence reports) are subject to disclosure under the CPIA, although Public Interest Immunity may be asserted.

9.3.2 Grading intelligence

An analyst receiving individual pieces of information, of which there may be many in any one information report, will not on plain reading be able to assess the accuracy of the information presented. Those providing information into an intelligence process must provide subsequent analysts and decision-makers with an indication of the quality of the information by indicating the nature of its provenance. Is the information known personally to the report-maker? If it has been received from a third party, is it known personally to that third party? Is that third party an individual who has previously supplied reliable information or is this a new, untried, and untested source? Does the information come from a partner agency? If so, what measures did that agency take to verify the accuracy of the information? Relevant to any of the above questions is the issue of how recent the information is. Is the information so old that it no longer has any currency for decision-making?

In order to bring uniformity to information assessment, a grading system has been devised to indicate the information report's assessment of the reliability of a given piece of information. The use of a grading system is helpful but the use of letters and numbers gives the appearance of an *objective* hierarchy when in fact, some of the values identified in this way are *subjective*. Originally the system used in the UK—and still in use throughout Europe—was the '4x4' system. The UK has subsequently adopted a '5x5x5' system.

> **Further information and reading**
>
> Much of the detail of these systems remains outside the public domain, but Bichard summarizes the two systems in the glossary to his report.
>
> **4x4 system**—a subjective alpha/numerical intelligence grading system used by most police forces to determine the reliability of a piece of information (on a scale of A, B, C and X) and the reliability of the source of the intelligence (on a scale of 1–4). Therefore, 'A1' means the intelligence source is highly credible and the intelligence is of a high standard.
>
> **5x5x5 system**—the successor to the 4x4 system of intelligence grading, incorporating the two factors above but including a judgment about who can have access to that intelligence (on a scale of 1 to 5).
>
> M Bichard The Bichard Inquiry Report (TSO, London, 2004) 157.

Grading should be recognized for what it is, a subjective evaluation of individual pieces of information. There are some important caveats. A single information report about a single individual may nevertheless contain a number of different pieces of information each of which could be evaluated differently depending upon the source for each piece of information. Failure to evaluate each individual piece of information within a single report may compromise future intervention if assumptions are made. Secondly, the use of numerical and alphabetical scales in attempting to assign a qualitative value implies a definitive hierarchy, may incline those using the evaluation to place too much reliance upon it. The evaluation will only be as useful as the contextual knowledge of the evaluator. The same source, for instance, may be assigned different reliability gradings from different investigators based upon their different knowledge of the source. Such an inconsistency will not be apparent to a subsequent user of the information because of source anonymization.

Information that is from a reliable source and which can be considered most probably accurate will not necessarily be any more useful to a decision-maker than information from a previously untested source the accuracy of which cannot be ascertained at the time of coming into the possession of the organization gathering the information. Each piece of information contributes to the wider picture and will inform further intelligence, prevention, or enforcement activity. Depending upon the nature of the information, for instance, it may be necessary to undertake an operation to check and corroborate the accuracy of information from an untested source.

Corroboration of a piece of information believed to be of a 'high standard' and from a 'highly credible' source (to draw on Bichard, see box above) would hardly seem to be necessary but its credibility and quality, whilst being good indicators, are not a guarantee of total accuracy. By the same token, a piece of information that cannot immediately be ascertained as accurate and which comes from a previously untested source, may well be entirely accurate, but its grading may incline readers of the report to assume it is of less significance. No one piece of information will be the whole picture. Decision-makers must assess each item and determine whether further action is required in respect of the information before it is used to inform an intervention.

This highlights the need for staff gathering information and providing the initial grading to be fully trained in the process and aware of its significance for decision-making at a later stage. At all times professional judgement should inform evaluation, rather than personal feelings. There is a danger that evaluation could be a means inappropriately to enhance 'the value' of a piece of information, which will compromise analysis and subsequent intervention. Intelligence unit operatives should follow up initial information reports which require further development and corroboration. This highlights the need for appropriately trained and resourced intelligence units.

9.3.3 Analytical tools and techniques

As previously discussed (Chapter 5), the NIM defines nine analytical tools and techniques (see Table 9.1).

Table 9.1 The NIM analytical tools and techniques

Tool	Purpose
Results analysis	To evaluate effectiveness of law enforcement activities, in particular of intelligence, prevention and enforcement operations undertaken
Crime Pattern analysis	To identify the nature and scale of emerging and current crime trends and patterns, linked crimes or incidents, and hotspots of activity
Market profiles	To analyse the criminal market around a given commodity or service in a specified geographical area
Criminal business profiles	To detail how criminal operations/business and techniques work at a micro (individual) or macro (thematic) level in the same way that legitimate businesses may be explained
Network analysis	To understand the nature and significance of the links between people who form criminal networks, or organisations that interrelate, together with the strengths and weaknesses of criminal groups or organisations
Target profile analysis	To provide sufficient detailed analysis to initiate a target operation or support an ongoing operation against an individual or networked group of individuals by identifying options for intervention or disruption

Tool	Purpose
Demographic/social trends analysis	To examine the nature of demographic changes and their impact on criminality, as well as the analysis of social factors that might underlie changes or trends in crime or offending behaviour
	To describe statistically the constitution of the population of a given area and the associated economic/social/environmental indicators with reference to law enforcement requirements
Risk analysis	To support assessment of the scale of risk posed by individual offenders, organizations or crime types to potential victims, the public generally, the law enforcement agencies or the criminal justice system
Operational intelligence assessment	To ensure that on-going investigations remain focused and are not side-tracked by new and unanticipated intelligence that may require a separate operational response

Their relevance to the NIM is presented in Chapter 5 above and they are also discussed in the ACPO *Guidance on the National Intelligence Model* (NCPE Centrex, Wyboston, 2005). These tools and techniques are labelled in terms of the products derived from the activity undertaken. A variety of software tools are commercially available to support such analysis, although the sophistication with which some of these are applied is variable. Gill notes that 'Geographical Information Systems (GIS) fed with crime data simply provide a high-tech (and very expensive) way of doing what police have long done—put pins representing crime occurrences in maps and observing resulting clusters' (2000: 220). Crime pattern analysis software, such as the Compstat methods employed in New York can, with sufficient quality data and analytical skill, provide information to support more sophisticated interpretation (Gill 2000: 220), although the style of policing known as zero tolerance, which is supported by Compstat, has been subject to criticism (M Moore 'Sizing up Compstat: an important administrative innovation in policing' *Criminology and Public Policy* 2(3) 469–94 (2003)); which draws attention to the fact that intelligence systems and the use made of intelligence are two related but distinct business areas which should not be confused. Pictures, it has been said, can paint a thousand words and in this vein mapping—a visual representation—can be seductively impressive. Innes et al captured contemporary perceptions of mapping within the police service (see box below).

Case study—analytical mapping

Pictures, it has been said, can paint a thousand words and in this vein mapping—a visual representation of 'hotspots'—can be seductively impressive.

'. . . one of the intelligence products most often requested by operational officers was a crime map—a visual representation that shows the spatial distribution of criminal incidents over a given territory . . . in order to identify "hot-spots", on the understanding that this will allow them to target their resources to these locations. . . . [Fieldwork research conducted amongst operational police officers established that] the maps that were produced served little functional purpose. Analysts often acerbically commented that they were merely producing wallpaper . . . There was no inferential interpretation conducted in an effort to identify what factors could be used to explain the clustering, beyond the obvious point that robbery was most prevalent around the main shopping streets in the borough. . . . crimes that were similar in terms of their execution, but occurred at different ends of the same street, were mot, according to this mode of analysis, identified as connected.'

M Innes, N Fielding, and N Cope 'The appliance of science? The theory and practice of crime intelligence analysis' *British Journal of Criminology* 45:48–9 (2005).

One hundred and fifty years ago Snow and Whitehead demonstrated that less mapping can often be more, and that it is not the map that is important but the interpretation of the information in context. They arrived at an understanding of the way cholera operates not by mapping the dead but by mapping the living (Johnson 2006: 193–5). Knowing the location of a crime is not unimportant, but successful detection, intervention, and prevention will depend upon understanding the movements (and the reason for them) of the protagonists up to the point of the commission and then afterwards. Equally, identifying links between different criminal associates is little more than an exercise in quantification unless there is additional information, analysis and intelligence to understand the quality of the relationship identified. This wider appreciation comes from the sophisticated use in combination of the various tools and techniques outlined above.

The nine tools and techniques that form part of the NIM are not unique. Read and Oldfield identified eight tools and techniques in their 1995 research for the Home Office. In North America, contemporaneously, Peterson identified 26 (1995). It suffices here to refer to those utilized within the NIM because that is the business model of choice employed in the UK.

Further information and reading

T Read and D Oldfield *Local Crime Analysis* Crime Detection and Prevention Series, Paper 65 (Home Office, London, 1995).

M Peterson *Applications in Criminal Analysis: A sourcebook* (Greenwood Press, Westport, Conn, 1995).

Subject to capacity, capability, and time, analysis is a continuous cycle of hypothesis-checking using these tools and techniques. It is worth reiterating that the value of analysis lies particularly in the ability of the profession to modify and inform prevailing assumptions. Investigators must expect to be challenged by analysis and be open-minded to such challenges. Analysis that is geared merely to reinforcing preconceptions undermines the theoretical basis of intelligence-led policing. For example, if analysis is used for nothing more than linking offenders to offences through apparent modus operandi, which then supports the use of prison-visits to identify offences that can be taken-into-consideration or provides the basis for sanctioned detections, then emerging criminals and crime trends will be missed and systemic knowledge errors created and perpetuated. It is a lesson Lord Butler highlighted (2004, paragraph 32) when suggesting that *analysis* can only be conducted by those expert in the subject matter. (*Assessment*, he continued, may be conducted separately or as a parallel process.)

> Assessment has to make choices, but in doing so runs the risk of selection that reinforces earlier conclusions. The risk is that uneven standards of proof may be applied; reports that fit the previous model are readily accepted, while contrary reports have to reach a higher threshold. This is not only perfectly understandable. It is the way perception normally operates. (2004, paragraph 33).

The box below details a test that analysts can use as a basis for reflective learning about their own work and in order to ensure that the manner in which they present their analysis is quality-assured.

Case study—Testing the presentation of analysis

John Grieve, building on the work of Ian Grant, has adapted the following check-list against which analysts can test the presentation of their work.

1. Presentation of thesis in a clear synopsis in a clear **abstract:**
   What is the problem? What has been proved and how? What next? From a clear abstract, all else follows. The **conclusions** should follow logically from the abstract.
2. What is the logic and structure of the argument being presented?
   Are the **generalizations** within the hypothesis logically, rationally and compellingly drawn? If the analysis is used like this, **then** the results will be this. . . .

---

3. Distinction between fact and value statements:

   What is **interpretation**, inference or evaluation? What is evidence or empirical data?

4. Status of information/intelligence/evidence:

   What is the **integrity** of information upon which the analysis has been based? What degree of confidence can be attributed to the available information? Is some information considered more reliable than other information? Why? What are the implications for its interpretation and action dependent thereon?

5. **Testing** of propositions:

   What information gaps remain which, if filled, could change the current interpretation? What has not been done? Why not—insufficient resources to gather possible information prior to analysis or no information to be had? What cannot be done?

6. What are the **limitations** to the conclusions being presented?

   Is an alternative interpretation possible based on the same intelligence? Does information/intelligence/evidence exist to dissent from the analysis being presented? Are there caveats that decision-makers must take into consideration?

7. Matters omitted:

   Is it believed that sources may have **withheld information**? Why have particular matters known from intelligence (and possibly known to the audience for the analysis) been omitted from the final presentation?

8. Check for any **bias**.

   Bias, epistemic imbalance is where some piece of testimony counts more than some other piece. Bias in the lay sense, typically refers to prejudice— literally prejudging an issue due to strong prior belief or motive. Such bias may be conscious or unconscious.

9. Does the author of the analysis identify with argument? Is the argument **compelling**? In other words has the author persuaded her-/himself and the reader?

Sources: John Grieve QPM, former Deputy Assistant Commissioner and former head of intelligence, Metropolitan Police Service (personal communication September 2007) following Ian Grant, Units 26 and 27 of module U202, *Inquiry*, The Open University.

9.3.4 Protective marking and the 'need to know' principle

The **Government Protective Marking Scheme** (GPMS) is intended to protect sensitive information collected, generated, and held within government and associated agencies. Its application is common to all agencies and government departments that have adopted it. The GPMS comprises the classification (marking) of

198

documents, the storing of material and audited handling, including destruction. Implementation of the scheme requires appropriately trained and vetted staff, with the correct equipment and storage facilities commensurate to the level of protection required. Correct handling and storage is as integral to GPMS operation as is correct document classification and processes need to be in place to ensure that properly trained staff are accurately complying with the scheme.

Proper implementation demonstrates to other organizations that any information they share will be appropriately handled. This fundamental confidence underpins partnership working. Without it partnership does not work.

The police service formally adopted it on 16 February 2001 although, rather like the NIM, its implementation within the service is neither universal nor consistent.

Access to certain categories of information are restricted to individuals who have undergone **security vetting**: counter-terrorism checks (CTC), security clearance (SC), and developed vetting (DV). This hierarchical framework determines who may access what. The **'need to know' principle** applies to ensure that, even within the framework, access to sensitive information is restricted to those who have a specific need to know.

Definition of 'need to know' principle

'A security principle which states that the dissemination of classified information should be no wider that is required for the efficient conduct of business, and should be restricted to those who have authorized access. A balance must be struck between making information as widely available as necessary to maximise potential benefits, and restricting availability to protect the security of sources, techniques and information. The development of systems helps to support the integrity and effectiveness of the intelligence environment.' (para 2.2)

ACPO *Guidance on the National Intelligence Model*
(NCPE Centrex, Wyboston, 2005).

Those who 'own' the information usually make the determination of who has a specific 'need to know'. In doing so they may not always be aware of whether others have a specific need to know a particular item of information or intelligence. 'Need to know' rightly focuses on the protection of sources, techniques, and information itself. This narrow perception, however, has the potential to sustain an overly restrictive approach.

There are two questions decision-makers have to ask themselves in applying the 'need to know' principle:

- Who 'needs to know' the information in the format in which it currently exists?

- Is it possible to sanitize the presentation of the information in its entirety or in part in order to share the intelligence without compromising sources, techniques, or other information?

These tests will determine the widest possible options in terms of information-sharing, which should minimize occasions in which information that could and should have been shared is withheld.

'Need to know' will be influenced by the classification assigned to information in order to minimise risks to individuals and organizations arising from improper information handling. The classification system underpinning the GPMS is founded upon an estimation of harm: if this information fell into the wrong hands, what damage would it cause?

Table 9.2 Government Protective Marking Scheme, adopted and implemented by ACPO, 16 February 2001

Top Secret	• threaten directly the internal stability of the UK or friendly countries • lead directly to widespread loss of life • cause exceptionally grave damage to the effectiveness or security of UK or allied forces or to the continuing effectiveness of extremely valuable security or intelligence operations • cause exceptionally grave damage to relations with friendly governments • cause severe long-term damage to the UK economy
Secret	• raise international tension • seriously damage relations with friendly governments • threaten life directly or seriously prejudice public order or individual security or liberty • cause serious damage to the operational effectiveness or security of UK or allied forces or the continuing effectiveness of highly valuable security or intelligence operations • cause substantial material damage to national finances or economic and commercial interests
Confidential	• materially damage diplomatic relations, that is, cause formal protest or other sanctions • prejudice individual security or liberty • cause damage to the operational effectiveness or security of UK or allied forces or the effectiveness of valuable security or intelligence operations • work substantially against national finances or economic and commercial interests • substantially undermine the financial viability of major organizations • impede the investigation or facilitate the commission of serious crime • seriously impede the development or operation of major government policies • shut down or otherwise substantially disrupt significant national operations

Restricted	
	• adversely affect diplomatic relations
	• cause substantial distress to individuals
	• make it more difficult to maintain the operational effectiveness or security of UK or allied forces
	• cause financial loss or loss of earning potential to, or facilitate improper gain or advantage for, individuals or companies
	• prejudice the investigation or facilitate the commission of crime
	• breach proper undertakings to maintain the confidence of information provided by third parties
	• impede the effective development or operation of government policies
	• breach statutory restrictions on disclosure of information
	• disadvantage government in commercial or policy negotiations with others
	• undermine the proper management of the public sector and its operations
Unclassified	All other material

Potential weaknesses of the classification element of the GPMS are the dangers of under- and over-classification. Over-classification is more likely given that individuals are risk-averse and more likely to 'play safe'. But, as the ACPO guidance below illustrates, over-classification creates its own significant problems.

Further information and reading

'Users should be made aware of the dangers of over-classification, which, in the experience of the armed forces and other Government organisations, quickly becomes endemic unless stringent controls are applied at local level. *Over-classification leads rapidly to a devaluation of the entire protective marking scheme.* It can also result in substantial, but largely unseen costs as a result of greater use of expensive secure channels of communication, a requirement for extra numbers of specially trained and vetted staff, waste of time and resources on unnecessary use of cumbersome document handling procedures, etc.'

ACPO memo (unclassified) to police forces, dated 16 February 2001, paragraph 5. (emphasis added)

Classification does not automatically exempt documents from duties to disclose under the Freedom of Information Act 2000. Material content should be considered and the relevant statutory exemptions applied only after consultation with the owner of the information and other relevant parties. The length of time that has passed since information was originally classified may be an important factor in considering whether restrictions are still necessary.

> **Further information and reading**
>
> ACPO *Freedom of Information Manual* (Produced on behalf of ACPO by
> Hampshire Constabulary, 2006).

In reviewing whether information and intelligence has been appropriately classified, it will be necessary to consider whether documents taken together warrant
a higher level of classification. For example, documents A, B, C, D, and E have
each individually been classified as 'restricted' in status. In preparing to share all
five documents as a collection with a partner agency, decision-makers will need
to decide whether the collection taken as a whole should be reformulated into
one dissemination document with a 'confidential' classification because of the
cumulative risk of harm should all the information taken as a whole fall into the
'wrong hands'.

Reclassification can also take place in the opposite direction. For example,
when a new piece of information becomes available from an open source, other
documentation could be declassified with no risk to what were previously considered closed sources; except, of course, the fact that the information was originally derived from a closed source.

9.3.5 Sanitization

Sanitization is a solution to the issue of sharing information without compromising individuals or techniques. It is defined in the Glossary for ACPO's *Guidance on
the National Intelligence Model* (NCPE Centex, Wyboston, 2005) as '**The practice
of removing or altering the content of a document with the aim of protecting sensitive sources and/or methodology to arrive at a form appropriate for
dissemination**'.

Sanitization is particularly important when seeking to assist decision-makers
in arriving at strategic, organizational, decision-making. For example, within a
strategic assessment, describing the impact of current operational activity in a
given area of risk without necessarily describing the details of operation subjects or tactics and techniques being deployed. The strategic assessment will have
a wide audience and therefore information within it needs to be shared in an
appropriately sanitized form to demonstrate impact and to facilitate decision-
making appropriate to the level of identified risk both in terms of resource allocation and partnership-working.

The watchword is sanitization rather than sterilization. The information
should be presented in such a way as protects that which needs to be protected
without robbing the information of that which will be significant for the partners to whom it is to be disseminated. For the originating agency sanitization
must be supported by an audit trail that can trace what has been sanitized and
why, as well as to whom the information in its redacted from has been passed.

9.3.6 **Dissemination**

Protective marking and sanitization facilitate, but cannot guarantee, the final information processing phase, effective dissemination. Dissemination is a two-part function that includes receipt as well transmission. Once intelligence is disseminated, the originator losses control over its interpretation. Analysts cannot guarantee that the intelligence shared will be used in the manner for which it was intended on in a way that is supported by the intelligence. The product may be subject to reinterpretation by decision-makers and investigators second-guessing the analysts or seeking to adapt the intelligence to a predetermined agenda. This may arise from the organizational cultural issues discussed above. It may be because the intelligence has been shared with a partner agency that is trying to 'fit' the intelligence into a different way of working. Responsibility for appropriate dissemination rests with the originator and, where required, the authorizing officer who permits the transmission. But responsibility for the use of disseminated product rests with the recipient. Subsequent results analysis should distinguish between the poor quality intelligence and the poor use of intelligence.

9.4 **Interpretation through Analysis**

> **Further information and reading**
>
> 'It is in the translation of raw information into operationally viable intelligence that analysis plays its crucial role.'
>
> N Cope 'Intelligence-led policing or policing-led intelligence? *British Journal of Criminology* 44 188–203, 201 (2004).

Inferential thinking takes harm reduction in all its forms (including police-work) beyond the reactive recording of past events, towards proactive intervention based on predictive analysis.

Performance data and crime/incident reports allow statements to be made: X numbers of incidents have taken place in area Y. This in itself is insufficient to allow informed planning. Analysis that facilitates inference adds value to the data by providing an intelligence context within which to view the data. In this way prevention as well as enforcement can be planned. This can linked throughout the NIM levels of criminality/response.

Inference should enable you to make best decision possible using intelligence analysed within the organization. For example, it may be asserted that in the period leading up to Christmas there will be an increase in domestic burglaries. This is a bald statement rather than inference. Can analysis demonstrate that there really is a link between Christmas and increased burglaries? And if so, what else can be analysed in order to draw added value inferences? Herein may lie intelligence gaps that need to be filled before further inferences are possible. What, for instance, can be learnt about the activity of criminals in the period leading up to Christmas? Do domestic burglars become more active at that time of year? Or do other criminals, who would not normally commit domestic burglaries, engage in burglary before Christmas? In either case, why? Is there a different market for the disposal of burgled property at different times of the year? Depending upon the answers to these questions, different intelligence, prevention, and enforcement tactical intervention options may be available.

Case study—illustrations of inferential analysis

A

It is evident from information received and analysed that the social practice of males in the X community to congregate in the town centre precinct is perceived by other community members as intimidating. It is possible that this perception will increase fear of crime and possibly generate disorder if other groups start to congregate in the similar area and engage in antagonistic interaction with the first group.

From this it can be inferred that the Control Strategy should address preventative measures and community cohesion, together with partner agencies, to reduce the fear of crime.

B

Intelligence analysis shows that the majority of organized crime groups supplying Class A drugs in the force area are also using firearms and violence to support and sustain their criminal enterprise.

From this it can be inferred that the Control Strategy should link Intelligence, Prevention, Enforcement (and Reassurance) activity for Class A drugs and criminal use of firearms.

As a cross-check of interpretation and analysis, it has been suggested that the police (and by implication other agencies and authorities) could do worse than consult the community on interpretational issues, thus providing a further role for the community in information acquisition and intelligence analysis.

In their consideration of terrorism and community relations, Parliament's Home Affairs Select Committee heard from a variety of witnesses. The enquiry was held in the aftermath of the terrorist attacks on London in July 2005, the subsequent police shooting of Jean Charles de Menezes mistaken for a suspected terrorist and the abortive raid on a suspected terrorist cell at house in Forest Gate, London: all episodes that had called into question the value of intelligence held by the authorities. The Muslim Council of Great Britain suggested 'the Muslim community should be involved in independent scrutiny of police intelligence', the purpose being to provide a wider context within which decision-makers could utilize intelligence in their possession. On behalf of the police service, Leicestershire's Chief Constable Matt Baggott responded: 'the issue of public confidence is such that if you could have some degree of confidential, independent assessment that did not undermine the fundamental human rights of the sources and other issues of grave operational importance we would be very open to that and support that'.

Further information and reading

'We believe that there should be independent scrutiny, involving the Muslim community, of police intelligence and its use as a basis for stops and searches and arrests.'

Recommendation in paragraph 115 of *Terrorism and Community Relations*. The 6th Report of Session 2004–5 (3 vols) Home Affairs Select Committee, HC 165 (TSO, London).

The quote from the Muslim Council appears in the summary on p 4 and also in Question 355 of the published evidence. Chief Constable Baggott's response is in Question 357 of the published evidence.

Agencies and authorities will understandably be nervous about any actions that could compromise sources and will have to demonstrate a duty a care towards those whose well-being could be imperilled through compromise. Criminals who are sufficiently intelligence- and surveillance-aware may take the opportunity to infiltrate groups likely to be consulted about intelligence interpretation.

Such caveats recognized, there will be occasions when it will be appropriate and valuable to seek corroboration and verification of interpretations placed upon intelligence, the better to understand available intervention options and their possible consequences.

9.5 **Conclusion**

The outcome of processing and analysing information will be the creation of intelligence which decision-makers will have to consider when planning what sort of intervention, if any, to initiate. Such decisions will have to be taken within a wider contextual environment that includes factors such as, but not exclusively, resource availability, political priorities, inter-agency partnership, and community cohesion. The response options will generally divide into three types: to act on the intelligence; to initiate further intelligence development following recognition that the available intelligence has itself highlighted new and significant intelligence gaps; or not to act at all because of the other factors that a decision-maker has to consider when determining a course of action.

No matter which response strategy is adopted, it will feed back into the planning of future intelligence-led intervention. Filling intelligence gaps will obviously provide new intelligence for consideration, and either active intervention or the decision to take no action at this stage will generate consequences which will need to be considered in subsequent results analysis in order to identify what, if anything, has changed and what, if anything, needs to be done differently next time. And overarching this whole process is the continuous reflection in which organizations need to engage in order to review whether their intelligent management is, to borrow a phrase currently in vogue, fit for purpose. To that subject, the next chapter now addresses itself.

10

Using Intelligence in 'Policing'

10.1 **Introduction**

> ### Case study—is intelligence-led policing working?
>
> 'Things are certainly changing but they are doing so unevenly. What is clearly changing is the language and rhetoric with which senior police managers, especially in the UK, have embraced new techniques. What is less clear is how far this is matched by actual change within enforcement agencies.'
>
> P Gill *Rounding Up the Usual Suspects? Developments in Contemporary law Enforcement Intelligence* (Ashgate, Aldershot, 2000) 243.

Implicit at various points throughout this consideration of intelligence and policing has been the hypothesis that the modern practice of intelligence-led policing currently is not working as well as theoretically it could. Possible reasons for this are varied and have been rehearsed in Chapters 2 and 5 in particular. So the question arises how any organization involved in policing, community safety, criminal investigation, or some form of central or local government regulatory function, knows that what it is doing is working? In part this is a question for researchers and longitudinal studies. Recent falls in crime reporting rates look encouraging but sufficient research already exists to demonstrate that such a decrease may be due to causes other than policing. But it is also a question for organizational leaders and intelligence managers, which can be addressed with more immediacy.

Reflective thinking and results analysis—perhaps evoked more widely in rhetoric than used in reality—are key to the way forward in breaking free from the constraints of intelligence-led policing and moving towards knowledge-based policing, in which knowing itself enables an organization truly to make informed decisions on the basis of intelligence both known and unknown. This chapter seeks to initiate debate about a reflective framework. It is a debate in which both practitioners and those with oversight (for instance the Association of Police Authorities, the Local Government Association) should also participate.

10.2 **The Reflective Framework**

The framework is founded upon a series of test questions overarching which is a basic test of the relationship between intelligence product and organizational action. Would a member of the organization selected spontaneously at random at any time of the day or night and faced with a multitude of actions to deal with, know which activities to prioritize in accordance with outstanding Control Strategy issues, and understand those in relation to the reduction of harm?

10.2.1 How does an organization know what works and what does not?

Organizations need to ask some fundamental questions about their ability to deliver intelligence-led work. The following questions provide a framework of focus to facilitate understanding about an organization's capability and capacity to provide appropriate support (through resources, accountability, and products) that will develop effective intelligence-led processes and reduce harm.

10.2.2 How does an organization know it is getting its intelligence management right?

To what extent, if any, is the intelligence function integrated with prevention, investigation, enforcement, and reassurance functions? Is the organization following and regularly reviewing the operation of a strategic model such as the Identify—Assessment—Management model? (see section 8.1 above). The better an organization becomes at working through this cycle, the more risk will be driven down or at least better managed. Identification and assessment should aim to become predictive to facilitate preventive management.

10.2.3 Does the strategic assessment focus on the right priorities?

Or is it confusing priorities with performance targets? Strategic priorities are sometimes phrased in terms of reducing harm. But reducing harm is an outcome in and of itself, not a strategic priority intended to achieve an outcome. Harm reduction echoes language used by politicians and so inevitably finds its way into the strategic priority idiom. But that still doesn't make it a strategic priority activity that will address identified issues. Indeed, to suggest that 'harm reduction' is a strategic priority creates a 'priority' that encompasses so much possible activity it actually achieves the antithesis of prioritisation and so reduces organizational focus.

Strategic Assessments should include predictive inferences about what is likely to happen founded upon skilled analysis. Which will then influence the management of information and the activity that needs to be put in place. This ensures that strategic assessments and control strategies are as much about prevention and community safety as about enforcement and crime investigation. The strategic assessment must include some consideration of organizational capacity and capability (for instance through a SWOT and/or PESTELO analysis) as well as consideration of the particular harms that the organization has to address. It is not always apparent that forces using NIM to arrive at a control strategy, then always review structure in order to assess its fitness for purpose in achieving the desired outcome. This would ensure that support departments are brought into being intelligence-led. Structural issues should not be static. There is little point in purporting to be working towards a strategic priority if the organization lacks the capacity and capability to achieve the objective. In such circumstances the strategic priority is to address capacity and capability gaps in order to be able to deliver the performance target in due course. Without the necessary resources, intelligence gaps cannot be filled.

10.2.4 Do the control strategy prevention, intelligence, enforcement, and reassurance priorities reflect the strategic assessment priorities?

If an organization identifies an area of significant risk and adopts a suitable strategic priority to reduce that risk then IPE&R requirements should be linked to that strategic priority in the control strategy. In order for the organization to track compliance with the requirement, owners for all aspects should be identified and a timetable for resulting activity should exist with a suitable accountability framework to monitor delivery.

10.2.5 How does an organization know what works and what does not?

The organization should witness changes in the intelligence requirement between each strategic assessment and its review. If there is no change then it is legitimate to ask what has been achieved in the interim. The control strategy priorities may remain the same but there should evidence of achievement and progress between each strategic assessment.

A permanent review process (to which results analysis contributes for example) is required for any intelligence-led organization. Such review can take any or all of four forms:

- Independent formal audit and inspection
- Peer review
- Internal audit and inspection
- Self-reflection by intelligence department staff

Obviously the latter is the weakest of these options. Self-reflection may not recognize all that needs to be recognized or ask questions that someone external to the organization might ask.

10.2.6 Are relevant intelligence gaps understood?

Why do gaps exist? Is it due to organizational capacity and capability or is due to not yet having identified appropriate information sources (which latter could be a consequence of insufficient capacity and capability in source identification and development)? How does the organization propose to fill the gaps identified?

10.2.7 Are realistic collection plans in place to close intelligence gaps?

Do these plans take into account capacity and capability issues? Are support services business plans aligned to ensuring these intelligence gaps can be filled (eg with appropriately trained staff in the right roles)?

10.2.8 Are organizational resources and assets capable of delivering strategic priorities?

Once the priority activity has been determined, there needs to be a mechanism for ensuring compliance throughout the organization. What processes are in place to ascertain that people are doing what it required, processes are facilitating this, and the desired products are being created and intervention activity, using the right tools and techniques, are taking place in order to achieve the overall outcome.

Where it has been identified that strategic priorities need to address organizational capacity and capability before and in order to ensure that intelligence strategic priorities can be achieved, are support services business plans aligned to fill these gaps and is a suitable accountability programme in place to ensure achievement? (A number of organizations have support services with three or five-year business plans focusing on the delivery of support services than upon the delivery of intelligence-led policing. By definition such long-term plans cannot be aligned to a six-monthly strategic assessment cycle and so cannot be intelligence-led.)

Have issues been identified that are beyond the capacity and capability of the organization? Are potential partnerships available that that might help address such issues? How would such partnerships impact upon the control strategy?

10.2.9 Are people accountable and held to account for their contribution to organizational intelligence activity?

What mechanisms does it have for capturing experiential learning? How are successes and failures recorded? What mechanism exists for holding plan owners to account for IPE&R? How are other senior staff held to account for contribution to supporting the plan owners? Is intelligence seen as a numerical performance indicator rather than a quality issue? How is feedback on intelligence given to sources? How do sources know whether information they have supplied is useful or the right sort of information? Have sources been lost to the organization in the previous control strategy period? If so why? (Does the organization know?)

10.2.10 Can the organization identify emerging issues and trends?

Are assets deployed to discover emerging threats? Emerging issues should be identified in the strategic assessment with associated intelligence requirements which when developed will provide decision-makers with sufficient information to determine whether the emerging issue should become a new control strategy priority. Are assets structured in a way that provides sufficient flexibility to respond to an emerging threat whilst being able to deliver against current threats? To what extent does an organization utilize open sources in identifying, assessing, and prioritizing threats/risks of harm?

10.2.11 Is there a fast-time procedure for emerging events that occur outside the tasking meeting framework?

Is the procedure robust and capable of taking into account ongoing activity and resources already committed and so unavailable? How will reprioritization and redeployment be achieved if necessary? At what cost?

10.2.12 How can performance be reviewed for activity for which numerical data may be insufficient?

For example, the number of arrests bears no relationship to the overall success or failure of intelligence management. Of more concern is the ability to measure how long it takes, following a successful prevention or enforcement intervention, for a void in general disorder, street crime, or organized crime to be filled by new offenders. Together with an understanding of how and why the void was filled will better inform future strategies. Successful prosecution of a criminal offender will make little or no significant long-term difference to the crime rate unless investigators have already identified the criminal who will fill the market void.

In the regulatory arena, successful intervention against one individual infringing regulations will be undermined if the misbehaviour identified is not prevented elsewhere and if the original offender is not prevented from evading the regulations in some new way.

10.2.13 How will reflection and review operate in a partnership environment?

To what extent is intelligence reflection and review is possible given the increasing reliance on partnership but taking into account different organizational remits and needs? For instance, how is such reflection undertaken within joint intelligence cells at the neighbourhood policing level or at level 2 in regional police cooperation? Will conformity of reflection be required or can a means be found of accommodating the different individual ways in which different organizations might undertake the reflection?

10.3 Conclusion

This framework is suggested as a basis for debate about how intelligence-led policing and partnership can be made effective and move towards the emerging concept of knowledge-based policing which, howsoever it comes to be defined, would appear to be a recognition that intelligence-led policing, a decade on, could be enhanced and improved by moving beyond its original narrow remit as the crime investigation tool articulated by the HMIC in 1997.

It is possible to give the appearance of being intelligence-led without actually being so. Through products and processes intelligence is a profession that can be relatively easily measured in terms of outputs. But ultimately the intelligence professionals have no control over whether outcomes are achieved. Outcomes depend upon the use to which intelligence is put by decision-makers at strategic, tactical, and operational levels.

Intelligence-led policing is a conceptual expression firmly associated with the public police service and conceived, at least by some of its early advocates, as the driving force for criminal investigation within the overall responsibilities of the public police service. Its potential is wider than that and the NIM was presented as a business process that served all policing functions, not just criminal investigation.

But with the notions of the extended policing family and the fact that a wide variety of organizations, agencies, and departments in both the public and private sectors can contribute to community safety through prevention, regulation, governance, investigation, enforcement and reassurance, 'intelligence-led policing' may have become less useful: an expression with specific lexical significance that constrains creative thinking about possible solutions and excludes potential partners. Dean and Gottschalk's continuum of knowledge management architecture is a useful visualization of the difference between intelligence and the wider concept of knowledge (2007: 5–6). Knowledge implies an extension beyond intelligence to inform the making of specific decisions. Knowledge, to which external partners contribute as much if not more than the internal intelligence professionals, is the context within which intelligence can be utilised. In so doing intelligence-led policing by the public police service to prosecute and reduce crime becomes knowledge-based policing engaged in by whichever partners are appropriate for the purpose, in order to achieve community safety through the reduction of harm.

In highlighting the connections between intelligence, investigation, the community and partnership, this book has sought to demonstrate the breadth of understanding needed for an holistic approach to intelligence management amongst all levels and roles within an organization, in an arena in which different practitioners assign different values and meaning to the label 'intelligence', and in which the label 'police' attached to certain public sector organizations, tends to invite the erroneous conclusion that the police service can deliver all policing activity and that all policing activity should involve the police service. In doing so this book may well have left readers with more questions than answers: welcome to the world of intelligence.

Appendix 1
NIM Code of Practice

Made by the Secretary of State for the Home Department under sections 39 and 39A of the Police Act 1996 and sections 28, 28A, 73 and 73A of the Police Act 1997.

Prepared by: National Centre for Policing Excellence, January 2005

Contents

1 Introduction

1.1 Purpose of the Code

1.1.1 The purpose of this code is:

1.1.1.1 to set out to chief officers of police the basic principles and minimum common standards for the National Intelligence Model

1.1.1.2 to promote compatibility of procedures and of terminology for the National Intelligence Model

1.1.1.3 to clarify the responsibilities of chief officers and of police authorities in relation to the application of the National Intelligence Model

1.1.1.4 to ensure that observance of these principles, and the standards for implementation, results in a systematic programme of continuous development of police policy, practice and capability

1.1.1.5 to identify and promulgate good practice.

1.2 Statutory Basis of the Code

1.2.1 This code of practice comes into effect on 12 January 2005.

1.2.2 This code of practice is made under:

1.2.2.1 section 39 of the Police Act 1996, which permits the Secretary of State to issue codes of practice relating to the discharge by police authorities of any of their functions;

1.2.2.2 section 39A of the same Act, as inserted by section 2 of the Police Reform Act 2002, which permits the Secretary of State to issue codes of practice relating to the discharge of their functions by chief officers for the purpose of promoting the efficiency and effectiveness of police forces in England and Wales;

1.2.2.3 sections 28 and 73 of the Police Act 1997, which permits the Secretary of State to issue codes of practice relating to the discharge by the National Criminal Intelligence Service and the National Crime Squad Service Authorities of any of their functions; and

1.2.2.4 sections 28A and 73A of the Police Act 1997, as inserted by Schedule 1 of the Police Reform Act 2002, which permits the Secretary of State to issue codes of practice relating to the discharge by the Director General of the National Criminal Intelligence Service and the Director General of the National Crime Squad of any of their functions.

1.2.3 It applies directly to the police forces maintained for the police areas of England and Wales defined in section 1 of the Police Act 1996 (or as defined in any subsequent legislation) and to the National Crime Squad and the National Criminal Intelligence Service.

1.2.4 The code of practice is issued by the Secretary of State in relation to the discharge of the functions of chief officers of police. A chief officer of police shall have regard to this code, as will the members of the police force for whom the chief officer of police is responsible.

1.2.5 In the case of the National Crime Squad and the National Criminal Intelligence Service, references in this code to chief officers of police apply to the Directors General of those organisations, and references to forces shall include the National Crime Squad and the National Criminal Intelligence Service.

1.2.6 Should the definition of police forces under section 1 of the Police Act 1996 change, and should there be changes to the present constitution of the National Crime Squad or the National Criminal Intelligence Service, the Secretary of State may revise this code to ensure the application of the code to the chief officers of those forces.

1.2.7 It is available for adoption by other police forces in England and Wales, and by other jurisdictions within the United Kingdom.

1.3 Diversity Issues Under this Code

1.3.1 In the application of the National Intelligence Model issues relevant to all areas of diversity and culture, such as race, religion, gender, disability, sexual orientation, gender identity and age, will be taken into account. This principle applies to equipment and personnel selection procedures and in the application of the business model.

1.4 Procedures Covered by this Code

1.4.1 This code applies to intelligence and information used to direct police activity through a planned and systematic business process.

1.4.2 Guidance on the use of covert human intelligence sources and dedicated source units is set out in the ACPO Manual of Standards for the Use of Covert Human Intelligence Sources and is not otherwise dealt with in this code.

1.5 Confidentiality

1.5.1 In laying this code of practice before Parliament, the Secretary of State declares that nothing in this code is of a confidential nature.

2 Scope and Status of this Code

2.1 Legal Considerations

2.1.1 This code applies within the framework of the domestic law of England and Wales and has been written in accordance with the principles of the Human Rights Act 1998, which incorporates the European Convention on Human Rights.

2.1.2 Statutes of direct relevance to the code include:

2.1.2.1 Police and Criminal Evidence Act 1984

2.1.2.2 Criminal Procedure Investigative Act 1996

2.1.2.3 Police Act 1997

2.1.2.4 Crime and Disorder Act 1998

2.1.2.5 Data Protection Act 1998

2.1.2.6 Regulation of Investigatory Powers Act 2000

2.1.2.7 Terrorism Act 2000

2.1.2.8 Anti-Terrorism Crime and Security Act 2001

2.1.2.9 Police Reform Act 2002

2.1.3 Nothing in this code alters the existing legal powers or responsibilities of any chief officer of police, or any other police officer.

2.2 Relationship of the Code to Other Guidance

2.2.1 The National Intelligence Model Minimum Standards document of April 2003 (and any successor document) sets out the criteria by which the model should be applied. Chief officers will ensure that the arrangements for applying the model within their force comply with that document (and with any successor document as directed by the Association of Chief Police Officers).

2.2.2 Chief officers of police will make arrangements under this code for the authorisation, registration, deployment and usage of covert human intelligence sources, taking account of relevant legislation and the operational guidance set out in the ACPO Manual of Standards for the Use of Covert Human Intelligence Sources.

2.2.3 The Code of Practice on Management of Police Information (once published) as recommended by the Bichard Inquiry and associated guidance, including the ACPO Manual of Standards on the Recording and Dissemination of Intelligence Material, set out national standards for the management of police information, including intelligence material, its physical security and security of sensitive material. They are the authority on all questions of integrity of intelligence material and must be included as part of the operating protocols of the National Intelligence Model.

2.2.4 Other manuals of guidance that are of relevance to the application of the National Intelligence Model are:

2.2.4.1 ACPO Manual of Standards for the Deployment of Undercover Officers

2.2.4.2 ACPO Manual of Standards for the Deployment of Test Purchase and Decoy Officers

2.2.4.3 ACPO Manual of Standards on Surveillance

2.2.4.4 ACPO Manual of Professional Standards in Policing

2.2.4.5 ACPO Kidnap Manual of Guidance

2.2.4.6 The Murder Investigation Manual

2.2.5 The Home Office has also issued Codes of Practice that should be taken into account along with the above Manuals. Those codes are for:

2.2.5.1 Covert Surveillance

2.2.5.2 Interception of Communications

2.2.5.3 Covert Human Intelligence Sources

2.2.6 The National Intelligence Model will impact on force policies and it will be necessary for forces to review their policies to ensure standardisation and compatibility. In particular chief officers will ensure that there is a corporate approach to the timing, content and circulation of National Intelligence

Model products and that there are established and consistent links between those products and the force planning cycle.

2.2.7 The code is not a policy document for forces or intended to prevent or constrain forces from developing new operational tactics.

2.3 Role of HM Inspectorate of Constabulary

2.3.1 HM Inspectorate of Constabulary will inspect police forces in England and Wales to ensure compliance with this code and with the Minimum Standards document of April 2003 (and any successor document).

2.4 Role of Police Authorities

2.4.1 Police Authorities should ensure that police forces are adequately resourced to deliver the National Intelligence Model.

2.5 Role of National Centre for Policing Excellence

2.5.1 The National Centre for Policing Excellence, or any successor body designated by the Secretary of State, has responsibility on behalf of the police forces of England and Wales for the management and development of the intelligence doctrine and, in that respect, will have responsibility in collaboration with the Association of Chief Police Officers (ACPO) and the National Criminal Intelligence Service for the continuing development of the National Intelligence Model.

3 Basic Requirements of this Code

3.1 A National Model for Policing

3.1.1 The National Intelligence Model is a business process. The intention behind it is to provide focus to operational policing and to achieve a disproportionately greater impact from the resources applied to any problem. It is dependent on a clear framework of analysis of information and intelligence allowing a problem solving approach to law enforcement and crime prevention techniques. The expected outcomes are improved community safety, reduced crime and the control of criminality and disorder leading to greater public reassurance and confidence.

3.1.2 At the heart of the business process is the Strategic and Tactical Tasking and Co-ordination Group Meetings. The process is conducted at three levels to correspond with the specified levels of incidents: Level 1 represents local crime capable of being managed by local resources (which may include the most serious crime) and anti-social behaviour; Level 2 represents force, inter-force and regional criminal activity usually requiring additional resources; and Level 3 represents the most serious and organised crime. The purpose of the Strategic Tasking and Co-ordination Group Meetings is to agree a control strategy which establishes the intelligence requirement and sets the agenda for intelligence, prevention and enforcement priorities. The purpose of the Tactical Tasking and Co-ordination Group Meetings is to apply a planned response to the control strategy.

3.1.3 The National Intelligence Model is not confined to or restricted for specialist usage. It is relevant to all areas of law enforcement: crime and its investigation, disorder and community safety. Overall, it is a model for operational policing.

3.1.4 As such, effective application of the National Intelligence Model should enable police forces to trace the continuum between anti-social behaviour and the most serious crime and then to identify those local issues in most urgent need of attention. The model is compatible with other operational policing methodologies, in particular those which focus on problem solving by using analytical techniques.

3.1.5 The National Intelligence Model is a tool that Crime and Disorder Reduction Partnerships should use to develop and deliver the strategic priorities in their three year crime and disorder and misuse of drugs strategies. The National Intelligence Model should also be used to inform the strategic priorities of Drug Action Teams.

3.2 Ownership

3.2.1 For the purpose of maintaining standards within each force chief officers will ensure that an officer of at least the rank of assistant chief constable, or equivalent, is appointed to take the lead within the force in relation to policy and practice for the National Intelligence Model.

3.2.2 Chief officers of police will ensure that an appropriate officer of ACPO rank will chair Strategic and Tactical Tasking and Co-ordinating Group (TCG) Meetings held at force level, and that there is appropriate ACPO level representation at Strategic and Tactical TCG meetings held on a regional basis.

3.2.3 At BCU level the responsibility for delivery of the National Intelligence Model will rest with the local BCU commander. The exercise of that responsibility should include the chairing of the BCU Strategic TCG meeting and overseeing of the Tactical TCG meetings. Chief officers will ensure consistency of operation of the National Intelligence Model within the BCUs for which they are responsible.

3.3 Assets

3.3.1 Assets are those resources available to forces that underpin the business process of the National Intelligence Model. There are four key asset areas.

    3.3.1.1 Knowledge Assets: the professional knowledge, procedural documents, policies, databases and codes of practice held by forces and by partner agencies that enable the delivery of core business within those organisations.

    3.3.1.2 Systems Assets: those products that provide for the secure collection, recording, reception, storage, linkage, analysis and use of information,

    3.3.1.3 Source Assets: information from a wide variety of sources relevant to policing, from community intelligence at neighbourhood level to intelligence on serious and organised crime and terrorism at a national and international level.

    3.3.1.4 People Assets: the specific functions and posts required to enable the National Intelligence Model to function. Detailed descriptions of the above assets are set out in the National Intelligence Model Minimum Standards document of April 2003 (and any successor document) and chief officers will ensure that their force arrangements comply with that document (and with any successor document as directed by the Association of Chief Police Officers).

3.4 Briefing

3.4.1 Chief officers will ensure that an appropriately resilient briefing model based on the principles of the National Briefing Model is in place throughout their force to ensure the communication of intelligence that informs and directs operational policing activity at both levels 1 and 2.

3.5 Information Technology

3.5.1 A standardised, consistent and secure electronic information management system is essential to the success of the National Intelligence Model. To meet their responsibilities for delivering the National Intelligence Model chief officers and police authorities will be required to adopt a national IT system to support police intelligence in line with recommendations from the Bichard Inquiry.

3.5.2 Chief officers should ensure that geographic crime and incident mapping technology is used to aid decision making, problem solving, communication and performance management within the National Intelligence Model business process.

3.6 Consistency and Compatibility

3.6.1 In order for the National Intelligence Model to function effectively at all levels, chief officers must ensure that there is consistency and compatibility of records and data sets. Forces will have in place the National Crime Recording Standard, and a standardised intelligence recording system as recommended by the Association of Chief Police Officers.

3.6.2 To enable the efficient transfer of information forces will ensure that secure data transference capabilities are established with other forces and partner agencies and that the appropriate data sharing protocols are in operation in accordance with the provisions of the Data Protection Act 1998.

3.7 Security

3.7.1 The integrity of the National Intelligence Model requires adequate standards of physical, environmental, technical and personnel security. The Government Protective Marking Scheme (GPMS) sets out common standards for the protection of sensitive documents and other material. Its principles also extend to data held on computer and electronic recording systems. The ACPO Manual of Standards for the Recording and Dissemination of Intelligence Material sets out the GPMS in detail and gives guidance on the key features of a secure intelligence environment.

3.7.2 The management of security issues in Information Technology is complex and usually requires specialist advice at design, installation and implementation stages. The Government has published a Manual of Protective Security as a guide to this subject.

3.7.3 Chief officers will ensure that appropriate security procedures are maintained for the National Intelligence Model.

221

3.8 Data Protection

3.8.1 Chief officers are responsible for the development and implementation of appropriate procedures and systems to ensure that personal information on individuals is held in accordance with the requirements of the Data Protection Act 1998, and any other relevant legislation. The management of information must be in accordance with the Code of Practice on Management of Police Information (once published) as recommended by the Bichard Inquiry. This could include the retention of the information for purposes other than that for which it was collected where retention of that information could be shown to be necessary for policing purposes or is in the wider public interest.

3.9 Health and Safety

3.9.1 Chief officers of police should ensure that, in applying the National Intelligence Model within their force, the identification and assessment of any health and safety risks has been conducted and that suitable preventative or remedial action has been taken.

4 Tasking and Co-ordinating Groups

4.1 Strategic Tasking and Co-ordinating Group (TCG)

4.1.1 The purpose of a Strategic Tasking and Co-ordinating Group operating at Levels 1, 2 or 3 is to consider the Strategic Assessment in order to set a control strategy and establish an intelligence requirement for the level at which it is operating. The control strategy is a document that sets the agenda for intelligence, prevention and enforcement priorities. As well as setting the control strategy for that level the Strategic TCG will ensure it contains relevant links to other levels.

4.1.2 Chief officers will ensure that appropriate procedures, compliant with the National Intelligence Model Minimum Standards document of April 2003 (and with any successor document as directed by the Association of Chief Police Officers), are in place for the effective operation of a Strategic TCG. The Strategic TCG will meet to set the control strategy and, thereafter, every six months to review and monitor progress, to adjust the control strategy and to maintain links with other levels of activity. In addition, chief officers will have regard to the protocols of the Regional TCG meetings.

4.2 Tactical Tasking and Co-ordinating Group (TCG)

4.2.1 The purpose of the Tactical Tasking and Co-ordinating Group is to implement the control strategy through a menu of tactical options and to manage any subsequent priorities that may arise. The Tactical TCG has three main roles:

4.2.1.1 to apply the tactical menu to the control strategy;

4.2.1.2 to respond to new problems; and

4.2.1.3 to monitor plans agreed from earlier TCG meetings.

4.2.2 The principal document that informs the Tactical Tasking and Co-ordinating Group is the Tactical Assessment.

4.2.3 The Tactical TCG will meet as frequently as is necessary in accordance with force policy.

4.2.4 Chief officers will ensure that appropriate procedures, compliant with the National Intelligence Model Minimum Standards document of April 2003 (and with any successor document as directed by the Association of Chief Police Officers), are in place for the effective operation of a Tactical TCG and for the management and auditing of tasks and operational activity emanating from the Tasking and Co-ordinating process.

4.3 Reviews

4.3.1 Reviews of the National Intelligence Model business process, in particular intelligence analysis and the use of standardised products and operational plans, are essential if the model is to operate efficiently and effectively. Chief officers will ensure such reviews are conducted on a regular basis.

4.3.2 Further reviews of operations should be conducted to inform future resource deployments and tactics employed.

5 Intelligence Products

5.1 Strategic Assessments

5.1.1 Strategic Assessments must be produced on a biannual basis and should be reviewed every three months to ensure they are current. Chief officers will ensure that they are developed against the national minimum standard template to ensure standardisation of procedures and products between forces in order to enable the setting of regional, force and local priorities.

5.1.2 The aim of the Strategic Assessment is to identify the medium to long term issues that are apparent or emerging and to determine resource, funding and communication requirements. In that respect force strategic assessments should be considered in the business planning process and available for consultation between chief officers and police authorities. A further aim is to ensure there are links covering Level 1, 2 and 3 criminal activities between local, regional and national agencies.

5.1.3 While BCUs and forces will produce strategic assessments covering Level I and Level 2 issues, and in certain police areas the production of a Level 3 strategic assessment, the UK Level 3 threat assessment shall be the responsibility of the National Criminal Intelligence Service.

5.2 Tactical Assessments

5.2.1 Chief officers will ensure that Tactical Assessments are produced to inform Tactical Tasking and Co-ordinating Group meetings, specifically with regard to decision making and the allocation of resources.

5.2.2 The aim of the Tactical Assessment is to identify the short-term issues which require attention and to monitor progress on current business in line with the control strategy. The areas the Tactical Assessment will cover will include appropriate interventions for intelligence gathering, enforcement and prevention activities; the identification of emerging patterns of crime and incidents; and a performance assessment.

5.3 Target Profiles

5.3.1 A target profile is a detailed analysis of an individual or network and should contain sufficient detail to enable a targeted operation or intervention against that person or network. It will also recommend operational intelligence requirements in order to secure the information required to implement a tactical response.

5.4 Problem Profiles

5.4.1 The purpose of a problem profile is to provide an assessment of a specific problem or series of problems which may be criminal, which may pose a threat to public safety or may be anti-social in context. The profile will include an analysis of the problem with recommendations for intelligence gathering, enforcement or prevention. Problem profiles are ideally suited for existing problem-oriented policing methodologies.

5.5 Proportionality

5.5.1 Chief officers will ensure that where these intelligence products impinge on an individual that the actions comply with the requirements of the Human Rights Act 1998, the Articles contained therein, and that the actions of the police force comply with the principle of 'proportionality'.

6 Training: Standards and Accreditation

6.1 Selection, Training and Maintaining Competence

6.1.1 Staff roles within the National Intelligence Model will have competencies required by the post profiled by the Integrated Competency Framework underpinned by National Occupational Standards. The Skills for Justice Organisation will determine those requirements. Chief officers of police will ensure that personnel in those posts are trained to those standards. There should be an annual assessment of personnel against the standards.

6.1.2 Where applicable, those attaining the required standards of competence will be entered on the relevant professional register as determined by the Skills for Justice Organisation. They will remain on the register in accordance with any provisions for re-assessment and re-qualification which may be required under the conditions set down for registration.

6.2 Independent Accreditation of Training

6.2.1 The body responsible for the approval and accreditation of training courses and of trainers for these purposes will be the Police Licensing and Accreditation Board or any successor body designated by the Secretary of State.

6.2.2 The National Centre for Policing Excellence, or any successor body designated by the Secretary of State, will accredit all training courses for intelligence analysts to a common recognised standard.

7 Monitoring, Evaluation and Promulgation of Good Practice

7.1 Monitoring and Evaluation

7.1.1 Chief officers will ensure that there are procedures in place throughout their force to monitor compliance with this code of practice and the National

Intelligence Model Minimum Standards document of April 2003 (and with any successor document as directed by the Association of Chief Police offi cers). Her Majesty's Inspector of Constabulary will inspect and report on those procedures.

7.1.2 For that purpose chief officers will ensure that regular reviews of the National Intelligence Model take place within their force, together with an evaluation of its effectiveness and efficiency.

7.2 Promulgation of Good Practice

7.2.1 Notwithstanding that this code and the Minimum Standards are specific, part of the purpose of the code is to encourage continuous development of police practices relating to the National Intelligence Model and to ensure that such developments are made available throughout the police service. Where there is a reason to believe that improvements have been identified in procedures these should be reported to the National Centre for Policing Excellence, or any successor body designated by the Secretary of State.

7.2.2 It will be the responsibility of the National Centre for Policing Excellence to ensure that any necessary action is taken as soon as practicable on such reports passed to them.

7.2.3 While recognising that police forces will seek to improve the operation of the National Intelligence Model, in order to secure a corporate approach chief officers will ensure that any departures from established practice are only implemented, subject to the agreement of the National Centre for Policing Excellence (or any successor body), and where it can be shown that the change is an innovation that has resulted in an improvement to the operation of the model.

7.2.4 It will be the responsibility of the Association of Chief Police Officers and the National Centre for Policing Excellence to ensure that any such changes are not a diversion from the overall aim of achieving national corporacy in the application of the National Intelligence Model.

8 Communication and Information Strategy

8.1 Communication and Information Strategy

8.1.1 The Association of Chief Police Officers and the National Centre for Policing Excellence should have in place a procedure by which police forces, other law enforcement agencies and relevant partner agencies may be informed of changes and developments to the National Intelligence Model.

8.1.2 Chief officers will have in place a communication and information strategy to support the National Intelligence Model. The purpose of such a strategy is to ensure that all members of a police force, practitioners and specialists, and other agencies with whom there is a partnership agreement are informed of relevant developments in the application of the National Intelligence Model.

8.1.3 The strategy should also be applied to assist forces to bring the National Intelligence Model into the mainstream of police activity in seeking to enforce the law and to protect the public.

Appendix 2
Code of Practice on the Management of Police Information

Made by the Secretary of State for the Home Department under sections 39 and 39A of the Police Act 1996 and sections 28, 28A, 73 and 73A of the Police Act 1997.

Prepared by: National Centre for Policing Excellence, July 2005

Contents

1. Introduction

1.1 Purpose of the Code

1.1.1 Police forces have a duty to obtain and use a wide variety of information (including personal information), in order to discharge their responsibilities effectively. They need the support and cooperation of the public in doing so. The purpose of this Code and associated guidance is to assist the police to carry out that duty.

1.1.2 The responsibility for the management and use of information within the police service rests with the chief officer of the police force which owns the information.

1.1.3 Chief officers of police must therefore ensure that their forces adopt practices for the management of information that ensure such information is used effectively for police purposes and in compliance with the law.

1.1.4 The purpose of this Code is to ensure that there is broad consistency between forces in the way information is managed within the law, to ensure effective use of available information within and between individual police forces and other agencies, and to provide fair treatment to members of the public.

1.1.5 This Code sets out the principles governing the management of information (including personal information) which the police service may need to manage and use including:—

(a) procedures to be applied in obtaining and recording that information;

(b) procedures to ensure the accuracy of information managed by the police;

(c) procedures for reviewing the need to retain information and, where it is no longer needed, to destroy it;

(d) procedures governing authorised sharing of information within the police service and with other agencies; and

(e) measures to maintain consistent procedures for the management of information within all police forces so as to facilitate information sharing and the development of service-wide technological support for information management.

1.1.6 In doing so, it recognises that effective use of information for police purposes requires consistent procedures to be in place throughout the police service.

1.1.7 The procedures and equipment to give effect to the principles set out in this Code may change. This Code will therefore be supported by more detailed and extensive guidance that will define information management standards required within forces. That guidance may change from time to time, but must be framed in compliance with the principles established by this Code.

1.2 Statutory Basis of the Code

1.2.1 This Code of Practice comes into effect on 14 November 2005.

1.2.2 Nothing in this Code alters the existing legal powers or responsibilities of any police authority, chief officer of police, or other person.

1.2.3 This Code of Practice is made under:
- (a) section 39 of the Police Act 1996, which permits the Secretary of State to issue codes of practice relating to the discharge by police authorities of any of their functions;
- (b) section 39A of the same Act, which permits the Secretary of State to issue codes of practice relating to the discharge of their functions by chief officers where it is necessary to do so for the purpose of promoting the efficiency and effectiveness of police forces in England and Wales;
- (c) section 28 of the Police Act 1997, which permits the Secretary of State to issue codes of practice relating to the discharge by the National Criminal Intelligence Service (NCIS) Service Authority of any of its functions;
- (d) section 73 of the Police Act 1997, which permits the Secretary of State to issue codes of practice relating to the discharge by the National Crime Squad (NCS) Service Authority of any of its functions;
- (e) section 28A of the Police Act 1997, which permits the Secretary of State to issue codes of practice relating to the discharge by the Director General of the NCIS of any of his functions; and
- (f) section 73A of the Police Act 1997, which permits the Secretary of State to issue codes of practice relating to the discharge by the Director General of the NCS of any of his functions.

1.2.4 This Code recognises that there is an existing legal framework for the management of information in legislation relating to data protection, human rights and freedom of information.

1.2.5 It applies directly to the police forces maintained for the police areas of England and Wales defined in section 1 of the Police Act 1996, and to the NCS and the NCIS.

1.2.6 It is available for adoption by other agencies including other police forces not covered by section 1 of the 1996 Act and law enforcement agencies within the United Kingdom that exchange information with the police service in England and Wales.

1.2.7 References in this Code to chi ef officers of police apply, in the case of NCS and NCIS, to the Directors General of those organisations.

1.3 Role of HM Inspectors of Constabulary

1.3.1 HM Inspectors of Constabulary will monitor police forces' compliance with this Code, associated guidance, and standards.

1.4 Role of the Central Police Training and Development Authority

1.4.1 The Central Police Training and Development Authority (CPTDA), or any successor body designated by the Secretary of State, has responsibility on behalf of the police forces of England and Wales for the development of guidance under this Code. Such guidance and any subsequent amendments will be prepared in consultation with the Association of Chief Police Officers, the Association of Police Authorities, and such other persons as the CPTDA thinks fit.

1.5 Consultation

1.5.1 Consultation has been carried out by the CTDPA in accordance with the statutory provisions.

National Centre for Policing Excellence 6 Code of Practice: Management of police information

2. The Management of Information for Police Purposes

2.1 The Management of Police Information

2.1.1 In this Code, references to the management of police information include the processes of obtaining, recording, storing, reviewing, deleting and sharing information, including personal information, for police purposes in accordance with principles governing those processes set out at 4 below.

2.2 Information for Police Purposes

2.2.1 In this Code references to information include data. All information, including intelligence and personal data obtained and recorded for police purposes, is referred to as police information.

2.2.2 For the purposes of this Code, police purposes are:—

(a) protecting life and property,
(b) preserving order,
(c) preventing the commission of offences,
(d) bringing offenders to justice, and
(e) any duty or responsibility of the police arising from common or statute law.

3. A National Framework for the Management of Police Information

3.1 National Guidance on Management of Police Information

3.1.1 Guidance under this Code will:—

(a) set out the strategic information needs of the police service in line with the National Intelligence Model ;
(b) direct the management of police information within police forces so as to ensure consistent procedures throughout the police service for obtaining, recording, storing, reviewing, deleting and sharing information; and
(c) identify the minimum standards required within police forces to provide a standard basis for common police IT systems for the management of police information.

3.2 An Information Management Strategy to be Applied within Each Police Force

3.2.1 Chief officers will establish and maintain within their forces an Information Management Strategy, under the direction of an officer of ACPO rank or equivalent, complying with guidance and standards to be issued under this Code unless that guidance is superseded by regulations made by the Secretary of State under section 53A of the Police Act 1996.

3.3 National System Requirements for the Management of Police Information

3.3.1 For the purpose of achieving throughout the police service the standards described at 3.1.1 above, guidance issued under this Code, unless superseded by regulations made by the Secretary of State under section 53A of the Police Act 1996, may specify procedures to be adopted within police forces for the management of police information systems.

3.4 Security of Police Information

3.4.1 Chief officers should ensure that arrangements within their forces for managing police information include procedures and technical measures to prevent unauthorised or accidental access to, amendment of, or loss of police information. Such procedures should comply with guidance issued under this Code unless superseded by regulations made by the Secretary of State under section 53 or section 53A of the Police Act 1996.

3.5 Training for Staff Engaged in Police Information Management

3.5.1 Guidance issued under this Code may identify key posts for the management of police information, and may specify the qualifications to be held by staff in those posts, and the training required for such staff.

3.5.2 Chief officers of police should arrange the selection and training of those to be appointed to such posts so as to ensure attainment of standards of competence.

3.5.3 Those attaining the required standards of competence for such posts will be entered on the relevant professional register. They will remain on the register provided their continued suitability and competence remain assured in accordance with provisions for re-assessment and re-qualification.

3.5.4 Training for these purposes is not only to ensure compliance with the legal framework for information management and the maintenance of high standards of competence, but also to ensure the consistency of police information management procedures throughout the police service.

3.5.5 The body responsible for the approval and accreditation of training courses and trainers for these purposes or any successor body will be designated by the Secretary of State. Training standards will be kept under review by the accreditation authority.

4. Key Principles Governing the Management of Police Information

4.1 Duty to Obtain and Manage Information

4.1.1 Chief officers have a duty to obtain and manage information needed for the police purposes described at 2.2 above.

4.1.2 Chief officers must ensure that arrangements within their forces for the management of police information comply with the principles set out in the following paragraphs, and with guidance issued under this Code to give effect to those principles.

4.2 Requirement for Police Information

4.2.1 Chief officers must ensure that arrangements to gather police information comply with the principles of the National Intelligence Model.

4.3 Grading and Recording of Police Information

4.3.1 Information should be recorded where it is considered that it is necessary for a police purpose. Chief Officers must establish recording procedures in accordance with guidance issued under this Code.

4.3.2 Where appropriate and in accordance with guidance to be issued under this Code, the source of the information, the nature of the source, any assessment of the reliability of the source, and any necessary restrictions on the use to be made of the information should be recorded to permit later review, reassessment and audit.

4.3.3 Information should be assessed for reliability in accordance with guidance to be issued under this Code.

4.3.4 The format in which the information is recorded should comply with standards agreed and applied across the police service by means of guidance issued under this Code, to facilitate exchange of information and processing within standard police IT systems.

4.4 Ownership of Police Information

4.4.1 Chief officers of police are responsible for information originally recorded for police purposes by their forces. They or their successors in the force retain responsibility for subsequent reviews and decisions to retain or delete that information. The related responsibilities of those who may share that information are set out at 4.10 below.

4.5 Review of Police Information

4.5.1 Information originally recorded for police purposes must be reviewed at intervals to be prescribed in guidance under this Code, which may prescribe different intervals for different categories of information.

4.5.2 At each review, the likelihood that the information will be used for police purposes should be taken into account. Chief officers should ensure that this process is audited.

4.6 Retention and Deletion of Police Information

4.6.1 On each occasion when it is reviewed, information originally recorded for police purposes should be considered for retention or deletion in accordance with criteria set out in guidance under this code.

4.6.2 Guidance will acknowledge that there are certain public protection matters which are of such importance that information should only be deleted if:

(a) the information has been shown to be inaccurate, in ways which cannot be dealt with by amending the record; or

(b) it is no longer considered that the information is necessary for police purposes.

4.7 Sharing of Police Information within the UK Police Service

4.7.1 Guidance under this Code may specify a protocol for sharing information.

4.7.2 Subject to any constraints arising from guidance based on section 4.9 below, the content and the assessment of the reliability of information recorded for police purposes should be made available to any other police force in England and Wales which requires the information for police purposes.

4.7.3 Subject to any constraints arising from guidance based on section 4.9 below, the same degree of access to information recorded for police purposes by police forces in England and Wales should be afforded to other police forces in the United Kingdom provided that the chief officer responsible for the record is satisfied that the police force seeking access to the information applies the principles set out in this Code.

4.7.4 Chief officers may arrange for the sharing of information with other police forces in the UK, in accordance with the two preceding paragraphs, to be carried out either

(a) by response to bilateral or multilateral requests for information to police forces, or

(b) by holding such information on IT systems to which police forces referred to above may be given direct access.

4.8 Sharing of Police Information Outside the UK Police Service

4.8.1 Chief officers of police will continue to comply with any statutory obligations to share information with bodies other than police forces in England and Wales.

4.8.2 In addition, chief officers may arrange for other persons or bodies within the UK or overseas to receive police information where the chief officer is satisfied that it is reasonable and lawful to do so for the purposes set out at 2.2 above. In deciding what is reasonable, chief officers must have regard to any guidance issued under this Code.

4.8.3 The procedures for making such information available, and the extent to which it is made available, must comply with guidance to be made under this code, and with any protocol (whether at national or local level) which may be agreed with persons or bodies needing to receive such information.

4.8.4 In circumstances not covered by any such protocol, a chief officer may give access to police information in response to a request from any person or body to the extent that the chief officer believes this request to be lawful and reasonable for the purposes set out at 2.2 above, and in compliance with guidance issued under this Code.

4.9 Protection of Sensitive Police Information and Sources

4.9.1 Guidance under this Code may provide for special procedures to be applied to a request for access to information recorded for police purposes, in any case where it is necessary to protect the source of sensitive information or the procedures used to obtain it.

4.10 Obligations of those Receiving Police Information

4.10.1 In making national or local agreements and protocols for the sharing of police information with persons or bodies other than police forces, or in responding to individual requests for information outside such agreements or protocols, chief officers should require those to whom information is made available to comply with the following obligations:—

(a) Police information made available in response to such a request should be used only for the purpose for which the request was made.

(b) If other information available, at the time or later, to the person or body requesting police information tends to suggest that police information is inaccurate or incomplete, they should at the earliest possible moment inform the chief officer concerned of such inaccuracy or incompleteness, either directly or by reporting the details to the managers of the central police system through which the information was provided.

4.10.2 The chief officer responsible for the police information concerned should then consider, and if necessary record, any additions or changes to the recorded police information.

Appendix 3
A 'Model' Code of Practice for the Recording and Dissemination of Intelligence Material

This Code of Practice was published and adopted in 2005 as a joint venture between ACPO, HMCE and ACPOS. It pre-dates the merging of the NCS, NCIS and parts of HMCE into the SOCA. To the extent that it makes reference to the NCS, NCIS and HMCE, this Code is now out of date. The principles espoused, however, remain valid and pertinent so it is reproduced as a model for information and guidance for those organizations without similar policy guidance. At time of writing (2007) a number of police forces have published their own policies in respect of the recording and dissemination of intelligence material and work is being undertaken nationally in relation to guidance on the recording and evaluation of police information.

Contents

1.1 This code of practice must be readily available at all operational police premises and offices of the National Crime Squad, the Scottish Crime Squad, the National Criminal Intelligence Service (NCIS) and HM Customs and Excise, for consultation and reference by police officers, customs officers, civilian employees of a police authority, persons detained in police or HM Customs and Excise custody and their representatives. Copies should be available for consultation by members of the public at all police stations and public offices of HM Customs and Excise.

1.2 Notes for guidance printed in this code are not part of the code unless indicated but are designed to assist police officers and others in its application.

1.3 This code applies to the recording and dissemination of intelligence material within and from the United Kingdom by the police, the National Crime Squad, the Scottish Crime Squad, the National Criminal Intelligence Service and HM Customs and Excise.

1.4 The code regulates procedures for the recording and dissemination of personal information for use in or derived from intelligence systems.

1.5 This code does not relate to:
- the disclosure between agencies of personal information, when it is conducted on a statutory basis, notwithstanding that the relevant disclosure may be effected confidentially (see *Note 1A*); or
- the disclosure of evidential material to foreign law enforcement agencies which takes place through mutual legal assistance channels, such as by way of *commissions rogatoire*.

1.6 The law enforcement agencies, in the prevention or detection of crime, have a duty to seek out, record and disseminate intelligence material relating to offenders and suspected offenders. By its nature most of this activity cannot be conducted openly if it is to be effective. Sections 28 and 29 of the Data Protection Act 1998 provide that there is no requirement for openness where openness would be likely to prejudice any of the following:
- the interests of national security;
- the prevention or detection of crime;
The Recording and Dissemination of Intelligence Material
- the apprehension or prosecution of offenders;
- the assessment or collection of any tax or duty or of any imposition of a similar nature.

1.7 Notwithstanding that the requirement for openness may be set aside in appropriate circumstances, the law enforcement agencies must have a legitimate basis for processing data and observe the data protection principles regarding data quality and security in their handling of intelligence material. In particular:
- information from intelligence sources will be subject to evaluation of reliability and worth before being recorded in intelligence systems;
- where it is necessary to keep the identity of the source of the intelligence confidential, a record will be separately maintained of that source's identity;
- intelligence material will be retained only for so long as it remains relevant;
- before intelligence material is disseminated, the risks to the data subject or source attaching to use of the intelligence, or to the likely result from the disclosure of the intelligence, will be assessed. Public interest immunity in respect of intelligence material will only be sought after such an assessment;
- access to intelligence systems will be restricted to authorised personnel;
- persons permitted access to intelligence material will only access and use it in connection with their official business.

Interpretation

1.8 For the purpose of this code:

    1.8.1 **Intelligence material** includes:

personal information of value to national security, the prevention or detection of crime or disorder, the maintenance of community safety and the assessment or collection of any tax or duty or of any imposition of a similar nature, other than that required to be held for legal or administrative purposes, which has been assessed for accuracy and relevance, or similar non-personal information which has been assessed for accuracy and relevance and in respect of which it is necessary to protect the identity of the source.

    1.8.2 **Standard grounds** means:

the grounds on which individual officers of the police, the National Crime Squad, the Scottish Crime Squad, NCIS and HM Customs and Excise may record and disseminate intelligence material without the necessity to seek higher level prior authorisation, except where provided for below at paragraphs 3.8, 4.5 and 4.6.

Standard grounds are established where:

- it is believed that the recording or dissemination of intelligence material is likely to be of value in the interests of national security, the prevention or detection of crime and disorder, the maintenance of community safety, the assessment or collection of any tax or duty or of any imposition of a similar nature, or otherwise serves a significant public interest; and
- the recording and dissemination of intelligence material does not include 'confidential material' as defined below, unless safeguards contained in paragraph 3.5 have been taken into account; and
- the recording and dissemination of intelligence material would be in compliance with the Data Protection Act 1998.

    1.8.3 **Agencies** means:

the police, the National Crime Squad, the Scottish Crime Squad, the National Criminal Intelligence Service, HM Customs and Excise, other bodies with statutory responsibility for the investigation or prosecution of offences, and the Security and Intelligence Services.

    1.8.4 **Authorising officer** means:

a police officer, or an officer of the National Crime Squad, the Scottish Crime Squad, the National Criminal Intelligence Service or HM Customs and Excise, or a designated employee permitted by this code to record or disseminate intelligence material, or a police officer or an officer of HM Customs and Excise or the equivalent in NCIS empowered to authorise the dissemination of intelligence material in accordance with this code of practice.

    1.8.5 **Serious crime:**

conduct shall be regarded as serious crime if, and only if:

    a) it involves the use of violence, results in substantial financial gain or loss, or is conduct by a large number of persons in pursuit of a common purpose; or

b) the offence, or one of the offences, is an offence for which a person who has attained the age of twenty one and has no previous convictions could reasonably be expected to be sentenced to imprisonment for a term of three years or more.

1.8.6 **Community safety:**

a threat to community safety includes criminal or anti-social behaviour which is intended or likely to spread the fear of crime or violence or which is intended or likely to corrupt or undermine the health and well-being of the young or other vulnerable sections of the community.

1.8.7 **Public interest:**

a significant public interest includes the maintenance of the security and integrity of law enforcement agencies or other public authorities.

1.8.8 **Confidential material: Matters subject to legal privilege:**

both oral and written communications between a professional legal adviser and his/her client or any person representing his/her client made in connection with the giving of legal advice to the client or in contemplation of legal proceedings and for the purposes of such proceedings, as well as items enclosed with or referred to in such communications. Communications and items held with the intention of furthering a criminal purpose are not matters subject to legal privilege.

Confidential personal information:

information held in confidence concerning an individual (whether living or dead) who can be identified from it, and relating:

a) to his/her physical or mental health; or

b) to spiritual counselling or other assistance given or to be given; and which a person has acquired or created in the course of any trade, business, profession or other occupation, or for the purposes of any paid or unpaid office. It includes both oral and written information and also communications as a result of which personal information is acquired or created.

Information is held in confidence if:

- it is held subject to an express or implied undertaking to hold it in confidence;
- it is subject to a restriction on disclosure or an obligation of secrecy contained in existing or future legislation.

Confidential journalistic material:

material acquired or created for the purposes of journalism and held subject to an undertaking to hold it in confidence, as well as communications resulting in information being acquired for the purposes of journalism and held subject to such an undertaking. (See *Note 1B*)

Notes for guidance

Note 1A *Disclosure of certain types of information between some government agencies is regulated by statute. For example, successive Finance Acts, the Customs and Excise Management Act 1979, the VAT Act 1994 and the Immigration Act 1991 variously require, permit and regulate exchanges of information, which may include personal information, in the interests of the efficient conduct of the particular business of HM Customs and Excise to which the specified information is relevant. For statutory disclosures within Europe see paragraph 4.1.*

Note 1B *More comprehensive definitions of the terms 'matters subject to legal privilege', 'confidential personal information' and 'confidential journalistic material' are contained in sections 98, 99 and 100 respectively of the Police Act 1997.*
This code adopts the principles set out in that Act.

Authorisation procedures—recording of intelligence material

2.1 Individual officers and designated employees of the police, the National Crime Squad, the Scottish Crime Squad, NCIS and HM Customs and Excise are authorising officers for the purpose of their duty to record intelligence material in accordance with the Data Protection Act 1998 and the conditions set out below.

2.2 Before recording intelligence material the officer must be satisfied that:
- the activity conforms to the standard grounds set out in paragraph 1.8.2;
- the intelligence material to be recorded into systems has been properly evaluated and the provenance established;
- where the intelligence material is to be recorded into systems for later action, it has been assessed for risks arising from its use or from its potential disclosure in court proceedings.

2.3 Before including 'confidential material', as defined in paragraph 1.8.8, in an intelligence system due account will be taken of any restrictions on the use or requirement for special handling imposed by the officer who authorised its collection.

Records—recording of intelligence material

2.4 Intelligence material collected for recording in criminal intelligence systems will additionally record, subject to paragraph 1.7, the evaluation of the intelligence and the source of intelligence.

2.5 A record will be made of assessed risks in the use of such intelligence material or in its potential disclosure in court proceedings.

Authorisation procedures—dissemination within the United Kingdom of intelligence material

3.1 Except as provided by paragraph 1.5, the police, the National Crime Squad, the Scottish Crime Squad, NCIS and HM Customs and Excise will disseminate intelligence material to other UK agencies in accordance with the provisions of this code and the Data Protection Act 1998.

3.2 Individual officers of the police, the National Crime Squad, the Scottish Crime Squad, NCIS and HM Customs and Excise are authorising officers for the purpose of their duty to disseminate appropriate intelligence material to other United Kingdom agencies in accordance with the provisions of this code.

3.3 Subject to the provisions contained in paragraph 3.4, an officer may disseminate intelligence material to:
- statutory United Kingdom law enforcement agencies;
- the Security and Intelligence Services;
- United Kingdom agencies, other than statutory law enforcement agencies, which are prosecuting agencies.

3.4 Before disseminating intelligence material in accordance with paragraph 3.3, the officer must be satisfied that the dissemination:
- conforms to the standard grounds for activity set out in paragraph 1.8.2;
- concerns intelligence material that has been properly evaluated and the provenance established;
- has, where further action is likely to result from the passage of intelligence material, been assessed for risks attaching to its use or from its potential disclosure in court proceedings.

3.5 Where the material includes 'confidential material', any proposed dissemination must take due account of any restrictions on its use or requirement for special handling imposed by the officer who authorised its collection. Limitations on the use of material obtained following authorisations given under Part III of the Police Act 1997 are set out in the legal Code of Practice for Intrusive Surveillance at paragraph 2.36.
The Recording and Dissemination of Intelligence Material

3.6 Where the dissemination occurs through the medium of computer database access, the system should have an audit trail capability.

3.7 Subject to the authorisation procedure and additional safeguards set out below, intelligence material may be disseminated within the United Kingdom to parties other than those set out in paragraph 3.3 where:
- the standard grounds set out in paragraph 1.8.2 apply; and
- the dissemination is only of intelligence material which is relevant to the purpose intended by the dissemination.

3.8 Authorisations for dissemination of intelligence material within the United Kingdom to parties other than those set out in paragraph 3.3 may be given by:
- in the case of the police, the National Crime Squad and the Scottish Crime Squad, an inspector;
- in the case of NCIS and HM Customs and Excise, an officer of equivalent rank.

Records—dissemination within the United Kingdom of intelligence material

3.9 Where intelligence material is disseminated to an agency specified in paragraph 3.3, a record will be kept of:
- any restrictions on use or further dissemination of the material imposed as a result of an assessment of risks required at paragraph 3.4;
- where the material is 'confidential material', any restrictions on use or further dissemination, and any requirement for special handling imposed by the officer who authorised its collection.

3.10 Where intelligence material is disseminated to a recipient specified in paragraph 3.7, a record will be kept of:
- the material disseminated;
- the addressee;
- the authorisation;
- the purpose of the dissemination;
- any restrictions on use or further dissemination of the material imposed as a result of an assessment of risks.

Dissemination outside the United Kingdom 4

4.1 This section relates to the dissemination of intelligence material to European and non-European law enforcement agencies. It does not relate to disclosures of customs information within the European Union where such disclosure is provided for by regulation for the purpose of the administration of customs laws and the prevention or detection of customs fraud and evasion, nor, as indicated at paragraph 1.5, does it relate to evidential material disclosed to foreign law enforcement agencies through mutual legal assistance channels, such as by way of Commissions Rogatoire. (See *Note 4A*)

4.2 The draft European Union Convention on Mutual Assistance in Criminal Matters (Covert Operations) and the Convention on Mutual Assistance and Co-operation between Customs Administrations permit the exchange of information on criminal matters without prior request where the disclosure might assist the initiation or carrying out of investigations. The dissemination of intelligence material in these circumstances is subject to paragraph 4.4.

4.3 The dissemination of intelligence material to countries outside the European Economic Area (EEA) takes place for the purpose of the prevention or detection of international crime and terrorism. The Data Protection Act 1998, through its eighth Principle, prohibits the transfer of personal data to countries or territories outside the EEA unless that country or territory ensures an adequate level of protection for the rights and freedoms of data subjects in relation to the processing of personal data, or a substantial public interest would be served by the transfer. The law enforcement agencies will ensure that the dissemination of intelligence material beyond the EEA is conducted after an assessment of the risks to the data subject and that the dissemination takes place through established secure liaison arrangements. NCIS, HM Customs and Excise and the Metropolitan Police maintain these liaison arrangements. (See *Note 4B*)

4.4 The dissemination of intelligence material to foreign law enforcement agencies will be conducted, subject to the authorisation procedures set out below, where:
- the standard grounds apply and the dissemination is deemed a necessary means to effect the desired results; and
- the dissemination does not concern 'confidential material' unless due account has been taken of any restrictions on its use or requirement for special handling imposed by the officer who authorised its collection; and
- if the recipient country is outside the EEA and is judged not to possess an adequate level of protection, an assessment of risks to the subject arising from the transfer of the intelligence material has been conducted.

Authorisation procedures—dissemination outside
the United Kingdom of intelligence material

4.5 Authorisations for dissemination of intelligence material to foreign law enforcement agencies within the European Economic Area may be given by:
  • in the case of the police, the National Crime Squad and the Scottish Crime Squad, an officer subject to the supervision of an inspector;
  • in the case of NCIS and HM Customs and Excise, an officer subject to the supervision of an officer of equivalent rank to inspector.

4.6 Authorisations for dissemination of intelligence material to foreign law enforcement agencies outside the European Economic Area may be given by:
  • in the case of the police, the National Crime Squad and the Scottish Crime Squad, an officer subject to the supervision of a superintendent;
  • in the case of NCIS and HM Customs and Excise, an officer subject to the supervision of an officer of equivalent rank to superintendent.

Records—dissemination outside the United Kingdom
of intelligence material

4.7 Where the dissemination of intelligence material takes place in accordance with paragraph 4.4, a record will be kept of:
  • the material disseminated, including restrictions on use or further dissemination;
  • the addressee;
  • where the material is 'confidential material', any restrictions on use or further dissemination, and any requirement for special handling imposed by the officer who authorised its collection;
  • the objective of the dissemination; and
  • in respect of a recipient country outside the European Economic Area which is judged not to possess an adequate level of protection, the assessment of risk to the data subject(s) concerned.

Notes for guidance

Note 4A *The countries of the European Union are Austria, Belgium, Denmark, France, Finland, Germany, Greece, Ireland, Italy, Luxembourg, The Netherlands, Portugal, Spain, Sweden and the United Kingdom.*

Note 4B *The countries of the European Economic Area are the fifteen members of the European Union, Iceland, Liechtenstein and Norway.*

5.1 Where it is believed that intelligence material or other material relating to the recording or dissemination of intelligence material could be relevant to pending or future criminal or civil proceedings, it should be preserved in accordance with the requirements, where appropriate, of the Criminal Procedure and Investigations Act 1996 and other relevant legislation. (See *Note 5A*)

5.2 The Data Protection Act 1998 requires that personal data should not be kept longer than is necessary for the purpose for which it was acquired. Intelligence material will be subject to regular review and weeding. Intelligence material that is no longer of intelligence value should, except where paragraph 5.3 applies, be destroyed.

5.3 Where it is believed that intelligence material or any other matter required to be recorded by this code should, notwithstanding the requirement of paragraph 5.2, be retained on the grounds of significant public interest, as set out in paragraph 1.8.7, the material may be retained subject to:
- a record being made of the reason for the retention;
- regular review of its continuing retention; and
- the imposition of additional safeguards concerning access.

Note for guidance

Note 5A The Criminal Procedure and Investigations Act 1996 does not fully extend to Scotland and Northern Ireland.

6.1 The law enforcement agencies will maintain the standards set out in this code of practice.

6.2 Contraventions of the Data Protection Act 1998 may be reported to the Data Protection Commissioner or the officers set out in paragraph 6.3.

6.3 Complaints concerning breaches of the code may be made to the relevant Chief Constable, the Commissioner of the Metropolitan Police, the Commissioner of the City of London Police, the Director General of the National Crime Squad, the Commander of the Scottish Crime Squad, the Director General of the National Criminal Intelligence Service or the Chief Investigation Officer, or the relevant Collector, of HM Customs and Excise, as appropriate.

Select Bibliography

This select bibliography of recent work (the one exception being Willmer's ground-breaking 1970 study of crime and information theory) is intended to assist readers wishing to study further particular aspects of intelligence and policing. To that end it is arranged thematically and work that has relevance to more than one theme is listed under each relevant theme.

Official Guidance, Reports and Studies in relation to Intelligence and Information Management

ACPO *NIM Regional Tasking and Co-ordination – Protocol / Procedures / Policy and Performance Framework* (NCPE, Wyboston, 2004).

ACPO *Guidance on the National Intelligence Model* (NCPE, Wyboston, 2005).

ACPO *Independent Advisory Groups: A Guide* (ACPO, London, 2005).

ACPO *Practice Advice on Professionalising the Business of Neighbourhood Policing* (NCPE, Wyboston, 2005).

ACPO *Practice Advice on Core Investigative Doctrine* (NCPE, Wyboston, 2005).

ACPO *Code of Practice on the National Intelligence Model* (NCPE, Wyboston, 2005).

ACPO *DNA Good Practice Manual* (ACPO, London, 2005).

ACPO *A Practitioner's Guide to Intelligence-Led Mass DNA Screening* (NCPE, Wyboston, 2006).

ACPO *Retention Guidelines for Nominal Records on the Police National Computer* (ACPO, Kings Worthy, 2006).

ACPO *Guidance on the Management of Police Information* (NCPE, Wyboston, 2006).

ACPO *Guidance on the National Briefing Model* (NCPE, Wyboston, 2006).

ACPO *Data Protection: Manual of Guidance* (ACPO, London, 2006).

Audit Commission *Tackling Crime Effectively* (Audit Commission, London, 1993).

Audit Commission *Detecting a Change: Progress in Tackling Crime* (Audit Commission, London, 1996).

Bichard M *The Bichard Inquiry Report* (TSO, London, 2004).

Butler, Lord *Review of Intelligence on Weapons of Mass Destruction* HC 898, (TSO, London, 2004).

HMIC *Policing with Intelligence: Criminal Intelligence – A Thematic Inspection on Good Practice* (HMSO, London, 1997).

HMIC *A Need to Know: Thematic Inspection of Special Branch and Ports Policing* (TSO, London, 2003).

HMI Probation *An Independent Review of a Serious Further Offence case: Anthony Rice* (HMIP, London, 2006).

Intelligence and Security Committee *Iraqi Weapons of Mass Destruction – Intelligence and Assessments* Cm 5972, (TSO, London, 2003).

Intelligence and Security Committee *Report into the London Terrorist Attacks on 7 July 2005* Cm 6785 (TSO, London, 2006).

John T and Maguire M *The National Intelligence Model: Key Lessons from Early Research* (London, Home Office RDS On-line Report 30/04, 2004).

Lander S *Review of the Suspicious Activity Reports Regime (The SARs Review)* (SOCA, London, 2006).

Sheptycki J *Review of the Influence of Strategic Intelligence on Organized Crime Policy and Practice* (Home Office, London, 2004).

Intelligence-led policing

Cope N 'Intelligence-led policing or police-led intelligence?' *British Journal of Criminology* 44 188–203 (2004).

Gill P *Rounding Up the Usual Suspects? Developments in Contemporary Law Enforcement Intelligence* (Ashgate, Aldershot, 2000).

Grieve J 'Developments in UK criminal intelligence' in Ratcliffe J (ed) *Strategic Thinking in Criminal Intelligence* (The Federation Press, Sydney, 2004), 25–36.

Harfield C, MacVean A, Grieve J, Phillips D (eds) *The Handbook of Intelligent Policing: Consilience, Crime Control, and Community Safety* (Oxford University Press, Oxford, 2008).

Heaton R 'The prospects for intelligence-led policing: some historical and quantitative considerations' *Policing and Society* 9, 337–55 (2000).

Home Office *Practical Lessons for Involving the Community in Crime and Disorder Problem Solving* (TSO, London, 2005).

Innes M, Fielding N & Cope N 'The appliance of science? The Theory and Practice of Crime Intelligence Analysis' *British Journal of Criminology* 45, 39–57 (2005).

Innes M and Sheptycki J 'From detection to disruption: intelligence and the changing logic of police crime control in the UK' *International Criminal Justice Review* 14, 1–24 (2004).

Maguire M 'Policing by risks and targets: some dimensions and implications of intelligence-led crime control' *Policing and Society* 9, 315–36 (2000).

Maguire M and John T 'Intelligence-led policing, managerialism and community engagement: competing priorities and the role of the National Intelligence Model in the UK' *Policing and Society* 16, 67–85 (2006).

Ratcliffe J 'Intelligence-led policing and the problems of turning rhetoric into practice' Policing and Society 12, 53–66 (2002).

Ratcliffe J *Intelligence-Led Policing* (Willan, Cullompton, 2008).

Ratcliffe J and McCullagh M 'Chasing ghosts? Police perception of high crime areas' *British Journal of Criminology* 41, 330–41 (2001).

Sheptycki J 'Organizational pathologies in police intelligence systems: some contributions to the lexicon of intelligence-led policing' *European Journal of Criminology* 1, 307–32 (2004).

Tilley N 'Community policing, problem-oriented policing and intelligence-led policing' in Newburn T (ed) *Handbook of Policing* (Willan, Cullompton, 2003) 311–39.

Law relating to intelligence issues and human rights

Ashworth A *Human Rights, Serious Crime and Criminal Procedure* (Sweet & Maxwell, London, 2002).

Carey P *Blackstone's Guide to the Data Protection Act 1998* (Blackstone's Press, London, 1998).

Harfield C and Harfield K *Covert Investigation* (Oxford University Press, Oxford, 2005).

Leigh-Pollitt P and Mullock J *Point of Law: The Data Protection Act Explained* (3rd edn, The Stationery Office, London, 2001).

Starmer K *European Rights Law* (Legal Action Group, London, 1999).

Wadham J, Mountfield H, and Edmundson A *Blackstone's Guide to The Human Rights Act 1998* (3rd edn, Oxford University Press, Oxford, 2003).

Williams V *Surveillance and Intelligence Law Handbook* (Oxford University Press, Oxford, 2006).

National Intelligence Model

ACPO *NIM Regional Tasking and Co-ordination – Protocol/Procedures/Policy and Performance Framework* (NCPE, Wyboston, 2004).

ACPO *Code of Practice on the National Intelligence Model* (NCPE, Wyboston, 2005).

ACPO *Guidance on the National Intelligence Model* (NCPE, Wyboston, 2005).

Flood B 'Strategic aspects of the UK National Intelligence Model' in Ratcliffe J (ed) *Strategic Thinking in Criminal Intelligence* (The Federation Press, Sydney, 2004) 37–52.

John T and Maguire M *The National Intelligence Model: Early Implementation Experience in Three Police Force Areas* (Cardiff, University of Cardiff School of Social Sciences Working Paper Series 52, 2004a).

John T and Maguire M *The National Intelligence Model: Key Lessons from Early Research* (London, Home Office RDS On-line Report 30/04, 2004b).

Kleiven M (2007) 'Where's the intelligence in the National Intelligence Model?' *International Journal of Police Science and Management* 9(3) (253–73).

Maguire M and John T 'Intelligence-led policing, managerialism and community engagement: competing priorities and the role of the National Intelligence Model in the UK' *Policing and Society* 16, 67–85 (2006).

Risk

Barker J and Hodes D *The Child in Mind: A Child Protection Handbook* (Routledge, London, 2004).

Billingsley R 'Duty of care for informers' *Police Journal* 78, 209–221 (2005).

Billingsley R 'Risk management: is there a model for covert policing?' *Covert Policing Review* [2006] 98–109.

Ericson R and Haggerty K *Policing the Risk Society* (Clarendon Press, Oxford, 1997).

Harfield C and Harfield K *Covert Investigation* (Oxford University Press, Oxford, 2005).

Home Office *The MAPPA Guidance* Probation Circular 54/2004, 14 October 2004.

Kemshall H *Understanding Risk in Criminal Justice* (Open University Press/McGraw-Hill, Maidenhead, 2003).

Langan J and Lindow V *Living with Risk: Mental Health Service User Involvement in Risk Assessment and Management* (Policy Press, Bristol, 2004).

General texts relevant to policing, intelligence, information and knowledge management

ACPO *Guidance on the Management of Police Information* (NCPE, Wyboston, 2006).

Andregg, M 'Intelligence ethics: laying a foundation for the second oldest profession' in L Johnson (ed) *Handbook of Intelligence Studies* (Routledge, London, 2007) 52–63.

Dean, G and Gottschalk P *Knowledge Management in Policing and Law Enforcement* (Oxford University Press, Oxford, 2007).

Fleming M *UK Law Enforcement Agencies and Suspicious Activity Reports: Towards Determining the Value of the Regime* (Jill Dando Institute, London, 2005).

Gill, P *Rounding Up the Usual Suspects? Developments in Contemporary Law Enforcement Intelligence* (Ashgate, Aldershot, 2000).

Goldstein H *Problem-oriented Policing* (McGraw-Hill, New York, 1990).

Haggert K and Ericson R 'The surveillant assemblage' *British Journal of Sociology* 51(4) 605–22 (2000).

Harfield C 'SOCA: a paradigm shift in British policing' *British Journal of Criminology* 46(4) 743–61 (2006).

Harfield C, MacVean A, Grieve J, and Phillips D (eds) *The Handbook of Intelligent Policing* (Oxford University Press, Oxford, 2008)

Heath, S 'Using Multi-Agency Data to Reduce Deaths From Drug Abuse in Scotland' *The Journal of Homicide and Major Incident Investigation 1(1)* 15–24 (2005).

Hislop D *Knowledge Management in Organizations: A Critical Introduction* (Oxford University Press, Oxford, 2005).

Home Affairs Committee *Terrorism and Community Relations*, 6th Report of Session 2004–05, HC 165 (3 vols) (The Stationery Office, London, 2005).

Hyland K 'Texts – rewarding the public spirited defendant or a recipe for abuse' *Covert Policing Review* [2006] 87–97.

Innes M 'Signal crimes and signal disorders' *British Journal of Sociology* 55, 335–55.

Johnson L (ed) *Handbook of Intelligence Studies* (Routledge, London, 2007).

Kennedy H *Just Law: The Changing Face of Justice and Why it Matters to Us All* (Vintage, London, 2005).

Kryton E and Haggerty K 'Review essay: intelligence exchange in policing and security' *Policing and Society* 16, 86–91 (2006).

Lander S 'British intelligence in the twentieth-century' Lecture at the National Archives, 21 June 2001 <http://www.mi5.gov.uk/print/Page211.html>, accessed 12 September 2005.

Manningham-Buller E 'The international terrorist threat and the dilemmas in countering it' Speech to the Dutch Security Service, The Hague, 1 September 2005, <http://www.mi5.gov.uk/output/Page379.html>, accessed 12 September 2005.

Ratcliffe J 'The effectiveness of police intelligence management: a New Zealand case study' *Police Practice and Research* 6, 435–51 (2004).

Ratcliffe J (ed) *Strategic Thinking in Criminal Intelligence* (The Federation Press, Sydney, 2004).

Rogers C *Crime Reduction Partnerships* (Oxford University Press, Oxford, 2006).

Smith K 'NCPE Crime Operations – Supporting Serious and Series Crime Investigations' *The Journal of Homicide and Major Investigations 2(1)* 39–52 (2006).

Stelfox P 'The Role of Confidants in Homicide Investigations' *The Journal of Homicide and Major Investigation 2(1)* 79–92 (2006).

Willmer M *Crime and Information Theory* (Edinburgh University Press, Edinburgh, 1970).

Young H, Richards L, and McCusker S 'Profiling Mentally Disordered Offenders to Inform Decision Making and Intervention Strategies' *The Journal of Homicide and Major Incident Investigation 2(1)* 3–32 (2006).

Investigation guidance

ACPO *Good Practice Guide for Computer Based Electronic Evidence* (ACPO, London, 2003).

ACPO *Guidance on Investigating Domestic Violence* (NCPE, Wyboston, 2004).

ACPO *National Investigative Interviewing Strategy* (ACPO, London 2004).

ACPO *Road Death Investigation Manual* (Centrex, Bramshill, 2004).

ACPO *Guidance on Investigating Child Abuse and Safeguarding Children* (NCPE, Wyboston, 2005).

ACPO *Guidance on Investigating Serious Sexual Offences* (NCPE, Wyboston, 2005).

ACPO *Guidance on Major Incident Room Standard Administrative Procedures (MIRSAP)* (NCPE, Wyboston, 2005).

ACPO *Murder Investigation Manual* (NCPE, Wyboston, 2005).

ACPO *Guidance on the Management, Recording and Investigation of Missing Persons* (NCPE, Wyboston, 2005).

ACPO *Practice Advice on Core Investigative Doctrine* (NCPE, Wyboston, 2005).

ACPO *Investigator's Guide to ANPR* (ACPO, London, 2006).

Home Office *Mutual Legal Assistance Guidelines: Obtaining assistance in the UK and Overseas (Second Edition)* (Home Office, London, 2004).

NSLEC *Practical Guide to Investigative Interviewing* (Centrex, Bramshill, 2004).

Index

Printed and bound by CPI Group (UK) Ltd, Croydon, CR0 4YY